W9-BUS-203

# Art of Latin America since Independence

*by Stanton Loomis Catlin, Yale University Art Gallery, Director of the Exhibition
and Terence Grieder, Department of the History of Art, University of Texas*

*Published by October House Inc. for
The Yale University Art Gallery and The University of Texas Art Museum*

## Sponsors

Kingman Brewster, Jr., President, Yale University

Harry Huntt Ransom, Chancellor, The University of Texas

The Concilium on International Studies, Yale University
    Leon Lipson, Executive Secretary
    Arthur F. Wright, Vice-Chairman; Executive Secretary (1961-1965)

The Institute of Latin American Studies, The University of Texas
    John P. Harrison, Director

The Council on Latin American Studies, Yale University
    Richard M. Morse, Chairman
    George Kubler, Chairman (1964-1965)

The Yale University Art Gallery
    Andrew C. Ritchie, Director

The University of Texas Art Museum
    Donald B. Goodall, Director

1 112

**Yale University Art Gallery:** January 27 – March 13, 1966

**University of Texas Art Museum:** April 17 – May 15, 1966

**San Francisco Museum of Art:** July 2 – August 7, 1966

**La Jolla Museum of Art:** August 27 – September 30, 1966

**Isaac Delgado Museum of Art, New Orleans:** October 29 – November 27, 1966

# Contributors

American Airlines
James H. Binger
Celanese Corporation of America
The Ford Foundation
The Grace Foundation
The Edgar J. Kaufmann Charitable Trust
The Samuel H. Kress Foundation
David B. H. Martin
The Aaron E. Norman Fund, Inc.
The Spanish Institute, Inc.
Arthur K. Watson

# Preface

The aim of this exhibition is to provide an introduction to the closer study of Latin American artistic and cultural evolution during the century and a half since Independence. It is addressed primarily to the North American university community, which, because of its resources in teaching and research, both interdisciplinary and specialized, has a unique capacity for cultivating knowledge within particular areas of scholarly and public interest.

Since this exhibition is a record of artistic achievement, artistic quality has been the primary criterion for selection. Its basic premise, however, is that art forms part of intellectual experience in general and can, therefore, reflect and often epitomize other aspects of culture. Thus, Neoclassical and Romantic art, no less than social-revolutionary art, project into philosophy, law, politics, and other fields, and any one may illuminate any other. Accordingly, selections for the exhibition represent discernible traditions or intellectual commitments to which these works of art owe basic ingredients or impulses of form and content. Such a premise has not been adopted to convert art into the handmaiden of intellectual history, much less to suggest that Latin American art cannot stand on its own. On the contrary, we hope to approach from a general intellectual perspective unfamiliar sources of artistic value, for which aesthetic criteria alone – so often conditioned purely by taste – offer too narrow a view, and also to help disclose deeper levels of the Latin American mind and sensibility.

Although historical summaries of this evolution have been written (for the most part as sections of multivolume world histories of art) and histories of national art are beginning to grow in number, both knowledge and interest have been limited even within Latin American countries themselves, and direct observation generally has not yet succeeded traditional or casual evaluation of significance and quality.

This exhibition is also the first stage and nucleus of an effort to reveal through art some of the characteristics of culture and sensibility that differentiate Latin American traditions from those of North America. It precedes a book to be published a year or two hence, which is planned as a scholarly source for the teaching of Latin American art of the nineteenth and twentieth centuries. In view of the meager literature and the few reproductions in this field in any one place, the exhibition seems necessary to provide a comprehensive base of reference for the specialists and regional authorities who will be asked to help to write the book. The exhibition may also draw attention to actual as opposed to remembered or photographed reference material, and to create a photographic record of consistent quality for the illustration of the exhibition's publications, as well as for teaching and other long-range purposes. Underlying these considerations is the need to promote interest and research activity over a broad front, in a field too long unexplored for lack of both resources and initiative. As a consequence of neglect, many monuments in this field, with their potential contribution to cultural and historical consciousness, lie in jeopardy.

In view of these overall purposes, an organization suitable for teaching has been adopted, even though we are aware of its arbitrary nature and its possible oversimplification. The results are offered as an introductory view to be filled out and revised by later exploration, stimulated partially, we hope, by this project.

The past one hundred and fifty to two hundred years of Latin American artistic and intellectual evolution have been conceived of as an integral cultural phenomenon, despite evident national and regional distinctions. For both the exhibition and the book which is to come, the period is divided into five chronological divisions corresponding roughly to the intellectual and cultural climates that (allowing for regional differences) affected all countries, although often with varying consequences. In this catalogue, each of these divisions is treated in a brief essay on the general conditions that provided the background for artistic activity, an equally brief review of some of the major manifestations in art, and a group of reproductions of works of art selected for the exhibition. In this scheme, it is assumed that the characteristics common to all countries outweigh the significance of national and regional differences, at least in historical terms. In the exhibition as well as in the book, therefore, the emphasis is on international rather than national traditions. In all cases, but especially in that of

Brazil – which fits such a pattern only if viewed permissively – it is hoped that further study will eventually lead to more revealing frames of reference.

Even so, this chronological division is by no means intended to obscure regional, national, or even local differences, and certainly not to sustain the conception of Latin America as an area of linguistic and cultural uniformity. On the contrary, the older, perhaps more unified colonial and pre-Conquest cultures are seen as background for a modern diversity of characteristics, which in turn have a common denominator in worldwide international currents.

The exhibition includes works of art in the media of painting, political caricature, architectural and mural design, drawing, and printmaking. With the exception of public monuments of an architectural character, which are shown by plans and photographs, sculpture was excluded for curatorial, as well as practical, reasons; its potential contribution, in the light of the purposes of the exhibition, was not considered significant enough to replace any of the other major media in this respect. All but sculpture were considered necessary to convey a reasonably accurate idea of quality and commitment within the artistic and intellectual life of each period. In the final selection, however, one condition applied: in no case were visual works selected solely to document currents of thought, no matter how significant. Thus, nineteenth-century positivism is represented by a single, perhaps borderline, work. Again, since artistic criteria were uppermost, the founding generation of Peruvian landscape, social scene, and social comment painting of the 1930s and 1940s was chosen to represent as well the only slightly modified continuation of this tradition by younger contemporary painters in Cuzco.

In order to include the best available examples of significant traditions and directions wherever encountered, neither all countries nor all eligible artists are represented in the exhibition. Not only would a selection presenting all exponents of a particular school or tendency have been impractical in terms of space and digestibility, it would have defeated the purpose of the project to create an intelligible structure for study. Moreover, it was impossible to cover all the geographical ground over such a long time span. It will also be noted that some artists are represented by single works, and others by several. Here the evaluation reflects a personal judgment in keeping with the exhibition's plan.

In these instances, as with the choice of all works of art in the exhibition, final decisions were made by one person, the director of the project. The one-man procedure, now well tested and generally accepted in the United States as a viable alternative to "committee juries," especially for group competitions among living artists, is less familiar in Latin America. This method of selection was chosen for the sake of a more closely governed structure according to the focus and objectives of the exhibition. The Latin American contributors graciously accepted this point of view.

To acknowledge the contributions of the myriad individuals and institutions in Latin America and the United States whose collaboration has made this exhibition possible, a separate publication would be required. Some idea of the extent of this collaboration may be gained from the persons listed in the formal acknowledgment section of this catalogue. But that covers only a fraction of the number of persons and institutional representatives who have played an essential part in the often intricate arrangements that have led to the appearance of the present synoptic display of Latin American art in this country.

The gratitude of the sponsoring institutions is expressed in the first instance to the lenders of works of art in all countries, a measure of whose generosity is indicated by their consent to entrust to us some of their most valued artistic treasures for the extraordinary period of fifteen and a half months. These include the trustees of National Patrimonies, museums, libraries, private collectors, artists, galleries, cultural institutes, and many others whose names appear in the list of lenders. To the departments, departmental heads, and their deputies within the Ministries of Education and Foreign Affairs, and the embassies in Washington, D.C., who assumed charge of arrangements at the official level, we express our gratitude. We are grateful to the directors and their associates and staffs of Latin American museums and universities, private and public cultural foundations, institutes of artistic extension and other professional bodies as well as independent scholars, collectors, and connoisseurs on whom has fallen much of the technical demand and time-consuming burden of practical arrangements in assembling, documenting, and preparing the works of art for shipment. In Latin America also, we thank the Cultural Affairs Officers, their superiors and staff of the United States Information Service, whose nonofficial but officially approved assistance has provided the principal bridge for establishing and maintaining the formal basis of collaboration between the private sponsors of the project and Latin American state agencies. In this, and in an infinite number of varied and varyingly demanding supporting tasks, the U.S. Foreign Service has played an indispensable role. We are also grateful to our own Yale alumni committee chairmen and their committee members who, without exception, responded to the request to serve in supporting capacities as the project's official representatives in their countries of citizenship and residence – a charge involving diverse activities and responsibility in services, communications, and arrangements at all levels of local organization over many months up to and including the actual shipment of the works of art to the United States. The loyal support of these members of the Yale alumni body was unfailing in all circumstances, and to them is due success in meeting many of the critical needs and problems that attend an undertaking such as this.

On the professional level in nearly all countries,

National Commissions and Yale Committees relied on the executive assistance of many persons. For their painstaking, persevering, and often brilliant work we should like especially to thank the following: Señora María Urquidi de Franco, in association with Señora Ana María Icaza de Xirau, Señora Elvira Gándara de Niro, and Señor Jesús R. Talavera, Mexico City; Señor Roberto González Goyri, Guatemala City; Señora Olga Zubieta de Oller, Panama; Señorita Mireya Zawadzky, Bogotá; Señora Germania Paz e Miño de Breilh, and Señora Laura de Crespo, Quito; Señorita Neda Prpic, Guayaquil; Señora Sara Lavalle, Lima; Señor Federico Assler, Santiago de Chile; Arq. Samuel Oliver, assisted by Señora Silvia Ambrosini, Buenos Aires; Senhora Rosalina Leão, Senhorita Dina Flüsser and Senhor Edson Motta, Rio de Janeiro; Mr. Alvin H. Cohen, São Paulo; and Señor Miguel Arroyo and Señor Gerd Leufert, Caracas.

Even such a summary review of the individuals and groups in Latin America to whom the exhibition is indebted would be incomplete without mention of the seventeen photographers who, in their respective countries, produced an aggregate of 1,500 negatives and 3,500 prints of subjects included in the preliminary selections. These photographs form a comprehensive black-and-white pictorial record of the material with which this long-range project is concerned. Reproduced photographs by these collaborators are credited in another section of this catalogue.

Turning to the United States, the director of the

# Contents

# Introduction

The history and art of Latin America fall naturally into three periods: pre-Columbian, colonial, and modern. Of the three, the modern period is least known to the world at large. Its approximate duration of one hundred and fifty years – dating from the era of Independence – does not compare with the millennia of pre-Columbian artistic culture, and its span is only half that of the colonial period. Nevertheless it encompasses artistic treasures and remarkable personalities that deserve to be more widely known.

The material of the present exhibition is of special interest for the United States since it comprises the work of fellow Americans. That they are indeed fellow Americans becomes clear as we examine the achievements of the various periods here considered. In general, artistic development in the Latin American countries in the nineteenth and twentieth centuries follows a course surprisingly parallel to the evolution of the arts in the United States. On the other hand, in view of the fact that Latin Americans have so often been described, by themselves as well as by others, as poetic and emotional, the objectivity of their images is surprising when compared with the romantic enthusiasm of their North American contemporaries. The prevailing preconception of the public in both North and Latin America is that each holds the advantage in art. Although the interest of such a question is more political than artistic, the claim of Latin American artists to our attention cannot be easily ignored.

The Latin American painters may bring to mind cognates in the art of the United States. For example, the Venezuelan Juan Lovera may remind us of his contemporary, Trumbull; Blanes may be compared to Homer and Sívori to Eakins. The dispassionately observed and conceptually controlled Mexican landscapes of Velasco make a striking contrast with the more poetic and emotional landscapes of Inness, Bierstadt, and Church. In some periods and styles there are no very direct parallels; for example, there are none for the strong Cubist-oriented school of the 1920s and '30s of Pettoruti, Guido, Spilimbergo, and Berni in Argentina.

Two points, however, clearly distinguish the Latin American art world from its counterpart in the United States, namely the acceptance of the principle of patronage of art by all levels of government and, again in principle, the widespread respect of the public for artists. The Latin American tradition of government patronage is inherited from the colonial period, when patronage was extended both by the royal courts of Spain and Portugal and by their representatives in the New World. The Mexican Academy of San Carlos and the Brazilian Academy, founded in 1785 and 1816 respectively, are the earliest of the Latin American national academies and represent continuations of the Spanish and Portuguese traditions of the national patronage of art schools. National art academies were founded in Chile (1848) and in other countries, the majority well before our own. If some of

1

these schools have lost their influence in recent years – with the notable exception of the National School of Fine Arts in Peru – their historical role has been impressive.

One of the results of government patronage is public esteem for the arts. Accomplished artists in Latin America, living or dead, are regarded as great men, and their profession is generally honored as a distinguished calling. In some cases, respect has perhaps been carried too far, as in the election, purely on his merits as an artist and great man, of Pedro Américo to the first Constituent Assembly of Brazil in 1890. (The excessiveness in this instance is evident by the fact that Américo did not perform his duties in the Assembly, but departed almost immediately for Florence to pursue his true vocation.) Other artists have held high political office, for example, José Guadalupe Zuno, governor of Jalisco, Mexico, and Pedro Figari of Uruguay. The presence of an Imperial court in Brazil from 1811 to 1889, which made Rio de Janeiro a major art center, also inspired a certain amount of emulation in other nations. But the tradition was well established in any case. In Mexico Porfirio Díaz, hardly an art lover, gave a special grant to the late Dr. Atl (Gerardo Murillo) for study in Europe when the young man approached him; and such stories are common in the artistic biographies from many nations. The artist who did not receive a government stipend for study in Europe is the exception, as a glance through the accompanying biographies will reveal – surely a situation that Homer or Eakins would have envied. Even governments that obviously could not afford to indulge in extravagances provided modest scholarships for art study abroad, as in the case of the Uruguayan government, which sent Blanes to Italy with such meager funds that he could not afford to travel from Florence to Rome. So large was the return on the investment in Blanes' case that it would be hard to calculate.

In addition to direct patronage of artists and academies, the continuation of the tradition established by the courts of Europe had other effects. It led to the beautification of cities, and especially of the public parks. The public interest, often neglected in social and economic terms, was unusually well served by handsome areas provided and tended by the government. Manifestations of the same tradition may also be seen in the importation of missions or individual artists from Europe to Rio de Janeiro in 1816 and to Buenos Aires in 1824 to design the public buildings of those cities, and to Peru in 1880 for Lima's Exposition Park, a spacious green bounded by wide avenues and containing circles lined with monuments. The vast sweep of the multiple malls of Brasília (1956) is in this same tradition.

The acceptance of public patronage in Latin America is at least in part the result of the academic tradition, which considers art a learned study. Hence, judgment in art matters has been reserved to those educated in art. A remark of the sort ''I don't know anything about art, but I know what I like'' is not unknown in Latin America, but the attitude expressed in it, historically speaking, has had less direct influence on important patronage than in our own country.

If the exhibition may be of special interest to North Americans for the light its comparison may shed on our art, it is of equal interest for the view it provides of European art and society of the times here represented. Perhaps unwittingly, we have accepted a picture of the nineteenth century that is far removed from the facts of European culture. Comparison of almost any major art gallery in North America with its Latin American counterpart reveals the relative wealth of the nineteenth-century collections of the latter as compared to the relative poverty of its twentieth-century collections. The reverse is the case in the North American museums, where the nineteenth century means the French Impressionists, with perhaps Ingres, Delacroix, Corot, and Courbet for good measure. Manet would perhaps be amazed, and not entirely gratified, by our overscrupulous selection of precursors of twentieth-century movements.

The revolution of taste against the Parisian Beaux-Arts tradition has been far less extreme and complete in Latin America. As we examine the collections of the Latin American museums, a phase of life and art is revealed that has been largely omitted from our frames of critical reference, but whose values and glories cannot be considered entirely transient. This phase was dominated by the sophisticated, luxury-loving, international monied aristocracy whose world centered on Paris, whose literary models were French novels, and whose artistic tastes were based on those expressed by the Paris Salons. The First World War destroyed this world so completely that only vestiges of it remain, and these vestiges are possibly more alive in the cities of Latin America than in Europe itself.

This world is revealed again in the paintings of Américo and Visconti in Brazil, of Tovar, Michelena, and Rojas in Venezuela, of Hernández and Baca-Flor in Peru, and of Pedro Lira and Valenzuela Puelma in Chile. This world's complacency and materialism are most remembered now; but its insistence upon technical quality and finish, its formality, its modes of sensibility, and its serious concern, at least in theory, for the noblest human sentiments – in short, its idealism and its high technical standards – are refreshing, and so out-of-date as to seem avant-garde. This was the stylistic ambiance of Europe in the period from 1875 to 1910, as most respectable Europeans knew it, and some of its foremost names – Bouguereau, Collin, Cabanel – were the teachers of the Latin Americans.

In Latin America the esteem in which art is held is just one facet of an intellectual approach that favors the aesthetic. The Latin American *pensador* is far more likely to write an *Aesthetics* (for example, Vasconcelos, Pedro Figari, and Antonio Caso and, in a sense, Ricardo Rojas under the title, *Eurindea*). The Mexican positivist, Francisco Bulnes, remarked in disgust "The great Latin delusion is the belief that art is the highest, almost the only object of national life." Thus, he says, by trying to be artists, they turn their religion into idolatry; they handicap themselves in industry; and in science they fail to understand the scientific method, all because "Latins lend every effort to being artists." Bulnes, writing before 1899, takes a negative view of what in humanistic studies can only be considered one of Latin America's chief glories: her poetry and belles-lettres. Yet, even among the positivist thinkers, a large and influential group in the last decades of the nineteenth century, we do not find the pragmatic approach but rather an exaggerated idealism. The famous Puerto Rican educator, Eugenio María de Hostos, who worked primarily in Santo Domingo and Chile, saw his mission in terms of an ideal society – an approach that may be considered aesthetic rather than utilitarian or pragmatic. And among Latin American thinkers generally, according to Crawford, many "were poets first, and nearly all wrote poetry."

It is a strange fact that the subjective and frankly "aesthetic" appears more frequently in the literary than in the pictorial arts of Latin America which, as mentioned earlier, are often objective. Some of the best Latin American work in "science" has appeared in pictorial form, such as the botanical drawings of Mutis' late eighteenth-century academy in Bogotá, the ornithological paintings of Joaquín Pinto, the paintings of the Comisión Corográfica in Colombia, and the volcano studies of Dr. Atl of Mexico. These, Bulnes would say, are examples of the confusion of art and science. Whether they succeed as science may be debatable, but their artistic value is hardly in doubt.

The cultural and geographical implications of the exhibition's title may again raise the question of the existence of an art that may properly be called Latin American. The creation of a "Latin American" art or a "National Art" has been a persistent concern among artists and critics in the Latin American world. As the complex problem of national identity that faces nations with highly diversified populations is cultural as well as political in nature, such concern on the part of artists is natural. This preoccupation cannot be discounted as a productive force when one considers artists such as Rivera, Siqueiros, Sabogal, Portinari, Mérida, Szyszlo, Obregón, and many others, whose works have reflected regional, national, or ethnic values. In our opinion, however, it is more valuable at this stage not to attempt to consider this question, but rather to examine the kinds of art produced by artists who have an identifiable relation with Latin America as a whole.

This is a broad category. In an area and during a period in which artists, styles, and ideas from abroad have played a constant role, borderline cases frequently occur. For example, the style of the majority of nineteenth-century reportorial artists remains European in the course of their American activity. Here their involvement in American subject matter, and the premise that their art may well have played a part in the formation of the Latin American image of itself are the deciding factors. Moreover, except for the accident of birth, it would almost seem that such figures as the Peruvian Baca-Flor and the Venezuelan Michelena should be eliminated from the American category because of their almost totally Europeanized styles. However, birthplace is still everywhere accepted in cultural history as a basic fact of identity, and in these and other cases the styles practiced were variations on an international approach that was widely accepted in their times in Latin America. There is also the reverse position of the European professionals who came to America under contract to governments to teach in state academies. Although many of these artists continued in directions already established, they played an important role in the for-

mation of new generations and in the shaping of the sometimes reactionary artistic climate in the countries where they worked. Not at issue, of course, is the position of foreign artists who came on their own in search of New World careers and who borrowed or modified their styles under American conditions.

There are more questions about Latin American art since Independence than there are answers, and if the exhibition brings into focus the questions, it will have served its purpose. The visual arts, literature and philosophy, and the natural sciences probably have been more closely interwoven in Latin America than anywhere else. The disclosure of their specific relationships promises invaluable insight into the realities of Latin American society as well as its art and the problems of the Hemisphere which we have in common.

Stanton L. Catlin     Terence Grieder

# Period I: 1800-1835

# Period I: 1800 – 1835

The Independence movements throughout the Western Hemisphere were the political result and, to some extent, the social response to a much wider phenomenon that made its appearance among the populations of nearly all regions bordering on the Atlantic Ocean from the latter half of the seventeenth century on. This was the intellectual revolution that has been named "The Enlightenment" or the "Age of Reason," when a civilization-weary Europe began to look to classical antiquity for new models of social morality and state organization, to social philosophers for ideas for the improvement of man's worldly condition, to nature for objective truth, and to primitive society for a new evaluation of human dignity. It gathered momentum after the mid-eighteenth century with the advance of skepticism and the inner decay of monarchical institutions. The growing power of the bourgeoisie, the rediscovery of ancient Greek and Roman monuments, the writings of dissident philosophers, and the findings of science and of naturalists' explorations of the non-European world all penetrated to the roots of society, not only in Western Europe, but the Spanish and Portuguese domains of the Western Hemisphere. A major effect of this trend was to loosen the absolutist grip on thought, which in turn provided the opportunity to transfer intellectual authority to the responsible individual conscience of free men.

The political climax of the first cycle of this change was reached in the American, French, and Latin American Revolutions. In the last instance, the ground was prepared partly by the liberalization of colonial policy within the Spanish Empire, which was also reacting to the impact of the new thought. During the regime of Charles III, the guarded relaxation of controls on thought, the establishment of art academies, and the introduction of new art forms as an adjunct to political and economic modernization and, after the succession of weak monarchs in the seventeenth century, the opening of new ports to international trade, furthered a general reorientation of perspectives and restlessness of mind in the vast but hitherto isolated and self-sufficient Ibero-American world. In a short fifty years, Spanish power had been vitiated and was overturned by the Independence armies of Simón Bolívar and José de San Martín. Another important factor for Latin American Independence movements was the Napoleonic invasion of the Iberian Peninsula. The abdication of Fernando VII opened the way for the destruction of Spanish monarchical authority and the substitution of republican principles in its western domains, whereas the escape of the Portuguese Crown to Bahía, in Brazil, set the stage for quite a different kind of evolution toward independence in that country in which the principle of constitutional monarchy continued to the last decade of the nineteenth century.

The dominant intellectual tradition of the Independence period may be characterized as Neoclassical. That is to say, the ideals of Greek and Roman antiquity in thought, custom, ethics, education, law, and institutional organization, as well as in art and architecture, became the models for a general reshaping of society. At the same time, reason and observation replaced faith and myth in principle. Although the image of the Mediterranean classical world had never been forgotten – its influence having continued unbroken from the end of the Roman Empire – its outward forms and inner meaning had been so changed by fifteen hundred years of European history that there was general interest in recovering its original character. The effect of this interest penetrated all levels and geographical reaches of the European-settled world. Among the most distant of these were the Spanish-speaking colonies of Spain, from Mexico to Chile, where its impact was felt in the provinces as well as in the major cities.

At the same time, Romanticism, the paradoxical concomitant of Neoclassicism, began to form a parallel tradition. The aspiration to freedom of action and expression, long contained in colonial Latin America, was stimulated anew by the writings of Rousseau, Schiller, and Chateaubriand, and released by general social change. It was particularly in America that it found new range of exercise, not only on the part of Creoles (American-born Europeans), but also by those who began to come to America in increasing numbers from all parts of the European world.

From the end of the eighteenth century, therefore, the Neoclassical and the Romantic trends developed side by side, and perhaps nowhere did the coextension of their careers, extending into the twentieth century, produce more variations or interactions than in Latin America.

Probably the most consistent artistic reflection of the Neoclassical aspect of the new intellectual orientation is to be found in architecture. All the American variations of the late "Baroque" manner were almost immediately succeeded by structures and remodelings in Neoclassical style, with stress upon the Greek and Roman orders, rational organization, clarity of plan, and restraint in detail. This stylistic redirection, which in certain areas was sponsored by royal and ecclesiastical authority prior to Independence, was rapid and complete, and it extended into nearly all building fields.

Probably the largest concentration of Neoclassical buildings in South America was begun in Brazil, where, after 1816, the new style was officially introduced by the Portuguese Crown from its new transatlantic base. There Grandjean de Montigny and other members of the Lebreton Mission of architects, artists, and engineers trained in French principles established a National Academy in Rio de Janeiro and began to design and ornament public buildings of many kinds. Over a thirty-five year period, these included the Imperial Palace of João VI, the National Library, the National Museum, the Seminary of São Joaquín, the Palacio de Comercio, the Botanical Gardens, and the facade of the new Academy of Fine Arts.

At a considerably earlier date, a very similar official effort was made by the rival Spanish Crown to introduce Neoclassical principles of design in Mexico. This began with the foundation of the San Carlos Academy in 1785, whose faculty soon included some of the ablest Spanish artists, among them the architect-sculptor, Manuel de Tolsá. Foremost among Tolsá's architectural works in Mexico is the School of Mines, which is one of the outstanding examples of Spanish-American Neoclassical building. The style was carried on in Mexican architecture by Francisco Eduardo de Tresguerras, whose buildings were largely in his native state of Guanajuato. Tresguerras' chief work is the Church of El Carmen in Celaya. In this and many other still anonymous churches, houses, theaters, and monuments in outlying parts of this state, one sees evidence of the penetration of the Neoclassical style into nineteenth-century life in Mexico.

Its extension into other parts of the Spanish-American world was not delayed for long. In Central America, major cathedrals were designed and constructed in Guatemala and Nicaragua, antedating Independence in the case of the former (1785–1815). In South America, Bogotá Cathedral (1806–1811) was designed by the Spanish Capuchin monk, Domingo de Petrés. In Lima, the stronghold of Spanish power in South America, a little-known architect, Matías Maestro, built the baldachino of the metropolitan cathedral, as well as the interior of El Milagro church and the altar of La Merced, all lesser but good examples of Neoclassical architecture. The extraordinary spread of this style is seen again at La Paz in the Cathedral of San Francisco (1835 on) and the cloisters of the Tercer Orden and of San Calixto, as well as in the Cathedral of Potosí.

In Chile, surviving evidence of late eighteenth- and early nineteenth-century Neoclassicism are almost nonexistent unless one considers Toesca's Santiago Cathedral (1780–1799), which was totally reconstructed in an academic eclectic manner in 1903. However, in Toesca's stately Moneda, now the Presidential Palace, the turn toward Neoclassicism in the late eighteenth century is anticipated in the reserved design and limited use of ornament by this Italian architect, whose magnificently subtle treatment combining grace and scale does not, however, depart from the aesthetic of the preceding style.

Beyond the high passes of the cordillera, on the eastern side of the continent, national development of the present regions of Argentina and Uruguay began from a minimal base. Lima, the chief South American viceregal capital for three centuries, through which all communication with the mother country had to be routed, was more than fifteen hundred miles away. Under these peripheral conditions, settlement was limited until the late eighteenth century, when, largely for military reasons, Buenos Aires became a port of direct contact with the European world. Thus, long isolated, thinly populated, and preponderantly rural at the outset of the nineteenth century, these regions had almost no history or local tradition of artistic interest. Even late colonial activity in building and sculpture, influenced by the highly developed Jesuit missionary centers in Paraguay and neighboring provinces to the north, was limited and provincial, and architecture of the following Independence era was chiefly in the hands of European emigré craftsmen or engineers. However, Neoclassical influences are marked in the facade of the Buenos Aires cathedral, a rigorous effort to emulate the dodecastyle of the Greek temple by Catelin, a French architect, commissioned by the early Argentine statesman, Rivadavia; and vernacular overtones of Neoclassicism can also be seen in Pellegrini's design for the dictator Rosas' palace in Palermo, now destroyed.

Latin American painting during the Independence period is no less a reflection of the Neoclassical ideal and artistic style than architecture. However, it seems more complex in its origins and aims and less constant in direction. Unlike architecture, it inherited no great tradition or institutional patronage from the colonial past. As with the early governments of Independence, painting had to begin at the beginning, without experience. In so doing, it was subject to a variety of influences, among which the following are most significant: (1) the Neoclassic principles of the Spanish and French painters and academic schools that were officially sponsored before Independence, and (2) the Romantic outlook brought in by the European costumbrista artists, who, in the interest of quasi-scientific,

quasi-exotic documentation, by the end of the 1830s were coming in large numbers. At the same time, colonial norms of portraiture continued to be influential, though usually modified by new treatment and content.

In general, influence of the standard European Neoclassic prototypes is felt most strongly in portraiture. A new emphasis on this genre is accompanied by a more precise linear quality, sobriety of color, clarity of tone, and a moral seriousness that is evident not only in the demeanor of the sitter, but also in the economy and precision of the artist's treatment. Among the outstanding examples of this type by non-American forerunners of the Neoclassic tradition is the portrait of Manuel de Tolsá by Rafael Jimeno y Planes, who left Spain for Mexico in 1795 to teach in the Academy of San Carlos. This work suggests the style of the German, Rafael Mengs, who as Court Painter to Carlos III played an important role in defining Spanish concepts of Neoclassic art. Another such work is the head of Jeanneton by Nicolas-Antoine Taunay, a Frenchman who accompanied the Lebreton Mission invited to Brazil by Emperor João VI shortly after the Portuguese monarchy moved its court across the Atlantic. Taunay's landscapes, heads of military officers, figure studies of women and children are perhaps more reminiscent of Chardin's style than that of the chief exponent of French Neoclassicism, Jacques Louis David; but in this case, it is once again a European artist who arrived before Independence under

Imperial aegis who typifies and sets the standard of the new style. Mexico and Brazil were the two centers where royal initiative established American academies in order to identify the colonial regime with progressive thought of the day. Although allied in other phases of their work to costumbrista art, Debret, a Frenchman who came to Brazil with the Lebreton Mission, and Pellegrini, a Savoyard invited to Buenos Aires by Rivadavia, represent further aspects of European Neoclassicism in America. Debret's paintings of the arrival and installation of the Portuguese monarchs in Brazil, *The Disembarkation of Princess Leopoldina* and the *Coronation of Dom Pedro I*, take as their models the ceremonial paintings of David's school; and Pellegrini's watercolor portraits of leading Argentine personalities of the Rosas era are done in the style of Ingres.

The first artistic manifestation in Latin America of the Romantic phase of the Enlightenment was costumbrista painting, which was a reportorial art of European nonacademic painters and draughtsmen concerned with recording the minutiae of the social and physical environment of a continent just recently revealed to European eyes. Its initial impulse came from the scientific desire for greater knowledge of this little-known world, and its development received great impetus from the explorations and writings of the German naturalist, Baron von Humboldt, who traveled widely in South America and Mexico at the turn of the eighteenth century under the auspices of the Spanish throne. One of Humboldt's followers, Johann Moritz Rugendas, became the best known of the foreign costumbrista painters. These artists were drawn from many parts of Europe, some independently, others attached to naval or diplomatic missions or associated with scientific voyages (for example, Martens with Darwin on HMS *Beagle*); many came with commissions for publications to satisfy a rapidly growing British and Continental curiosity about the Western Hemisphere, made possible by the new process of lithographic reproduction. In increasing numbers for a period of fifty years, they traversed the coastal regions and much of the interior of the then defined Latin American world, from the West Indies around the Straits of Magellan to California. Their most concentrated activity, however, seems to have been in the central region of the Rio de la Plata – Argentina and Uruguay – and on the east coast of Brazil, where expertly selected and documented, and sometimes zealously guarded, private collections of the best of this material are evidence today of the wealth and importance of this still neglected phase of the American artistic past. This art had a formative influence on European conceptions of Latin American life and society, and it also seems likely that through printed reproductions it had a similar influence on Latin American conceptions of itself. Its real relation to the art of American-born artists, as a source of artistic as distinct from social influence, awaits investigation. But the works of Debret and Landseer in Brazil; d'Hastrel, Martens, and Grashof in Uruguay; Vidal and Pellegrini in Argentina; Gay, Graham, and Giast in Chile; Mark in Colombia; Linati, Catherwood, and Nebel in Mexico; and the ubiquitous, prolific Rugendas, followed by the expeditionary lithographers, Fisquet and Blanchard – to name only a few – clearly constitute one of the richest and most interesting chapters in the history of nineteenth-century art in America.

It is in the work of the largely self-taught Creole or American-born painters of the period that variations upon the standard European Neoclassical prototypes occur. Here some of the first cross-influences become evident.

The portraits of García del Molino in Argentina, for example, render personality within the Neoclassic compositional framework, but the artist's sensibility is more attuned to the person and a local standard of value than to international style. The same may be said of Morel's *Portrait of Señorita Macedonia Escardo*. The influence of the costumbrista concern for everyday events and local history is manifested in that same artist's paintings of boisterous tavern scenes and cavalry combats, although in the latter case, the cue may come more from the Napoleonic battle picture in the French style set by Baron Gros.

The continuation of colonial standards of painting is marked in Ecuador throughout the first half of the nineteenth century, where religious subject matter continues its sway, and mystic concepts of reality are emphasized, often with ingratiating lyricism, as in Manuel Samaniego's *La Divina Pastora*. Or landscape is perceived detached from allegory and given independent existence as a reflection of patria, as in the view of Quito attributed to Rafael Salas.

Fusion of colonial and Neoclassical standards is evident in the formal portrait painting of the early Independence period in many areas. The work of Juan José Rosales of Guatemala and José María Vázquez in Mexico, for example, continues to show interest in decorative detail, background anecdote, and the lettered descriptions of colonial portraiture, but these attributes are subservient to the closer definition of personal character, a generally more reserved treatment, and the introduction of Neoclassical style in dress and surrounding properties. On the other hand, in paintings of revolutionary figures of the Independence campaigns, the Peruvian, José Gil de Castro, used the traditional basic colonial portrait type as a vehicle of popular vision, which became through his treatment the first consistent art style of Latin American republican idealism. Static in form, naïve in its fascination with the trappings of military dress, and repetitiously stylized, his work depicts with admiration and visual accuracy the personalities of Bolívar and his military contemporaries in Peru, Chile, and Argentina, with a conviction and freshness that seem to be an authentic reflection of the popular heroic spirit of Latin American Independence.

In his early career, the Guatemalan miniaturist,

Francisco Cabrera, painted high colonial officials with a purity of line and color and a directness of characterization that suggests a potential renewal, in diminutive form, of a waning tradition. After Independence, however, he turned to naturalistic observation as the basis of his work and, with sure taste and instinct for style, produced during the first third of the nineteenth century one of the finest series of portraits in this medium encountered in the course of the present survey.

S. L. C.

Plate 2. Gil de Castro. *The Martyr Olaya.* 1823

Plate 3. Cabrera.
*Gobernador General Don José Bustamante y Guerra.*

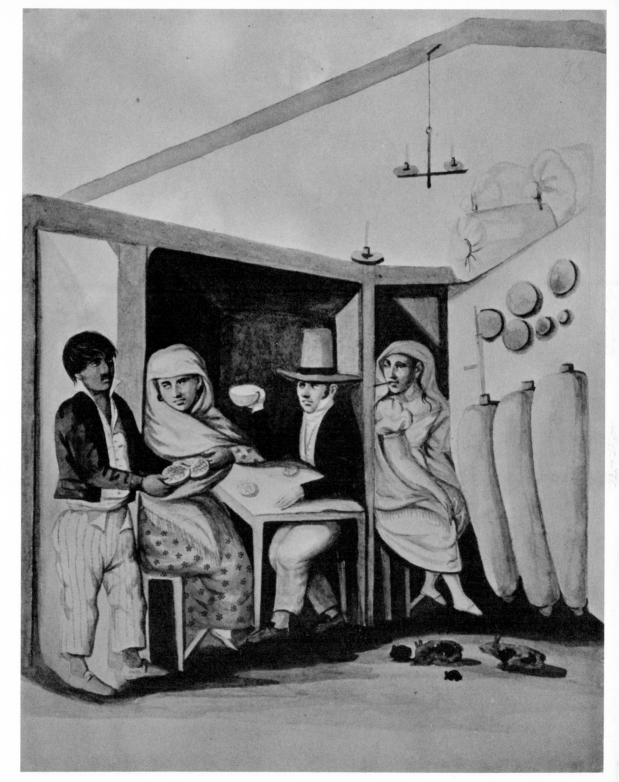

Plate 4. Anonymous.
*Piquantería.*

Plate 5. Gil de Castro. *Portrait of Bolivar.* 1823 *(left)*

Plate 6. Anonymous. *Solemn and Peaceful Entrance of the Trigarantine Army.*

Plate 8. Rodríguez de Sá. *Portrait of Dom Pedro I.* 1823 *(right)*

Plate 7. Debret. *Landing of Doña Leopoldina, First Empress of Brazil.*

Plate 9. Morel. *Cavalry Battle.* 1830 *(left)*

Plate 10. Pellegrini. *Sra. Agustina Rosa de Mansilla and her Son.*

Plate 11. Descalzi.
*Lady in front of the Mirror.*

Plate 12. N.-A. Taunay. *Portrait of Jeanneton*.

Plate 13. Pueyrredón. *A Rest in the Country*. 1861

Plate 14. Vidal. *Country Race.*

Plate 15. Debret. *Dance of the Savages from the Mission of Saint Joseph.*

Plate 16. Catherwood. *Ruins of Uxmal.*

Plate 17. Grandjean de Montigny. *Plan for the Exchange Building, Rio de Janeiro.*

Plate 18. Petrés. *Plan and Profile of the Cathedral Church of Santa Fe.*

Plate 19. St. Aulaire, after Sarokins. *View of Veracruz.*

Plate 20. Besnes e Yrigoyen. *The Priest Doctor Pérez Castellano.*

# Period II: 1835-1875

Plate 21. R. Salas (attr.). *Quito. (overleaf)*

The period between 1835 and 1875 may be characterized as the era of liberalism and political reform. In no country was Independence followed by any basic change in the social and economic order carried over from the colonial period, and restlessness and dissatisfaction were widespread. "Caudillismo" in the postrevolutionary decades was typified by the military dictatorships of Santa Ana in Mexico, Rosas in Argentina, López in Paraguay, and Flores in Ecuador. Violence, repression, and chaotic conditions were the outward manifestations of political problems. These included inexperience in government and in the application of constitutional principles inherent in the ideals of the Independence, and reliance upon force by shifting political groups who responded alternately to the desires of elements striving for constitutional stability and to the claims of the propertied classes. By mid-century, these conditions had led in Mexico to the rise of the Reformist party and to a general civil war, interrupted by the French Intervention. In Argentina, the struggle for a viable system satisfactory to both the centralists and the regionalists was resolved, at least temporarily, with the final defeat and exile of Rosas in 1852. International wars ensued, often over boundary issues, which can be traced to dictatorial ambitions, the scramble for economic resources (in which expanding foreign powers were often involved), and the desire to divert attention from difficulties at home. The principles of law and human right inherited from the Enlightenment were, however, slowly filtering through the educated upper and middle classes and, in Mexico and countries on the west coast, through the mixed white and Indian populations as well. Consequently, Latin American society began to be more aware of its own problems, of the deficiencies of social and economic conditions, and of the need to improve upon them. This phenomenon was parallel to, and received impetus from, developments in Europe and North America, such as the 1848 revolutions in France and Central Europe, and the comparatively late appearance of the Emancipation issue in the United States Civil War. There was, at the same time, a growing awareness of economic potentiality, aspects of which included an increased receptivity to the exploitation of national wealth by foreigners, and the beginnings of the desire to use and to keep up with the results of technological progress in the outside world. These tendencies were accompanied by intensified promotion of nationalism and universal insistence by liberal and reformist parties on the principle of free speech, which was frequently the subject of the brilliant political caricature of this period.

The fact that Mexico, under the leadership of Juárez, warred with Louis Napoleon, overthrew Maximilian, and institutionalized the Reform movement with a new and more socially equitable constitution, was the vindication and in a sense the culmination of the Reform period. Elsewhere, liberalism was in the crucible, and even in Mexico the legal and adminis-

educated European artist that the Uruguayan painter, Juan Manuel Blanes, had in his formative years. Yet Blanes' talent was announced early in his long career, and subsequently developed into one of the most formidable in nineteenth-century American art. Not only was he wide-ranging in interest, versatile in technique, accurate in observation, and sustained in performance, he also possessed true insight into the dramatic contrasts and psychological subtleties of the social and political scene of the Banda Oriental.

The Brazilians, Pedro Américo and Vítor Meirelles, transposed their academic training acquired in Rio de Janeiro and Europe to patriotic treatment of scenes and subjects of national history. In contrast, their contemporaries, Amoêdo and Almeida Júnior, applied their Romantic inclinations to the idealization of national qualities through less glorified but no less patriotic subjects, such as the resting woodchopper in Almeida Junior's *Derrubador*, and Amoêdo's *Marabá*. The Romantic qualities of both Américo and Meirelles are seen on a more intimate and expressive scale in Meirelles' *A Questão Christie* and Américo's *Paz e Concordia* (1895).

Beyond the limits of the present period, an extension of the same Romantic tradition may be found in the late nineteenth century in the murals of Tovar y Tovar depicting battles of South American Independence in the northern regions of the continent in the cupola of the Sala de Ceremonias (Congreso Nacional, Caracas) and in his superb portraits, the quality of which, with those of Blanes and Pueyrredón, establishes a nineteenth-century apogee in this field.

S. L. C.

Plate 22. Mark. *Bogotá Square.*

Plate 22a. Mark. *Bogotá Square*. (Detail)

Plate 23. **Pallière.** *Landscape of the Jungle of the Argentine Missions.* 1864

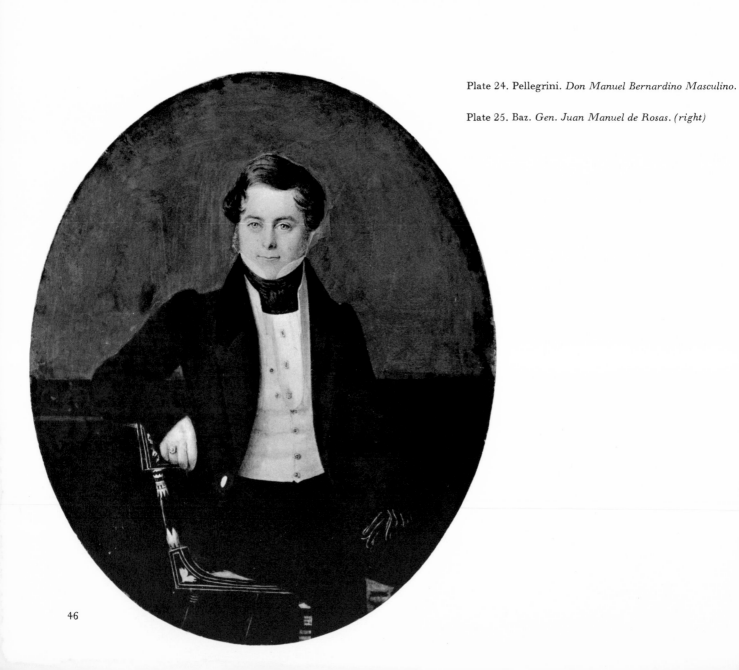

Plate 24. Pellegrini. *Don Manuel Bernardino Masculino.*

Plate 25. Baz. *Gen. Juan Manuel de Rosas. (right)*

84.

Plate 26. Laso. *Indian Potter*.

Plate 27. Monvoisin. *Portrait of Don Andrés Lamas.*

Plate 28. Ramírez Rosales. *Landscape with Palm Trees.*

Plate 29. Rugendas. *Plaza de Armas.*

Plate 30. Fisquet. *Humble Dwellings by the Sea.* 1836

Plate 31. Catherwood.
*The Well at Bolonchén, Yucatán.* 1843

Plate 32. Pinto. *Study of a Bird.*

Plate 33. Pancho Fierro. *Juanita Breña. (right*

Plate 34. Blanes. *The Assassination of Gen. Benancio Flores.*

Plate 35. Blanes. *The Two Ways.*

Plate 36. Tovar y Tovar
*Juana Verrue.* 1877

Plate 37. Egerton. *Real del Monte.* 1840

Real del Monte
D.T.Egerton 1840.

Plate 38. Clavé. *Benito Juárez.*

Plate 39. Anonymous (Xalapan). *Portrait of Miguel Pérez Amador.*

Nº 2.

Olhae d'este burrinho,
Cegou c'o muito estudar;
He chronica esta cegueira,
Não se pode mais curar

Traz o seu preço na testa,
Valor por que foi comprado.
Tem espirito de gente,
Escreve como um letrado.

Essa he a Rocha Tarpeia,
Prodigio da nossa terra:
Ao **metal** nunca resiste,
Cede á lima ao malho...a cerra

Plate 40. Araújo Pôrto Alegre (attr.).
*Caricature of Justiniano José da Rocha. (left)*

Plate 41. Anonymous.
*Benjamin, Chinese Writer.* 1868

Plate 42. Garay. *Portrait of a Lady*. (Detail) *(overleaf)*

Although it remained largely dependent on foreign centers of power, most of Latin America underwent major commercial and industrial development during the years between 1875 and 1910. Economic prosperity was enjoyed by the business and landholding classes; at the same time, immigration was significantly on the increase. The notable exception, Paraguay, remained in economic decline after its devastating war with Brazil, Uruguay, and Argentina. Bolivia and Peru, however, gradually recovered toward the end of the century following their conflict with Chile. This was the period in which cattle-raising and the export of beef were built into significant industries in Argentina, when coffee was established as an important export crop for Brazil, and when Chilean nitrate became significant in the world market. In many countries this was an era of railroad construction and of the development, almost entirely by foreign interests, of mines and banana plantations.

The classes that profited from these developments looked to Europe for safe and respectable cultural values. They acquired works by Italians, Frenchmen, and Spaniards, and sometimes they imported the artists as well, for example Landesio and Fabrés, who taught in the Mexican Academy. French ideas, especially the positivist philosophy of Auguste Comte, were dominant throughout Latin America during the earlier years of the period; and their role can be seen in the writings of many important philosophers (among them Bulnes in Mexico, Varona in Cuba, Lastarria in Chile, and Bomfim in Brazil), in which were expounded notions of scientific experimentalism and objectivity with regard to social problems.

More likely to appear in the arts than in governmental policy was national consciousness, which sometimes took the form of reexamination of the colonial past, as in the *Tradiciones* of Ricardo Palma in Peru. Palma's circle included the painter, Teófilo Castillo, who produced dream-like evocations of the colonial period. National consciousness of a more earthy nature is an ingredient of the popular art of Posada in Mexico. The Brazilian literary classic by Euclides da Cunha, *Os sertões*, creates a vast panorama of Brazil's Northeast through its account of a frontier rebellion. In caricature, we often find parallels both to the irony and pessimism of the Brazilian novelist Machado de Assís, and to the passionate political invective of Ecuador's Juan Montalvo, these two men representing the literary poles of the period.

For the arts, this era can be characterized as a period of consolidation rather than as one of innovation. The Neoclassic and Romantic traditions merged in Latin America to produce an idealistic academic style. Throughout the period, Parisian training was considered all but indispensable, and European experience resulted in a technical polish and critical sophistication that had been absent for the most part during the earlier periods. Portraits, battle paintings, narratives, and genre pictures were the main categories of painting. Paintings of battles produced by

Blanes in Uruguay, Américo and Meirelles in Brazil, and Tovar y Tovar in Venezuela, and many others were a major expression of patriotism and pride in the new nations. It was in subject matter rather than in style that a national expression asserted itself.

The style of the Spanish painter Ignacio Zuloaga, which was independent of the Parisian tradition, created a following of its own in Latin America. Intensely Spanish in mood, it carries on the tradition of Goya. Among the many who absorbed Zuloaga's style are Arturo Gordon in Chile, Saturnino Herrán in Mexico, and Tito Salas in Venezuela.

Newer European styles entered Latin America during the period. The Colombian, Epifanio Garay, brought home from Paris a dignified realist style in portraiture and religious figure painting. In Argentina, Eduardo Sívori introduced a stark French Realism in his famous *La Levée de la bonne* (1887), which shocked Argentine eyes accustomed to idealized renderings. Although both Garay and Sívori were instrumental in the establishment of art institutions in their countries, the Realistic style had few followers in Latin America, where it was generally considered tasteless. Sívori himself turned later toward a more colorful style, of which the portrait of his wife is a well-known example.

The two dominant currents discernible in the painting of this period are an academic style based on conservative Parisian training, which looked to the Paris Salons for the standard of quality, and the style of a number of independent painters whose expressions were related to Impressionism. The former style is most thoroughly displayed in the work of the two Peruvians, Daniel Hernández and Carlos Baca-Flor, who entered international society through their talent in portraiture. A similar style was used by many artists: Pedro Américo in Brazil, Pedro Lira in Chile, and Martín Tovar y Tovar and Arturo Michelena in Venezuela are a few figures from a widespread tradition. Characteristic are feminine portraits of remarkable finish and elegance, in contrast to the portraits of national heroes typical of earlier periods. The late work of Juan Manuel Blanes, the Uruguayan master, includes the triumphant portrait of *Carlota Ferreira de Regunaga*. Rodolpho Amoêdo's sensuous nude study of an Indian girl, *Marabá*, turns the academic style to the expression of local subject matter. The Indian girl becomes an evocation of the primitive beauty of the American land, just as *Sra. Luisa de Mesones* by Hernández evokes the sophisticated international drawing room.

Landscape was not neglected. Joaquín Pinto in Ecuador, a versatile painter, created accurate studies of snowy Andean peaks. *Chimborazo*, painted in 1901, just five years before his death, is a dashing treatment of his forbidding subject. José María Velasco, who is the outstanding landscape painter of his century and region, dedicated himself to an objective recording of the Valley of Mexico. The view eastward toward the great volcanoes, painted in 1900, is a late work. The objectivity of the image derives from the prevailing philosophy of positivism, and his occasional paintings of trains reflect positivist thought in their implied attitudes toward material progress.

Impressionism arrived in almost every Latin American country directly from France. During this period the style remained an importation, unnaturalized, and it was only in later years that a native Postimpressionism developed from it.

Impressionism as it was practiced in France, emphasizing vision and light, found few adherents. Collivadino in Argentina, Blanes Viale in Uruguay, and Clausell in Mexico are rare examples. More imaginative and coloristic Impressionistic styles, with diverse European connections, were practiced by Andrés de Santa María in Colombia, who reflected strong Expressionistic affinities, and Martín Malharro in Argentina. These artists, whose styles are more accurately classified as Postimpressionist or Expressionist, are probably more representative of long-term Latin American aesthetic preferences than their more rigorous European contemporaries, but they found scant encouragement from Latin American society, whose cultural choices depended on the certainty of the most conservative Parisian approval. The accomplished academic styles employing broken color used by Cristóbal Rojas in Venezuela, Eliseu Visconti in Brazil, and Edwardo Sívou in Argentina were more popular because they reflected the European taste of the period.

Architecture in this period was characterized by the entry of eclectic Italian and French architectural styles, and by the rapid expansion of urbanization following French ideas. Typical are the Palacio de Bellas Artes in Mexico City by the Italian architect, Adamo Boari, and the Paseo de la Reforma with its monuments to Independence and the Aztec hero, Cuauhtémoc, also in that city. Other representative structures are National Congress buildings in Buenos Aires, Montevideo, Bogotá, Caracas, and Santiago; the grandiose Buenos Aires town houses in Belgian Beaux-Arts style of the Norwegian emigré Christopherson; the great theaters of São Paulo, Rio de Janeiro, Buenos Aires, and even far provinces in many countries. In Lima the Plaza Bolognesi, a *glorieta* (circular plaza with radiating streets) by Marquina, dates from the last years of the nineteenth century. At this time, the European Art Nouveau style also makes its appearance in commercial buildings as well as residences of major cities and their suburbs.

T.G.

Plate 43. Bondat. *Battle of Pacocha.* 1877

Plate 44. Hernández.
*Sra. Luisa de Mesones.* 1883

Quito 1901 _____

Plate 45. Pinto. *Chimborazo. (left)*

Plate 46. Lira. *Love Letter*.

Plate 47. Velasco. *The Valley of Mexico.* 1900

Plate 48. Sívori.
*Portrait of the Wife of the Artist.*

Plate 50. Rojas. *Study of the Balcony. (right)*

Plate 49. Della Valle. *The Return from the Raid.* 1892

Plate 51. Américo. *Peace and Concord*. 1895

Plate 52. Amoêdo. *Marabá*. 1882

Plate 53. Amoêdo. *Bad News.* 1895

Plate 54. Michelena. *Sick Boy*. 1886

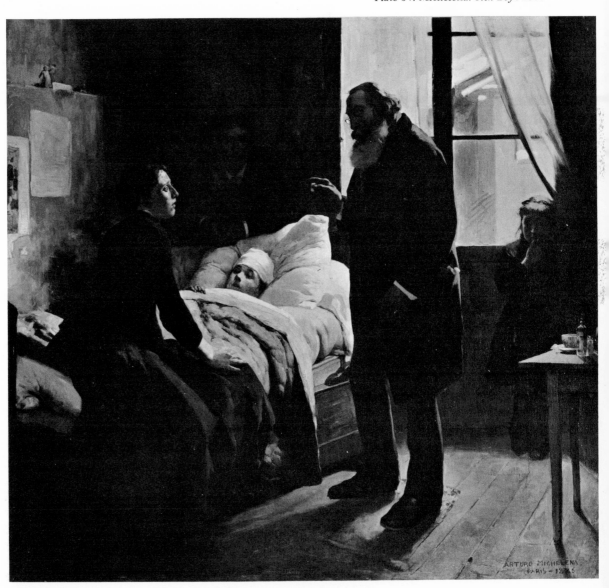

Plate 55. Baca-Flor. *Couple*. 1900

Plate 56. Gordon. *The Drunks*.

Plate 57. Herrán. *The Christ of the Granadas.*

Plate 58. Ruelas. *Criticism (Self-Portrait)*.

Plate 59. Posada. *Female Dandy*.

Plate 60. Demócrito II. *Don Quixote.* 1891

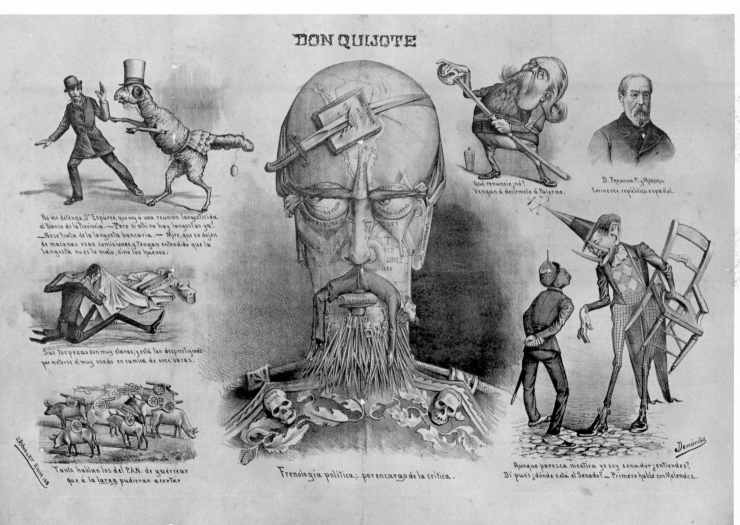

Plate 61. Pettoruti. *The Quintet. (overleaf)*

# Period IV:  1910 – 1945

The period between 1910 and 1945 was one of dramatic struggle for social justice, even in nations where the outcome was a totalitarian dictatorship. The Mexican Revolution of 1910 resulted in sweeping social reform, and in Uruguay the second administration of Batlle y Ordóñez (1911–1915) established the eight-hour day, workmen's compensation, minimum wages for rural labor, and the abolition of capital punishment. The nationalist, Indian-oriented, and socialist program of the Aprista party in Peru, although it never came to fruition, is characteristic of the period. Perhaps even more typical of the period as a whole is the nationalist state-socialist dictatorship of Getulio Vargas (1930–1945) in Brazil. In spite of rapid industrialization, the landed gentry retained great power in all Latin America, so that (the Uruguayan case notwithstanding) reform generally did not include legislation regarding rural labor and landholding.

Industrialization and economic reform were only one side of the story of progress. The university reform, a continent-wide movement begun at Córdoba in 1918, resulted in political autonomy and academic freedom in the universities. On quite another front was the new concern for the Indian element of the population. This was to some degree the result of the archeological rediscovery of the glories of the Indian past, which made a vast and pervasive contribution to the intellectual and general cultural life of Mexico in particular, and to a lesser extent, also of Guatemala and Peru. In all the nations with significant Indian populations, the integration of the Indian into national life was seen as a primary goal, especially as communicated in the arts, for example in the work of Saturnino Herrán in Mexico before 1918 and in the music of Carlos Chávez. A national though not Indianist, expression is found also in the music of Heitor Villa-Lobos of Brazil.

The academic tradition of Parisian Salon art survived into this period and retained for a time its hold on patronage, as evidenced by the selection of Daniel Hernández as first director of the Peruvian Escuela Nacional de Bellas Artes in 1919. The academic tradition was most successfully challenged by Impressionist and Postimpressionist styles. In Venezuela the Circulo de Bellas Artes, organized in 1912 and including Rafael Monasterios and Armando Reverón, dedicated itself to Impressionist views of the native landscape. An Impressionistic aesthetic of light, atmosphere, and color was espoused by Juan Francisco González and Pablo Burchard in Chile; Dr. Atl and Joaquín Clausell in Mexico; and in Brazil by Eliseu Visconti and others. The Impressionist insistence upon vision, as opposed to imagination, as the foundation of art, found less following among Latin Americans, who turned increasingly toward imaginative compositions and color. It would in fact be more precise to regard the movement as a whole as Postimpressionist in view of their imaginative and expressionistic tendencies.

More than any other feature of Impressionism, its liberation of color won it adherents in Latin America. One of the closest followers of French Impressionism was Armando Reverón, whose training was largely academic. His softly brushed landscapes and nude figures, frequently in white or wine-color schemes, are a thoroughly personal version of the style. In the art of Juan Francisco González the clear color appears in a heavy impasto, usually in landscape or flower subjects. Like Reverón, his training was academic; his style was a personal creation, not the outcome of any direct Impressionist influences.

A glowing, sensuous color is the main appeal of the nude figures and interiors painted by Miguel Carlos Victorica, a member of the Argentine Postimpressionist school. Far from being a record of vision, Victorica's paintings are compositions in the most abstract sense, not only giving line, plane, and color full value, but the leading role.

Several varieties of European Modernism began to enter Latin America just before 1920. German Expressionism was first seen in Brazil in the 1913 show of the work of Lasar Segall, who settled in that country ten years later. Anita Malfatti's exhibition of 1917 introduced examples of Fauvist art by a native Brazilian painter. The new styles were firmly established in 1922, despite much public outcry, by the Modern Art Week in São Paulo, of which Emiliano di Cavalcanti was a leader. Cavalcanti's style was based on Cubist models discovered in Europe, but his use and development of the style have a purely Brazilian tropical sensuousness.

Modernism, in a Synthetic Cubist form was brought to Buenos Aires by Pettoruti in 1924, again to the mystification of the public. His style was developed in Milan under Futurist stimulation and in Paris, where he was particularly close to Juan Gris. Despite long years of public disapproval, Pettoruti has remained a steadfast practitioner of the style. The Cubist–Purist–Concretist facet of the Modern movement has remained very important in Argentina, reinforced by Pettoruti's example. The more conservatively representational and often regionalist art of Guido, Spilimbergo, and Berni in the 1930s was powerfully conditioned by the Cubist aesthetic.

The great Uruguayan Constructivist, Joaquín Torres García, practiced his art in Europe and the United States during this period, returning to his homeland only in 1945. His many writings, as well as his paintings, have established him as a major figure of modern American art. His international reputation and influence is still increasing following his death in 1949.

The expression of social ideals was a major aim of art in the period between the two world wars. The most important manifestation of this tendency was the Mexican Revolutionary art of Dr. Atl, Orozco, Rivera, Siqueiros, and others. Mexico, in 1921, in the person of the Minister of Public Education, José Vasconcelos, called her artists home to participate in a national artistic revival and the redefinition of Mexican ideals following Indo-American models. The next decade saw the rise of the influential movement known as the Mexican Renaissance. The European experience of several major participants – with the notable exception of Orozco – was absorbed in a rapidly forming national style. Italian Renaissance art, Cubism, and Art Nouveau were principal ingredients of the new style, which, however, transcended its sources. That the movement expressed itself in murals was in part the inspiration of Dr. Atl, who for many years had been advocating a revival of Renaissance mural painting. That it turned ever more toward Indian themes is largely the result of the corporate work of the Syndicate of Painters at the National Preparatory School, 1921–1922, and the personal rediscovery of Mexico and its archeology by Diego Rivera and his assistants.

The influence of the Mexicans was far-reaching. Mural schools developed in Peru under the leadership of José Sabogal, and in Brazil, where Candido Portinari was the best-known practitioner. Mexican Revolutionary art, unlike that of any other Latin American country, has had a profound and continuing influence in the United States.

The architecture of the period was concerned in part with eclectic neocolonial styles. It is in the coun-

tries whose colonial pasts were most glorious that the majority of the best examples are found, such as the Archbishop's Palace (1924), the Presidential Palace (1938), and the Municipal Palace (1945), all in Lima, and the Palace of Justice (1941) in Mexico. It appears also in the Guatemala National Palace (c. 1935).

The versatile Brazilian painter–architect–writer, Flavio de Carvalho, anticipated later architectural movements in his early Purist-style buildings, such as the Government Palace of São Paulo (1927) and his cement house of the same period. The work of another Brazilian of the same period, Gregorio Warchavchik, was equally advanced. Their work, and that of other avant-garde Brazilian contemporaries of the late '20s, prepared the way for the famous Ministry of Education and Public Health building in Rio de Janeiro, begun in 1937. Le Corbusier came as consultant to the Brazilian architects in 1936 and his influence is paramount in the design. This impressive building was noticed throughout the world and established Lucio Costa, Oscar Niemeyer, Reidy, and the other Brazilian followers of Le Corbusier as the leaders of Latin American architecture. The Brazilian example was followed in many countries after 1945.

T. G.

Plate 62. Visconti. *Youth.*

Plate 63. Victorica. *Nude.* 1923

Plate 64. Juan Francisco González. *Roses*.

Plate 65. Santa María.
*Portrait of a Lady.*

Plate 66. Rivera. *Portrait of a Man.* 1913 *(left)*

Plate 67. Barradas. *The Miller from Aragón.* 1919?

Plate 69. Cavalcanti, *Five Young Ladies from Guaratinguetá.* 1930 *(right)*

Plate 68. Reverón. *Landscape.* 1929

Plate 70. Carvalho. *Portrait of Elsie Houston*. 1932

Plate 71. Tamayo.
*The Flute Player.* 1944

Plate 72. Alfaro Siqueiros. *Portrait of Amado de la Cueva.* 1920

Plate 73. Tarsila do Amaral. *EFCB.* 1924 *(right)*

Plate 74. Chiappini.
*Portrait of Toussaint L'Ouverture.* 1941

Plate 75. O'Gorman. *Memory of Los Remedios.* 1943

Plate 76. Urteaga. *The Betrothed*. 1937

Plate 77. Rivera. *Flower Vendor*. 1935 (*right*)

Plate 78. Poleo.
*The Three Commissaries.* 1942

Plate 79. Torres García. *Constructive Ship "America."* 1943

Plate 80. Cúneo.
*The Moon over the Ranch.* 1934

Plate 81. Spilimbergo. *Figures*.

Plate 82. Covarrubias. *The Lindy Hop.* 1936

Plate 83. Lasansky. *Dinner.* 1937 *(right)*

Plate 84. Carlos González.
*The Death of Martín Aquino.* 1943 (*left*)

Plate 85. Borda.
*Leonor González and José Borda.* 1920

Plate 86. Méndez. *Vision*. 1945

Plate 87. Orozco. *Head of Quetzalcoatl*. 1932-34 (*right*)

# Period V: 1945-1965

Plate 88. Antúnez. *Composition: Sun.* 1965 (*overleaf*)

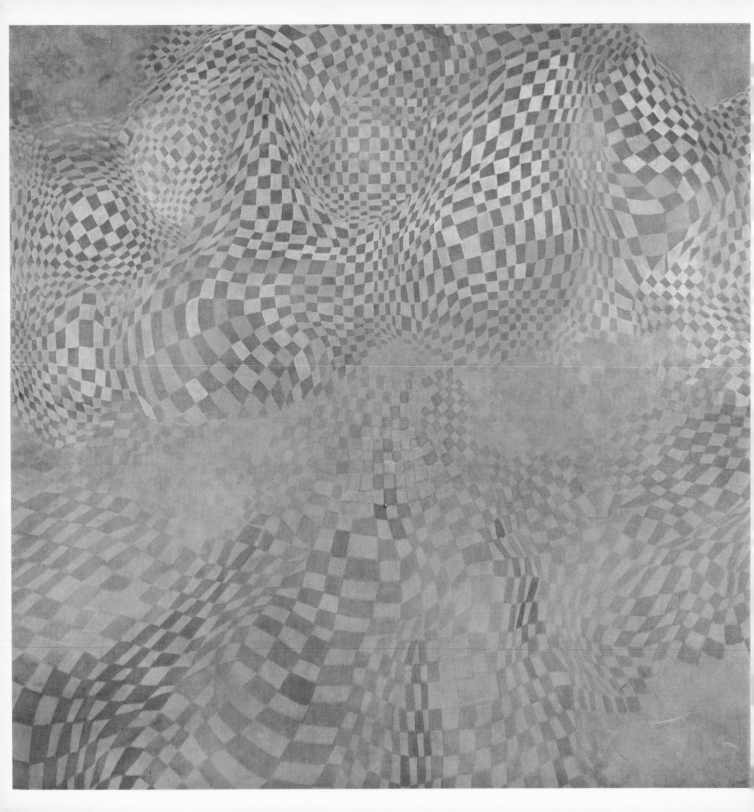

# Period V: 1945 – 1965

Period V, the contemporary period, has seen the triumph of internationalism in Latin American art. Present internationalism, born in Europe and given impetus from the United States, is not a universal style, but rather a new language in which many styles have been formulated. The full range of the phenomenal world has been accepted as the legitimate area of interest, both as subject matter and medium, limited only by the unity of the work of art in itself and its expressive organization. The general acceptance of this new language by artists, critics, and connoisseurs in Latin America reflects a world trend, and was made possible by the fact that Latin America has been involved in the traditions of the societies and of the centers of innovation and experimentation in which this new language took shape. It nevertheless represents a radical and abrupt departure from previous standards.

Since World War II, the evolution of artistic internationalism in Latin America has been marked by numerous trends, nearly all of European or North American origin. Among the earliest was Concretism, the nonobjective abstract art in the Constructivist tradition that was elaborated by the Dutch and Russian schools of the second decade of this century, institutionalized by the German Bauhaus in the 1920s, and varied by the Parisian Nouvelle Réalité group of the 1930s. Highly theoretical, and with close affinities to architecture and typography, this tradition demanded strict observance of canons of method and value and aspired to a universal purist order of art. It took hold in Argentina in the late '40s, partly under the influence of the Uruguayan master, Torres García, and found a serious following in Brazil. It was the avenue on which the artistic revolution to modernism in Venezuela achieved momentum, and it has inspired individuals in Cuba and, lately, in Chile. Only in Argentina and Venezuela, however, were there group attempts to apply strict Constructivist tenets with continuity and rigor, and even here a number of its most able exponents soon began to develop independent personal variations. In all these countries the tradition continues today more freely in individual directions. Furthermore, it plays a dominant role in the work of architects and in architectural planning where, as in the new city of Brasília, the university complexes of Caracas and Mexico, the gardens of Roberto Burle Marx, and Vázquez' new museums in Mexico City, it has provided the rational basis for carrying out the concept of "integration of the arts" on a grand scale. Perhaps nowhere in the Western Hemisphere has a large-scale architectural scheme involving this concept been put into operation more effectively than in Carlos Raúl Villanueva's Central University of Venezuela in Caracas.

Informalism, the most common term in Latin America for the international tradition of free, intuitive abstraction, began to attain its position of near-universal dominance toward the end of the 1950s. Taking its models variously from Italian, North European, North American, Japanese, and Spanish painting, this basically expressionist manner provided a direct avenue for the uninhibited exteriorization of personal emotion and has been embraced more widely by Latin American artists than any other formal mode since the beginning of the period covered by the present exhibition. An identifiably individual artistic style, often esoteric, sometimes involving impulsive, automatic, or accidental methods of execution, but requiring the organic consistency of artistic form and the allusive quality of poetic metaphor, generally became and remains the prevailing objective among a majority of contemporary Latin American painters today. Among the successful exponents of this trend are Mabe in Brazil, Pucciarelli and Testa in Argentina, Morales in Nicaragua, María Luisa Pacheco in Bolivia, and de Szyszlo in Peru.

Informalism has had the virtue of furthering a deeper exploration of instinct and a wider exercise of sensibility among Latin American artists, liberating them from clichés of older tradition, and at the same time encouraging creative self-reliance and closer communication with contemporary artists throughout Latin America and the international art world beyond. On the other hand, it has tended to produce a rhetoric of its own, and a superficial responsiveness to the fashions of international taste, which have often impeded Latin American artists from coming to closer grips with their artistic and intellectual problems.

In addition to the several outstanding Latin American individual informalist styles that have made their way into prominence on the world scene, this trend may be considered the matrix of one of the strongest postwar national schools of the hemisphere, that of the Argentine neo-figurists of which Deira, Macció, de la Vega, Noé, and Seguí are the chief representatives. Ranging from near-abstract configurations of line and color sweeping dynamically over large canvases to monster images derived from television and billboard advertising, the work of these painters characterizes with new savagery barbaric instincts that they see below the surface of modern civilized personality.

Related to this school is the work of a large number of artists who emphasize grotesque aspects of modern man. An international trend that has a wide following with many variations in Latin America, it may be an artistic projection of existentialism. The image of man as a distorted being, hopeless and ridiculous, is not merely a self-image; it is an image of all men, and may be seen as an expression both of self-examination and of social protest.

With the spread of the influence of internationalism, a reaction has set in against the schools of social revolutionary, social scene, and social comment painting which, emanating from Mexico, prevailed during the 1930s and early 1940s, especially in Guatemala and the northwest countries of South America: Colombia, Ecuador, Peru, and Bolivia. In these and other countries, abstract art has to a great extent replaced the social reformist or revolutionary interpretation of themes from Indian life as well as proletarian social motifs in general. In some of these countries, however, particularly in the highlands of Peru and Bolivia, many artists maintain their interest in the latter, to some degree abstracting or stylizing their images, but preserving indigenous appearance and nearly always emphasizing indigenous meaning. Nevertheless, although this trend continues, its representatives are isolated and little understood. International Modernism has prevailed and, as a result, the way has been opened to the development of many of the styles that have captured attention in principal foreign centers.

The long-standing interest in an "American art," however, continues to appeal to even the most articulate sponsors of international Modernism. Among the first and most important exponents of abstraction in the first postwar generation were Alejandro Obregón of Colombia, and Fernando de Szyszlo in Peru. Continuing to work in variants of the Cubist and Expressionist traditions respectively, they have been recently heralded in some quarters as the foremost younger representatives of a new American style, in part because of the freshness of their interpretation of American themes.

Similarly, the official Mexican school continues to emphasize indigenous values, although in terms of its more national definition of these values and of the formal norms established by Rivera and Siqueiros during the nineteen twenties and thirties.

Of the previous generation of artists who sought expression of indigenous meaning through modern international formal terms, the Mexican Rufino Tamayo, the Cuban Wifredo Lam, and Carlos Mérida, a Guatemalan also identified with Mexico, are the living patriarchal figures.

The latest movements on the international scene, Pop and Op, have evoked widespread interest in most South American countries. Except, however, for the work of Antúnez in Chile who as early as 1952 applied undulating checkerboard patterns to obtain the effect of vertigo, these movements have had success in only two countries. In Argentina, the work of Minujín, Carlos Squirru, and others, has achieved an authentic variation on Pop principles with strong overtones of social irony, while in Venezuela Otero and Soto have led the way in developing highly refined variants on retinal art.

The tradition of the Paris Salons has been resurrected since World War II in a new guise: the international biennial exhibition. These have so proliferated that their standing as arbiters may be in danger of dilution. In Latin America alone, there have been important biennial exhibitions in São Paulo, Mexico City, Córdoba, and Buenos Aires, not to speak of many important annual exhibitions. The large annual and biennial exhibitions set international standards of judgment today, just as the Paris Salons did in their day.

The tradition of patronage took a new lease on life with the establishment of important new museums and art galleries in São Paulo, Rio de Janeiro, Caracas, Buenos Aires, Lima, Bogotá, and Mexico City. This is partly the result of the participation of Latin American countries in prevailing international cultural competition, the arts today being regarded as an expression of national development and national pride. Large corporations and their foundations, notably the Instituto Torcuato Di Tella in Buenos Aires, International Petroleum in Colombia, Kaiser in Córdoba, and General Electric in Montevideo, have also entered the field of patronage of the arts, rivaling and, in some cases, taking over from the national and provincial governments.

Latin American artists from the late nineteenth century on have shared the concerns of their contemporaries in other countries over the problems of western man in a changing civilization. Since World War II, they have played an increasing part in efforts to explore and resolve these problems through redefinitions of reality based on new knowledge and the transfusion of their viewpoints, through art, into society. In the main, their efforts fall into two kinds of artistic statement: the formal and the social. In the first, with much of the rest of the world, they have approached renewal of value inwardly and experimentally, exploring the cohesive properties of nature on the plane of phenomenal existence; in the latter, perhaps more persistently than elsewhere, they have approached the same problem through artistically organized comment on and criticism of the outward forms of social organization, usually on the plane of subject matter. Both directions have been pursued now for over half a century, sometimes separately, sometimes overlapping, usually under the influence of ideological or long-standing cultural affinities, with multiplying adherents, and today with realism added to idealism. This activity is one of the most promising reflections of the beginning of a new era in Latin American cultural history. In the parallel concern of many Latin American artists for regional values, in the pride of being "American," it also anticipates the preservation of those special qualities of tradition, character, and talent of their magnificient part of this hemisphere. New conditions of communication have helped make it possible for them to make their presence felt on the world scene for the first time in history. This is a presence, all too belated, which can only augur well for the future development of art, creative thought, and culture generally.

S. L. C.

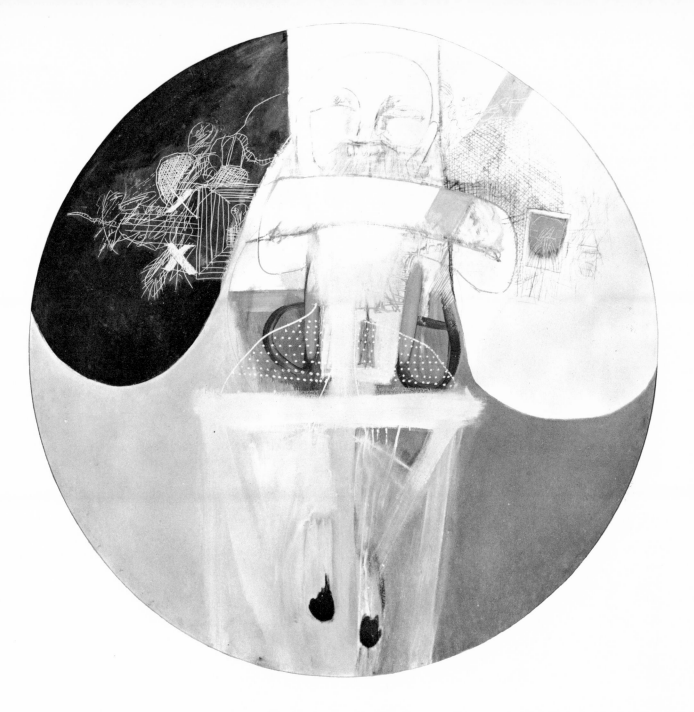

Plate 89. Macció. *To Live A Little Each Day*. 1963

Plate 89a. Macció. *To Live A Little Each Day*. (Detail) 1963

Plate 90. Obregón. *Carnivorous Flowers.*

Plate 91. Mabe. *Conquest of the Circle*. 1963 *(left)*

Plate 92. Morales. *Landscape*. 1964

Plate 93. Matta. *Birth of America.*

Plate 94. Renart. *Untitled*. 1964

Plate 95. Szyszlo. *Cajamarca*. 1963 (*left*)

Plate 96. Portocarrero. *Cathedral*. 1961

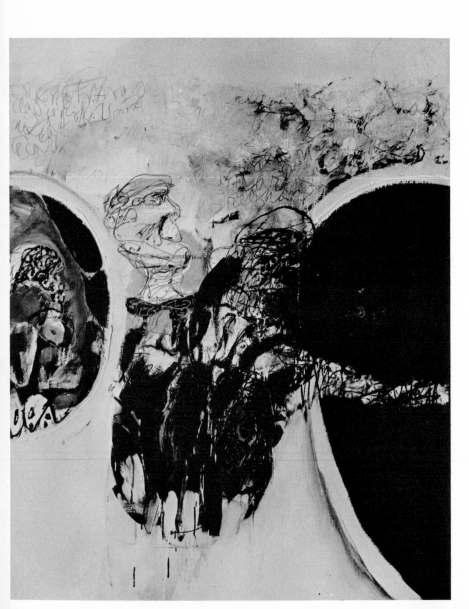

Plate 97. Deira. *Around Thought A (No. 2)*. 1964

Plate 98. Gerzso.
*Mythological Personage.* 1964

Plate 100. Caride. *Configuration. (right)*

Plate 99. Faz. *Stick Roast.* 1952

Plate 101. Arnal. *Tambo*. 1960

Plate 102. Souza. *Purgatory*. 1965

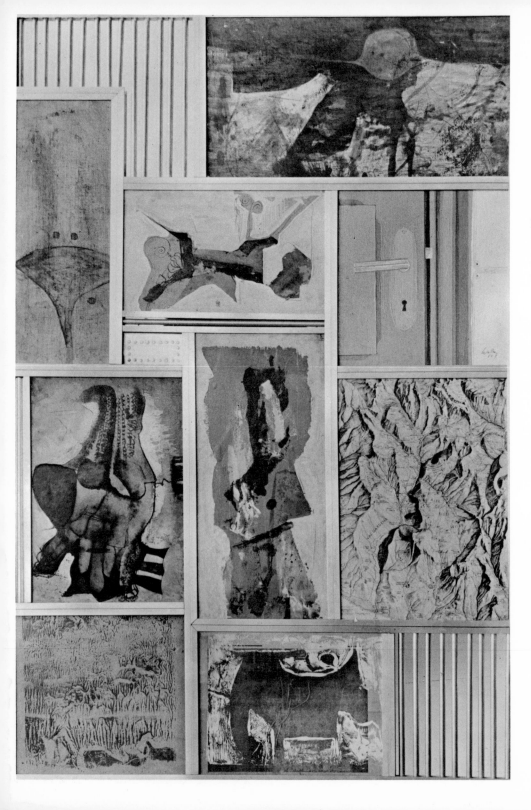

Plate 103. Lee. *Porta Factum*. 1965

Plate 104. Sabogal. *Dealer in Antiquaries.* 1949

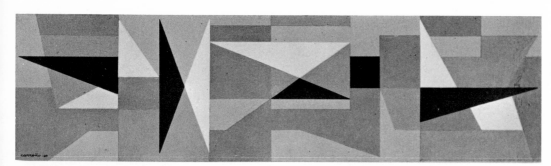

Plate 105. Carreño.
*Homage to Fra Angelico.* 1959

Plate 106. Pablo Burchard (Father).
*Landscape*. 1960

Plate 107. Goeldi. *Old Age*.

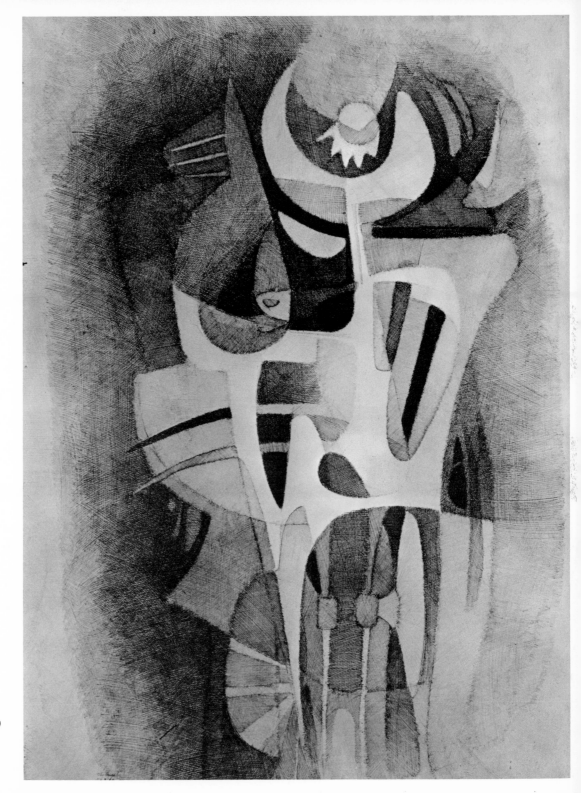

ate 108. Abularach. *Courtesan.* 1959

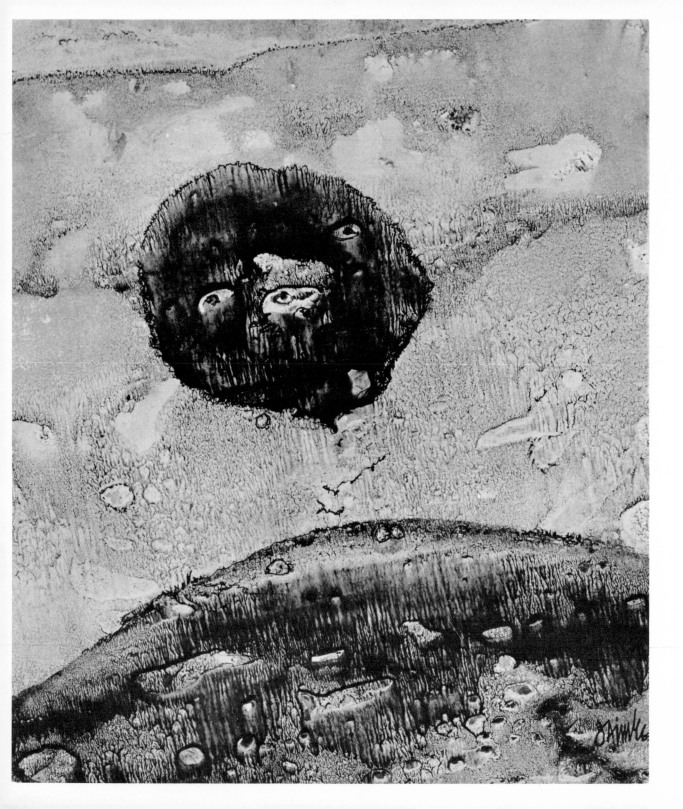

Plate 109. Jaime González. *Cover I for "Altazor" by Vicente Huidobro.* 1961 (*left*)

Plate 110. Grassmann. *Untitled.* 1961

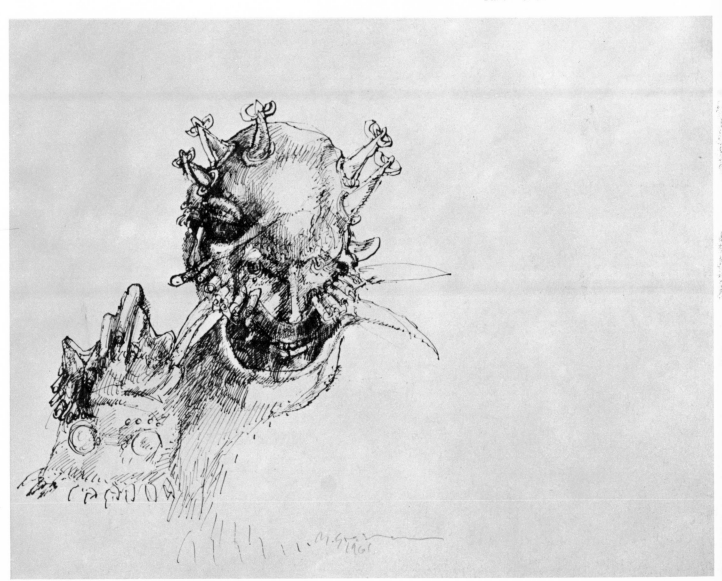

Plate 111. Carreño.
*Petrified World.* 1965

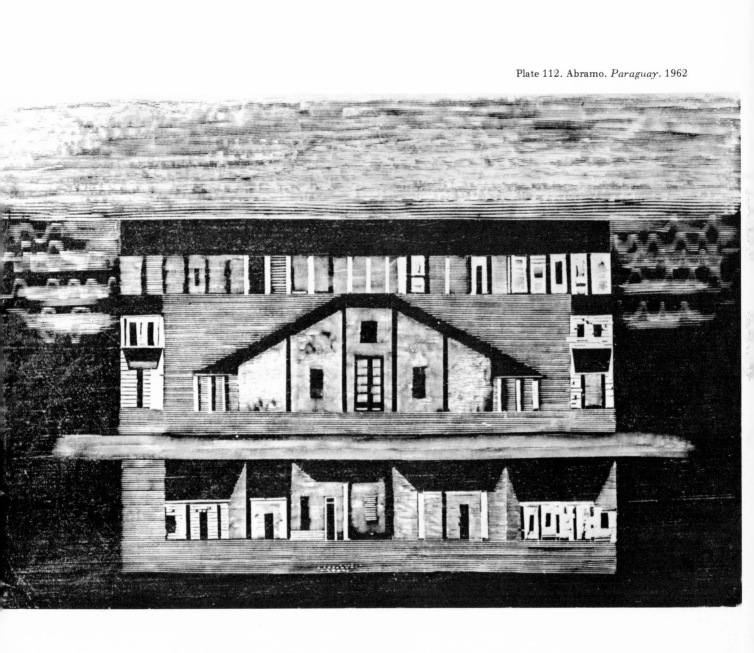

Plate 112. Abramo. *Paraguay*. 1962

Plate 113. Palacios. *Persistence of Rose.* 1964 *(left)*

Plate 114. Zachrisson. *Witch's Funeral.* 1963

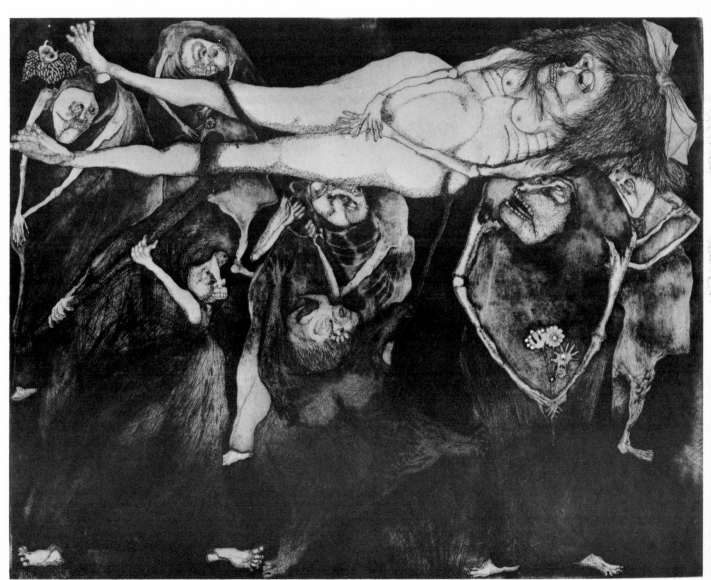

Plate 115. Fernández Muro. *Flag*. 1963 *(left)*

Plate 116. Hanné Gallo. *Maternity*. 1962

# Biographies

The biographical material in this section has been assembled and prepared by Yale graduate students under the supervision of Assistant Professor Terence Grieder of the University of Texas. Specific authorship is usually indicated by the following initials at the end of each entry:

DD  David Davidson, *History*
JD  John Deredita, *Spanish Literature*
CF  Charles Faulhaber, *Romance Philology*
TG  Terence Grieder

Biographies of several artists whose work is not represented in the exhibition are also included. Conversely, several artists whose works are included in the exhibition do not appear.

**Abarca, Agustín** [Talca, Chile, 1882 – Santiago de Chile, 1953]. Agustín Abarca grew up in the country, where he developed a lifelong love of landscape. He studied at the *liceo* in Talca and later became a clerk in the Tesorería Fiscal there. He became acquainted with the painter Pablo Burchard, who offered to teach him to paint. His supervisor in the Tesorería told him: "No sea loco, hombre, los pintores chilenos se mueren de hambre." In spite of this advice, he left his job to study art. In 1904 he went to Santiago and enrolled in the Academia of the Universidad Católica de Chile, where he was taught by Pedro Lira and Alberto Valenzuela Llanos. In 1907 he exhibited in the Santiago Salón de Independientes, and won first prize in drawing in the Academy show. This was the beginning of a long series of awards. In 1909 he returned to studies with Fernando Alvarez Sotomayor. He spent a period at Victoria, a fertile time for his art. Almost exclusively a landscape painter, Abarca's first love was the rugged hills of southern Chile. Among Chilean painters he is unusual in that he never studied in Europe. His style is nevertheless entirely in European tradition, following an Art Nouveau–Symbolist landscape style. He is notable for his color, poetic sensibility, and especially for his dramatic treatment of trees. TG

**Abramo, Livio** [São Paulo, 1903–    ]. Abramo, a self-taught artist, held his first one-man exhibit in 1942. In 1948 he exhibited in Rome and in 1950 in São Paulo. He won a coveted travel prize in the Annual Fine Arts Exhibit in Rio de Janeiro and took part in the first three São Paulo Bienals (1951–1955), as well as the Venice Biennials of 1950, 1952, and 1954. In 1953, at the 2nd São Paulo Bienal, Abramo won the first prize for Brazilian engravers. His work has been shown in Brazilian exhibitions in various parts of the world. DD

**Abularach, Rodolfo** [Guatemala, 1933–    ]. Rodolfo Abularach changed from architecture to painting during his studies at Pasadena, California. Later, in Mexico, he continued to study painting. After working in Guatemala, he returned to the United States on a fellowship. He presently works in New York. He has had six one-man shows and has participated in some twenty group exhibitions. His works are owned by numerous private collectors, as well as by the Museum of Modern Art in New York, the Museu de Arte Contemporánea of the University of São Paulo, and galleries in Washington, Guatemala City, and La Paz. TG

**Acuña, Luis Alberto** [Suaita, Colombia, 1904–    ]. Acuña left his home town to study sculpture at the Escuela de Bellas Artes in Bogotá. In 1924 he received a government grant to study in Paris. He spent six years in Europe traveling extensively. He worked formally at the Académie Colarossi with Bouchard and Landowsky. Returning to Bogotá in 1930 he taught at the Universidad Nacional. In 1938 he finished a book on the pre-Columbian art of Colombia. The following year he joined the Colombian mission in Mexico where he stayed three years. Acuña is now Director of the Museum of Colonial Art in Bogotá. He has also been Director of the Teatro Colón in the Colombian capital. Major influences on Acuña's work have been his early training as a sculptor and his stay in Mexico. His paintings have a quality of plasticity realized through divided brushwork and classical standards of compo-

157

sition and form and have long shown an interest in indigenous subject matter.   CF

**Adam, Alberto** [active Buenos Aires, 1867]. Nothing is known of this draftsman and lithographer except that he was active in Buenos Aires in 1867. Adam succeeded Enrique Meyer as illustrator for the newspaper *Correo del Domingo*, a position he held for only a few months.   TG

**Agostini, Ângelo** [Vercelli, Piedmont, Italy, 1843–1910]. Ângelo Agostini spent his childhood in Paris, where he studied painting before moving to São Paulo at the age of seventeen. His brilliant mind and generous spirit soon found themselves at home amid Brazil's idealistic younger generation, and he joined ardently in the campaign to abolish slavery. With Luiz Gama and Sizenando Nabuco, Agostini co-founded, in 1864, the satirical humor journal *Diabo Coxo* (*Lame Devil*), which enjoyed great success. The magazine, which later became known as *O Cabrião* (*The Billy Goat*), afforded Agostini a sounding board for his lively satire and mordant criticism of conditions of the day in Brazil. He succeeded as well in making numerous enemies in São Paulo and, after several reverses, he moved to Rio de Janeiro. There, in 1868, he founded *A Vida Fluminense* (*Life in Rio*), and later, *O Mosquito*. In 1876 he started the *Revista Ilustrada* where he created the popular character Zé Caipora. Agostini imparted to his painting the same verve and emotion that characterized his social satire and activism. His landscapes show a steady line, dense coloring, and poetic feeling for nature. Agostini's concern for Brazil – for its natural beauty as well as its social problems – earned him the respect of his contemporaries. In recognition of this concern, Joaquim Nabuco, one of Brazil's leading abolitionists and statesmen, told him: "Ângelo, in the name of your companions in the struggle [for abolition], in the name of liberty, in the name of Brazil, I declare you a Brazilian."   DD

**Aizenberg, Roberto** [Entre Rios, Argentina, 1928–    ]. Roberto Aizenberg studied from 1950–1953 with Juan Batlle Planas, the major exponent of surrealist art of his generation. Aizenberg follows in that tradition. He began exhibiting in 1954 and, since that time, has participated in numerous group shows. In 1958 he had a one-man show in the Galería Galatea. His work is generally small, exceedingly precise, with strong psychological overtones.   TG

**O Aleijadinho.** See: Lisboa, Antônio Francisco

**Alfaro Siqueiros, David** [Chihuahua, 1898–    ]. Siqueiros studied both at the Academia de Bellas Artes in Mexico City and at the Escuela de Pintura al Aire Libre in Santa Anita.

Afterward, in 1913, during the Mexican Revolution, he joined the faction of General Venustiano Carranza. Five years of military and political activity convinced him of the need for a fundamental change in the arts as well as in the social structure of Mexico. After Carranza became President of Mexico, Siqueiros was sent to Europe, where he engaged in diplomatic and artistic activities. He met Rivera in Paris, and in Madrid he founded a magazine, in which he published a "Manifesto to the Artists of America," urging the creation of a public, human and monumental art inspired in the example of the prehispanic cultures. He returned to Mexico in 1922 and became a leader of the Syndicate of Painters and Sculptors, publishing another Manifesto, which was the first voice of the muralist school. Siqueiros painted his first murals in the Escuela Nacional Preparatoria in 1922. Since 1924 he has been active in orthodox world Marxism, attending congresses in various parts of the world and acting as spokesman of social revolutionary theories in which art is allied to political action. He was an officer in the Spanish Republican Army in 1938. His political orientation has on occasion taken him to prison. Siqueiros' art has always projected revolutionary principles with fervor. Dissatisfied with the development of the mural movement, he went on to evolve a personal style in which landscapes and portraits as well as proletarian themes are rendered. On occasion he has with dramatic force made use of exaggerated perspective, surrealist themes, montage techniques, and various optical devices to heighten plastic effect and to reinforce ideological meaning.   JD

**Almeida Júnior, José Ferraz de** [Itú, Brazil, 1850 – Piracicaba, Brazil, 1889]. José Ferraz de Almeida Júnior's gift for sketching and painting became evident in childhood. Of poor parents, he grew up in the countryside among simple folk, where he was imbued with a strong love of his nation, its customs, and its historic legends. This *alma brasileira* later found expression in the themes of his painting. In 1869 Almeida Júnior entered the Académia de Belas Artes in Rio de Janeiro, where he studied with Julio Le Chevrel and Vítor Meirelles. He was awarded a gold medal upon his graduation in 1872 and, three years later, received a stipend for European study from the Emperor Dom Pedro II, who met the painter on a visit to Itú. In 1876, Almeida Júnior went to Paris to study with Alexandre Cabanel of the Académie des Beaux Arts. After six years of serious study, nostalgia for his homeland led him to return to Brazil. Almeida Júnior's passionate love of homeland is reflected in the lyrical mood of his landscapes and paintings of daily life. His *Caipiras negaceando* (*Backwoodsmen Setting Traps*), *Picando fumo* (*Chopping Tobacco*), and *Amalação interrompida* suggest a current of telluric mysticism that flows just beneath the surface of his fundamentally academic style and realistic subject matter. His works exude a realistic odor of red earth and virgin forest, which is conveyed with romantic élan. The painter was murdered while at work at his easel in Piracicaba on November 13, 1889.  DD

**Alonso, Carlos** [Mendoza, Argentina, 1929–     ]. Carlos Alonso is known both as draughtsman and painter. He studied with Gómez Cornet and, for a somewhat longer time, with Spilimbergo. In 1957, he was honored by an award from the Emecé publishers, Buenos Aires, to illustrate the second part of their publication of *Don Quixote*. His recent work has turned toward earth-colored figure compositions that lean toward abstraction. There has been a continuing tendency toward social comment in his art.  TG

**do Amaral, Tarsila** [Born Capivarí, São Paulo, active since 1920s]. Tarsila do Amaral began her studies in drawing and painting with Pedro Alexandrino and Elpons in São Paulo. In 1920 she went to Europe and studied in Paris with Emile Rénard at the Académie Julien, and later with Lhote, Gleizes, and Léger, from whom she learned the basic tenets of Cubism. Tarsila exhibited her first painting in 1922 in the Salon des Artistes Français. She had her first one-man show in Paris in 1926 at the Galerie Percier. On this occasion she won praise from numerous reviewers, and was honored by having one of her works bought by the Grenoble Museum. Tarsila had a second exhibition in Paris in 1928, in which she displayed her "*antropofágica*" composition *O Aboropú*, a Cubist interpretation of Brazilian themes. *Antropofagismo*, or Cannibalism, was soon adopted by such Brazilian intellectuals as Oswald de Andrade, Raúl Bopp, Guilherme de Almeida, and many other leading avant-garde figures, as the keynote for one phase of Brazil's nativist, ultramodern movement in arts and letters, the social sciences, and politics.  DD

**Américo de Figueiredo e Melo, Pedro** [Paraíba do Norte, Brazil, 1843 – Florence, Italy, 1905]. Born of a cultured family, Pedro Américo was something of a child prodigy, painting at the age of seven, and being appointed by the President of his province as official sketcher for a scientific commission at the age of nine. In 1856 he entered the Académia de Belas Artes in Rio de Janeiro, where he was recognized as a brilliant student. Three years later, with the aid of Emperor Pedro II, he went to Paris. There he studied with Ingres, Cognat, Flandrin, and later, Horace Vernet. His insatiable appetite for learning and travel took him later to Florence and England before he returned to Brazil in 1864, when he was awarded the chair of drawing at the Académia. In 1865 he went back to Europe where, again, he traveled extensively. During this time he wrote *O Holocausto*, a philosophic novel criticizing Brazilian customs and institutions. Again in Paris, the artist encountered severe financial problems and was forced to sell many of his medals and awards, even facing arrest when the police suspected that he had stolen them. Pedro Américo then moved to Brussels, sketching in cafés to support his studies at the University of Brussels, where, in 1868, he received the degree of Doctor of Natural Sciences. During the next three decades, on various trips between Paris, Florence, and Brazil, he continued to write on a wide range of subjects and to exhibit his paintings on both continents. In 1890, he was elected to the Constituent Assembly of the new Brazilian Republic. Not long afterwards, he retired in Florence. Pedro Américo was one of the outstanding figures in Brazilian art of the nineteenth century. A master of composition, he fluently designed sweeping historical themes on canvases of immense proportions. He favored biblical, as well as historical subjects, and an heroic mode. His colors were joyful, as in *Rabequista árabe* (*Arab Fiddler*), and at times luminous. The success of his work and his imaginative spirit made Pedro Américo the most popular Brazilian artist of his time.  DD

**Amoêdo, Rodolfo** [Rio de Janeiro, Brazil, 1857–1941]. Although the son of a poor Portuguese actor, Rodolfo Amoêdo managed to acquire his schooling at the Colégios Vitório and Pedro II in Rio de Janeiro. His need for money led him to take a job with Albino Gonçalves, a "pintor de letras," with whom Amoêdo first developed his talent for drawing. In 1873 he entered the Liceu de Artes e Ofícios under the tutelage of Sousa Lôbo and Vítor Meirelles, transferring in the following year to the Académia de Belas Artes, where he received instruction in painting from Zeferino da Costa and Agostinho da Mota. Amoêdo's *O sacrifício de Âbel* (1878) won for him a trip to Paris and the opportunity to study with Cabanel, Paul Baudry, and Puvis de Chavannes. He returned to Brazil in 1890, after a productive period during which three of his oils were exhibited in various Salons in Paris. On his return he was first named Professor of Painting and later Director of the Escola Nacional de Belas Artes. His continued activity in Brazil earned for him a prize at the Chicago Exposition of 1893 and a Medal of Honor at the Brazilian Exposição Geral of 1917. He also decorated the foyer of the Teatro Municipal, the Biblioteca Nacional, the Palácio do Itamarati, the Casa da Moeda, and the Supremo Tribunal, all in Rio de Janeiro. Considered one of the leading Brazilian artists of his time, Amoêdo is perhaps best appreciated for his mastery of technique and his ability to achieve a harmonious equilibrium of tonalities within the bounds of French academic realism.   DD

**Antúnez, Nemesio** [Santiago, Chile, 1918–    ]. Like many of Chile's contemporary artists, Nemesio Antúnez received his basic training in the School of Architecture of the Universidad Católica de Chile in Santiago. In 1943 he went to New York City to study architecture at Columbia University, and to work under and later to assist Stanley Hayter in his Workshop 17. When Hayter moved to Paris in 1950, Antúnez went with him. He returned to Chile in 1953 and, three years later, organized the Taller 99 in Santiago. In 1962 he became Director of the Museo de Arte Contemporáneo of the Universidad de Chile. He is presently serving as Cultural Attaché of the Chilean Embassy in the United States. Antúnez has been a restless artist of unusual lyric sensibility. His art has echoed the work of his countryman, Roberto Matta, and also that of Paul Klee, of Surrealism and Neorealism, in the process of acquiring a style of his own. Working in oils, watercolors, and engraving, he has examined minute parts of natural objects and telescoped immense natural processes to achieve, in both cases, a near abstract art expressed in the plastic dynamism of unstable planes and converging lines. In his "Earthquake" mural in the Nilo cinema, Santiago (1958), he anticipates the effects of Op art, although his purpose is expressionistic rather than retinal.   CF

**Arnal, Enrique** [Catari, Bolivia, 1932–    ]. Arnal, a self-taught painter, has lived in Argentina, Chile, and France. He now works in La Paz. In 1955 he participated in the 3rd Bienal of São Paulo. In the same year he received the Grand Prize for Painting in the Salon of Bolivian Art.   CF

**Arrieta, José Agustín** [Puebla, Mexico, 1802–1879]. Arrieta is perhaps the best known of the painters of Puebla, where he studied the academic style at the Academia de Bellas Artes. His paintings present typical Mexican costumbrista themes, particularly the customs of his native city. He has a good sense of composition and he seems to delight in close descriptions of objects and social types.   DD

**Baca-Flor, Carlos** [Islay, Chile, 1867 – Neuilly-sur-Seine, France, 1941]. Although Baca-Flor spent only eight years of his life in Peru, he considered himself Peruvian, and is so considered by Peruvians. He was born in the little port town of Islay, then in Peru. When the town was closed in 1871, the family moved to Santiago, Chile. At the age of fifteen, he entered the School of Fine Arts where he studied for five years under the Italian Giovanni Mochi, and the Chilean Cosme San Martín. In 1887 he was awarded a scholarship to study in Rome on condition that he give up his Peruvian citizenship. Baca-Flor refused, and shortly thereafter moved to Lima. He became intimate with the high society of the city, and painted members of the family of President Cáceres. He began to specialize in the portraiture that was to make him famous. In 1890 he was awarded six thousand *soles* by the Peruvian government to study in Rome. He left immediately, accompanied by his mother, and he never returned to Peru. In Rome, Baca-Flor studied under the Spanish artist Pradilla in the Royal Academy of Fine Arts. Unable to support his mother, he sent her home, then moved to Paris in 1893 where he continued his studies under Jean-Paul Laurens and Benjamin Constant. He stayed there perfecting his technique, refusing all commissions until 1907, when one of his portraits won first prize in the Salon des Artistes. Fame swiftly followed. J. P. Morgan commissioned a portrait, agreeing to pay the artist's passage to the United States in order to complete the sittings which Baca-Flor felt were necessary. In the remaining thirty-odd years of his life, the artist traveled extensively in Europe, producing one hundred and fifty portraits for each of which he received approximately $20,000. Among his subjects was Eugenio Pacelli, later Pope Pius XII. Baca-Flor's detractors usually grant that he painted "technically competent portraits"; but they are more than that. His composition is generally impeccable and at times brilliant. He frequently achieved an amazing physical resemblance. Except for several excellent informal oil sketches of student colleagues and Parisian cafe and theater life now in the Lima Museo de Arte, Baca-Flor ignored the artistic currents of his time, remaining content to practice his technical mastery according to accepted 19th-century canons.   TG

**Bacle, César Hipólito** [Versoix, Switzerland, 1794 – Argentina, 1838]. Bacle arrived in Buenos Aires about 1828 and, with his wife, immediately opened a printing establishment. The enterprise proved successful and, within a year, the Bacles became official lithographers to the national government. One production of outstanding quality is *Trajes y Costumbres de la Provincia de Buenos Aires* (1833). Frequent difficulties with the Argentine government led Bacle to consider moving to Chile, a move prevented by his arrest, on false evidence, by the dictator Rosas. Bacle was imprisoned from March 4, 1837, to the end of that year, when he was released without explanation. His imprisonment had completely broken his health, however, and he died on January 4, 1838, a few days after his release. His contribution to Argentine art and cultural life during the early years following Independence was considerable.  TG

**Barradas, Rafael Pérez** [Montevideo, 1890 – Montevideo, 1928]. Son of the painter, Antonio Pérez Barradas, Rafael Barradas shared the artistic leanings of his father and began to paint at an early age. After a brief career in journalism, during which time he founded the periodical *El Monigote*, Barradas left for Europe in 1913, visiting Italy, France, and Switzerland. He settled in Spain where he held exhibitions in Zaragoza, Barcelona, and Madrid, and became a member of a group of Spanish intellectuals that included Ignacio Zuloaga and Joaquín Torres García. Barradas also did numerous illustrations for journals and books, as well as backdrops for productions in the Teatro de Arte. In 1923 he sent three of his works to the Salon de Primavera, organized by the Círculo de Bellas Artes in Montevideo, and in 1925 entered the International Exposition of Paris. In failing health, Barradas returned to Montevideo in 1928, where he died a few months after his arrival. Rafaél Barradas' work is intensely personal. Although he participated in the European currents of artistic innovation of the first quarter of the century, he developed his own particular forms of expression, as in his *Vibrationism*, *Clownism*, and *Mystic Painting*. It is likely that he had an influence on the art of his friend and companion in Spain, Joaquín Torres García. His drawings, caricatures, illustrations, and oils reveal a depth of bitterness beneath his frequent humor.  DD

**Barreda, Ernesto** [Paris, 1927–   ]. Born abroad of Chilean parents, Ernesto Barreda returned to Chile for his education, graduating in 1952 from the Escuela de Arquitectura de la Universidad Católica de Chile. He began exhibiting in 1947 in Santiago and won international notice in the late 1950s through exhibitions in Buenos Aires and New York. He was named Chilean Painter of the Year by the Association of Chilean Art Critics in 1960. In 1962 he was awarded second prize in the 1st American Biennial at Córdoba, Argentina. He is best known for his tortured paintings of dilapidated buildings and architectural features such as doors and windows. He works in oil, within a limited range of very dark colors, sometimes characterized by strong highlights, giving an effect of apparition to irrevocably dead and abandoned objects, perhaps an Existentialist interpretation of human condition.  CF

**Bayot, Adolphe Jean-Baptiste** [Alessandria, Italy, 1810– ? ]. This genre painter and lithographer of costumbrista views did all of his work in France, where he exhibited in the Paris Salons from 1863 to 1866.  CF

**Baz, Ignacio** [Tucumán, Argentina, c. 1820–1887]. Born in Tucumán about 1820, Ignacio Baz was interested in art from childhood. His father brought him and his brother to study art with Pablo Caccianiga at the University of Buenos Aires, where, in 1835, he won a drawing prize. His studies there may have been interrupted by Rosas' closing of the school the same year. Later Baz returned to Tucumán. He was settled in Córdoba by 1845, then went back to his home town when his father died. Between 1847 and 1860, he spent short periods in Buenos Aires, in Chile, and in Lima, supporting himself by painting portraits. Traveling outside the country to escape the tyranny of the Rosas regime, many of Baz's portraits are of fellow refugees, although he did draw the striking head of the dictator in this exhibition. From 1860 until his death in 1887 he settled in Tucumán, earning his living by painting portraits and by teaching as professor of drawing in the Colegio Nacional de Tucumán. His ability as a miniaturist is reflected in the precision of his portraits in larger scale. Baz's portraits are done both in pencil and in oil.  TG

**Berni, Antonio** [Rosario, Argentina, 1905–   ]. Antonio Berni studied art in Rosario until the Jockey Club of that city gave him a scholarship to study abroad. This was continued by the government of Santa Fe Province. He went to Europe in 1925, traveled in several countries, and finally settled in Paris where he studied with Othon Friesz and André Lhote until 1931. Berni's earliest paintings were impressionist landscapes. However, his Parisian training produced a sculpturesque style, based on the Purist and Cubist influences of his teachers. This first became apparent in the paintings he sent to the National Salon in Buenos Aires in 1927. In 1941 Berni was sponsored by the Comisión Nacional de Cultura to engage in studies of pre-Columbian art and to paint American themes. From a visit to Peru, Mexico, Bolivia, and the United States, he produced a number of paintings of Indian life. An influential figure in Argentina, he has been president of the Asociación Argentina de Artistas Plásticas, and taught from 1936 to 1951 in the Escuela Nacional de Bellas Artes M. Belgrano. Continuous renewal has marked his style in recent years. He has realized group portraits of proletarian families in a paint-collage technique carried out on a very large scale, comic collage subjects, and large relief and intaglio prints, impressing found-subjects to produce both inked and embossed designs of striking impact. TG

**Besnes e Yrigoyen, Juan Manuel** [Spain, 1788 – Uruguay, 1865]. Juan Manuel Besnes e Irigoyen, a native of the Basque country in Spain, arrived in Uruguay in 1809, a skilled calligrapher and filigranist. He was instrumental in the promotion of social services in the nascent Uruguayan Republic, dedicating himself to the advancement of elementary education, charities, orphanages, and the establishment of Lancaster schools. In addition, he became a founding member of the Institute of Public Instruction and vice-president of the Commission of Public Instruction. In 1850 he was made a member of the Consejo de Notables, and in 1856 the president of the Topographic Commission. He also found the time to serve in the military, teach drawing, and act as inspector of public schools. Besnes e Irigoyen left a large collection of watercolors, sketches, and lithographs of Montevideo and its surrounding countryside, a record also of the development of the city. His rural scenes, views of gaucho and ranch life and of the taming of wild horses, had a formative influence on the young Juan Manuel Blanes, Uruguay's first great artist, as well as on a whole generation of Uruguayan costumbristas. He did many oils, a number of watercolor portraits and caricatures on historical subjects and military themes, and several elaborate calligraphic compositions which he donated to the young Museo de Bellas Artes. In 1946 the Uruguayan government organized a commemorative exhibition of his works. DD

**Blanes, Juan Manuel** [Montevideo, 1830 – Florence, Italy, 1901]. Juan Manuel Blanes was the founder of Uruguayan painting. Blanes taught himself to draw while still a child, and began to paint while working as a typographer for the Uruguayan daily, *El Defensor de la Independencia Americana*. In 1860 the Uruguayan government recognized the young painter's talents and awarded him a stipend for study in Europe. After studying with Antonio Ciseri in Florence, Blanes returned to Uruguay where he worked tirelessly on canvases depicting the heroes and episodes of his country's history. Blanes returned to Europe in 1879, 1880, and 1898, and he also visited parts of Chile and Argentina. He died in Florence during his last trip to Europe. Blanes exhibited works in the Exposición de Santiago de Chile in 1875, and in the Exposición Continental de Buenos Aires in 1882. In 1884 he decorated the rotunda of the Cementerio Central, and later, at the request of the Dirección General de Correos, painted *El Gauchito*, which figured in stamps issued in 1895–1896 and 1897. His works are found in museums throughout Argentina and Uruguay. His *La Fiebre amarilla* (*Yellow Fever*), depicting the terrible epidemic of yellow fever that ravaged Buenos Aires in 1857, was received with acclaim in that city. Blanes also received critical acclaim in Santiago de Chile where the paintings *La Revista de Rancagua* and *Los ultimos movimientos de Carrera*, were exhibited. Juan Manuel Blanes was Uruguay's first painter and one of its greatest. His oeuvre includes historical paintings, portraits, and scenes characteristic of his country's customs and human types. He displays a mastery of technique, a balanced light and color, and above all, a sense of the character and reality of his subject matter. DD

**Blanes Viale, Pedro** [Mercedes, Uruguay, 1879 – Montevideo, 1926]. Pedro Blanes Viale took his first lessons in drawing and painting as a child with the Catalonian artist Jaume y Bosch. He moved to Spain with his entire family to study at Madrid's Academia de San Fernando. He later frequented the workshop of Joaquín Sorolla, then went to Paris to study in the Académie Benjamin Constant. In 1899, after traveling through Italy and Mallorca, he returned to Uruguay where he discovered and painted the landscape of his native land. He soon returned to Paris where he established a workshop and studied with enthusiasm the work of Puvis de Chavannes, Lucien Simon, Henri Martin, and Whistler. He developed a deep respect for Impressionism, the Italian Renaissance masters, and the Spaniards, El Greco and Velázquez. He is one of the most accomplished American exponents of luministic painting, a variety of Impressionism which had a wide following in Latin America. Blanes Viales is most remembered for the sympathetic reflection of benign aspects of nature. His landscapes record with shimmering freshness the fields, rustic settlements, and the gardens of ranches and farms that surrounded Montevideo in his day. They have been called "symphonies of color" in which light and color, as well as a sense of ambience and time, clothe a subtle geometry. DD

**Blas, Camilo** [Cajamarca, Peru, 1903 –      ]. Blas studied in the Escuela Nacional de Bellas Artes in Lima, where he later became a teacher. He served as artist for the Museo de Arqueología Peruana, which led him to work with indigenous Peruvian motifs and styles. Between 1925 and 1927 he studied in Cuzco with José Sabogal, learning about that highland region and its people, the descendants of Inca civilization. The result of this experience was twofold: his personal style was strongly influenced by Sabogal's simplified social and ethnic realism, and with Sabogal he helped describe horizons for a new Peruvian art based on Indian values. The work of Camilo Blas was widely exhibited during the 1930s and '40s: in Seville, at the 1937 International Exposition in Paris, in San Francisco, and in New York.　TG

**Boggio, Emilio** [La Guaira, Venezuela, 1857 – Venezuela, 1920]. Half-French and half-Venezuelan, Boggio went to France at the age of fifteen to complete his general education, then returned to Venezuela to enter business. Interest in art caused him to return to France, where he enrolled in the Académie Julien and worked under Jean-Paul Laurens and later Henri Martin. Boggio spent most of the rest of his life in France and Italy, returning to Venezuela the year before his death. A friend of Sisley and Pissarro, Boggio first exhibited in the 1887 Salon des Artistes Français. His style went from the academism of Laurens through Impressionism to an almost Pointillist technique. His themes changed from religious works and interiors full of chiaroscuro to landscapes painted in the open air.　CF

**Borges, Jacobo** [Caracas, 1931 –　　]. Jacobo Borges received his early artistic schooling in the Escuela de Artes Plásticas of Caracas between 1949 and 1951. In the latter year he transferred to the Taller Libre de Arte. In 1952 he was awarded a fellowship to study at the Salon de Jeunes Artistes of the Musée de l'Art Moderne of Paris. He remained in Paris until 1956, when he returned to Caracas and held a one-man show. He has won prizes in Venezuelan and international exhibitions with regularity since 1957, when he received Honorable Mention at the 4th São Paulo Bienal. In addition to his main work in oils, he has designed settings for a number of plays produced in Venezuela, among them Tennessee Williams' *Glass Menagerie* and García Lorca's *Blood Wedding*. Starting with the idea of the artist as a person with social responsibilities, Borges has evolved toward a figurative expressionism reflecting various influences: Goya, Daumier, Picasso, José Luis Cuevas, and de Kooning, from the latter's famous series on Women. Nonideological, he seeks to bring to painting the general significance of reality and to express the humiliation of the individual in mass society.　CF

**Botero, Fernando** [Colombia, 1932–　　]. Fernando Botero began his studies in Colombia and later continued them in Italy, France, and Spain. He has a long record of exhibitions all over the world: New York, Venice, São Paulo, to mention a few. He has received eight major awards. His style, of a distinctively massive and grandiose representational character, in which emphasis on the grotesque is relieved by gently hu-

morous satire and by an ingratiating plastic and color sensibility, has remained consistent, identifiable, and independent of international trends.　TG

**Brambila, Fernando** [Milan, Italy, ? – Madrid, 1832]. Brambila joined the Malaspina Expedition at Acapulco, Mexico, in 1791. During the long voyage of this last exploratory mission sponsored by the Spanish Crown, Brambila produced many drawings, water colors, and prints, among them views of Buenos Aires. His later life was spent in Spain, where he produced paintings and a series of prints.　TG

**Bru, Roser** [Barcelona, Spain, 1923–　　]. Roser Bru moved to Chile after the final collapse of the Republican army during the Spanish Civil War in 1939. She worked and studied in Santiago's Escuela de Bellas Artes. Married in 1942, she continued her artistic work in watercolor, fresco, and painting. However, recognition came slowly. She held her first exhibition in 1955 and, in the following year, worked in Nemesio Antúnez's Taller 99. One-man shows in Mexico City, Bonn, Barcelona, and Stuttgart followed, along with prizes in Barcelona (1958), Santiago (1959, 1960) and at the 1st American Biennial, Córdoba, Argentina (1962). In 1960 she was commissioned to do a large mural for the Liceo del Coronal in Santiago. Señorita Bru currently prefers to work in the graphic arts, in which she increasingly emphasizes texture and line. Her favorite subject is the human figure, particularly that of women engaged in domestic occupations.　CF

**Burchard, Pablo** [Santiago, 1873 – Santiago, 1960]. Pablo Burchard, Padre, studied architecture with his father, Teodoro, who introduced the Gothic Revival into Chile around 1855. The son studied painting with Pedro Lira and Miguel Campos in the Escuela de Bellas Artes of Santiago. Later he was influenced by the Impressionistic style of Juan Francisco González. Although Burchard never left Santiago until late in life, he was surprisingly open to European innovations. He became the leader of the Montparnasse group of Chilean artists. His style evolved from Impressionism through Constructivism to a refined Fauvism – simple colors, abstract harmonies, and virtual suppression of subject matter. In 1903 he became Professor of Drawing in Talca and later moved to the Escuela de Bellas Artes, which he directed from 1932 to 1935. His long activity in Chilean art was at last rewarded with the Prize of Honor at the Santiago Centenary Exhibition in 1941 and with the National Art Prize in 1944. Of exquisite sensibility within his range of pale hues, which he controls with true instinct for lyric character, Burchard Padre is one of the foremost exponents of American painting in the Post-Impressionistic spirit. CF

**Burchard, Pablo A.** [Santiago de Chile, 1919–    ]. Pablo A. Burchard, Hijo, the son of the renowned Chilean artist, Pablo Burchard, studied at the Universidad Católica de Chile and in the United States under Abraham Rattner. His first mature easel works showed themes reflecting the monotony of suburbia and the poverty of cities. These are exposed with expressionistic pathos. Burchard's expressive spirit was compassionate but pessimistic. During the 1950s, he began to move from Neorealism to a less representational art. He maintained his preoccupation with pathetic themes, but sought now to evoke them more abstractly. Among the fruits of this style are the mysterious and forbidding forms in *Darkness in the Earth* (1959) and the dynamic expressionism of *Fire Abyss* (1961). He has executed several large mural paintings in public areas of Santiago, including The Banco Central. Burchard has had one-man exhibits in Chile and the United States. He continues to work as an architect and is Professor of Architecture at the Universidad Católica de Chile. JD

**Burle Marx, Roberto** [São Paulo, 1909–    ]. Burle Marx grew up in Rio de Janeiro and, at the age of nineteen, was sent to school in Berlin. In Europe, Burle Marx discovered the works of Picasso, Klee, and Kandinsky, and was deeply impressed by them as well as by the Dahlem Botanical Garden of Berlin, which exhibited Brazilian plants he had never seen before. In 1930 he returned to Rio, enrolled in the School of Fine Arts, and began to build his own botanical collection with a special interest in the visual effects of the plants. The architect and city planner, Lúcio Costa, a neighbor of the Marx family, arranged for Roberto Burle Marx to design a garden in 1933. The design was so successful that many other commissions followed, including the design for the public gardens of Recife. In 1937 he collaborated with Portinari on murals for the new Ministry of Education building, for which Burle Marx also designed the gardens. A bachelor, Burle Marx resides in Leme, a suburb of Rio de Janeiro, where he is considered the indispensable designer of gardens. In 1948 he was a representative from Brazil at the Venice Biennial and has since been awarded many honors and important commissions, including the American Institute of Architects Fine Arts Medal in 1965. TG

**Butler, Horacio** [Argentina, 1897–    ]. This noted Argentine painter studied first in the Academia Nacional de Bellas Artes and then in Europe, where he seems to have been repelled by avant-garde art and its forerunners, with the exception of Cézanne. He spent six months studying in Germany, but returned to Paris, where he spent his formative years working under Othon Friesz and the Cubist, André Lhote. In Argentina, Butler is regarded as one of the most important painters of his generation. For the most part, his subjects are figures, genre, and landscapes, often based on the life and surroundings of El Tigre, a picturesque middle-class suburb of Buenos Aires that still preserves its late Victorian character. *La Despedida* (*The Farewell*) (1938) has a strong synthetic Cubist or Purist base that gives presence to natural appearance invested with nostalgic human association. Recently he has made quilted hangings of sewn cloth, also based on El Tigre themes. TG

**Cabré, Manuel** [Caracas, 1890–    ]. Born into a family of artists – both of his parents were sculptors – Cabré received his early training at the Academia de Bellas Artes in Caracas. He was a member of the School of Caracas, an anti-academic group established about 1913, and later studied at the Académie des Beaux-Arts in Paris during the 1920s. The artist's major theme is the valley of Caracas in all its moods and weathers. He is particularly sensitive to the play of color in landscape; but his coloristic tendencies are restrained by a rigorous sense of form and composition. CF

**Cabrera, Roberto** [Guatemala City, 1939–    ]. Roberto Cabrera studied at the Escuela Nacional de Bellas Artes in Guatemala and received scholarships for study in Panama and Mexico. He is active both in painting and in printmaking, has exhibited and has received prizes in numerous international shows, including an honorable mention in São Paulo and a first prize in painting in the Valencia International Salon. He teaches at the Universidad Popular in Guatemala. TG

**Calder, Alexander** [Philadelphia, Pa., U.S.A., 1898–    ]. Alexander Calder, who executed the ceiling baffles for Carlos Raúl Villanueva's Aula Magna in the Ciudad Universitaria of Caracas, went to Stevens Institute of Technology, graduating in 1919. Following in the family tradition – both his father and grandfather were sculptors and his mother a painter – Calder studied drawing at night school in New York and later at the Art Students League. In 1926 he went to Paris and began to work with wire sculpture. In 1931 he experimented with abstract figures in motion. He returned to America in 1933 and settled on a farm near Roxbury, Connecticut. It was Marcel Duchamp who gave Calder's moving sculptures the name "mobiles." In the mid-1930s, Calder developed his best-known variant of this genial art form, the hanging mobile, a flexible arrangement of biomorphic metal shapes in suspension, balanced to respond to shifting air currents. Later he evolved sculptural compositions of metal planes in fixed rather than mobile arrangement, calling them "stabiles." In the ceiling for the Aula Magna, Calder utilizes giant organic shapes in controlled suspension, thus serving acoustical as well as aesthetic ends.  CF

**Camino Brent, Enrique** [Lima, Peru, 1909-1960?]. Enrique Camino Brent studied under José Sabogal at the Escuela Nacional de Bellas Artes and later became Professor of Drawing and Painting there. During his career he has had exhibitions in Buenos Aires, Santiago de Chile, and Lima and was a member of the National Council for Conservation and Restoration of Historical Monuments. Like most of Sabogal's pupils, Camino Brent is an indigenist painter. His subjects, the Peruvian Indians of the Andes and their highland villages and landscape, are painted with a freshness of color and with a native eye for character. He is the most optimistic and least tragic of the painters of his school.  CF

**Caride, Miguel P.** [Buenos Aires, Argentina, 1920–     ]. Caride is a self-taught artist who has shown in the Argentine National Salons since 1950. He has also had several one-man shows in Buenos Aires, including those in the Galería Rubio, in the Museo Histórico y de Arte in Morón, and in the Galería Rubbers. He is one of the most accomplished of the surrealist painters of Latin America today.  TG

**Carreño, Mario** [Havana, 1913–     ]. Carreño studied at the Academia San Alejandro in Cuba until 1932, when he left for Madrid. He spent three years there, traveled briefly to Mexico, and then lived in Paris from 1937 to 1939. The outbreak of World War II sent him back to Cuba by way of the United States. In 1944 he returned to New York to become a professor of painting at the New School for Social Research, a post he held until 1948. He has been living in Chile since 1958.  CF

**Carrera, José Miguel** [1785–1821]. Under the pretense of heading off a royalist plot to restore colonial rule to Chile, Carrera seized dictatorial power in 1811 and ruled until 1813 as the first President of Chile. Bernardo O'Higgins and other members of the Chilean aristocracy revolted against him and the two factions carried on a series of skirmishes until the approach of Spanish troops caused them to bury their differences and join forces. They met the Spanish at Rancagua in 1814 and were soundly defeated. Both sought safety across the Andes in Mendoza, Argentina. Carrera was subsequently banished to Buenos Aires and never returned to Chile. During 1815–1816 he went to the United States, secured three ships and some volunteers, but was blocked by Argentine authorities when he attempted to land in Buenos Aires. He and his two brothers were executed in Mendoza, probably on O'Higgins' orders, after having participated in the opening phases of the Argentine civil wars. Little is known about his artistic career except for a number of caricatures of contemporary figures traditionally attributed to him.  CF

**Carril, Delia del** [Argentina, ? –     ]. After leaving Argentina, Delia del Carril studied in Paris and later in Chile, where she worked in the Universidad Católica's Taller 99. She has had one-man exhibitions in Santiago, Buenos Aires, Paris, and Moscow. She works chiefly in drawing and printmaking.  CF

**Carvalho, Flávio de Rezende** [São Paulo, Brazil, 1899–     ]. Flávio de Carvalho, who began his studies in Paris and London, has led a rich and variegated life as an artist, designer, architect, social psychologist, playwright, civil engineer, and essayist. His work in architecture won him recognition as the initiator of modern architecture in Brazil, and Le Corbusier's praise as a "revolutionnaire Romantique." In the early 1950s, he became a critic of painting and dance, and then dedicated himself to the study of psychology, which resulted in his book *Experiência no. 2*. In 1931 Flávio de Carvalho dedicated himself to painting and sculpture and exhibited in the Salão Nacional de Belas Artes. In 1932, he won a prize for his *Monumento do Soldado Constitucionalista*, and was a founder of the Clube dos Artistas Modernos. The following year he founded the Teatro da Experiência, which was closed by the police after a few showings of his play, *O Bailado do Deus Morto*. In 1934 Flávio de Carvalho had his first one-man show in São Paulo, exhibiting some 150 oils and metal sculptures. The exhibition was also closed for its daring unorthodoxies, although a court order permitting it to be reopened was subsequently obtained. In 1952 he achieved what is probably his best-known work, *A Série Trágica*, a series of drawings on the death of his mother. Since the early 1950s, Flávio de Carvalho has been continuously active in architecture, painting, and stage design. Flávio de Carvalho is a member of many associations, among them the Institute of Engineering of São Paulo and the Institute of Architecture of Brazil. He has written widely on many subjects, and his works include *L'aspect psychologique et morbide de l'art moderne*, *Os ossos do mundo*, and various writings on art, history, and psychology in the form of books and articles. His paintings have appeared in exhibitions in Rome, New York, Paris, and numerous cities in Spanish America and Brazil. He was awarded a special room in the 7th Bienal de São Paulo, held in 1963. His *Self-Portrait* was painted for the present exhibition.   DD

**Castellanos, Julio** [Mexico City, 1905–1947]. Julio Castellanos first studied at the Academia de San Carlos in Mexico City. Afterwards he studied and traveled in South America, the United States, and Europe. The Mexican artist Manuel Rodríguez Lozano imparted to his work of the '20s and early '30s both classical and surrealist influences. From 1933 on, Castellanos created a distinctive style of his own. Among the first manifestations of the strange world of innocence and expectation that became his characteristic expression are his murals at the Escuela Melchor Ocampo in Coyoacán, completed in 1933. In this and later oils, such as *El Baño de San Juan* (1939), Castellanos saw the people of Mexico in their austere and impassive aspects. To his fine sense of technical detail he often added surrealistic elements, such as the oversized Dalíesque butterfly of *El Bohío* (1946). Castellanos' production was small, but of consistently high quality. One of the reasons he was not prolific was the effort he devoted to the improvement of art education and public artistic facilities in Mexico. He was able to realize many of his plans as Director of the Federal Department of Plastic Arts, a post he held from 1946 to his death the following year.   JD

**Castillo, Teófilo** [Lima, 1857–1922]. Castillo had become a devotee of Ricardo Palma, the author of *Tradiciones Peruanas*, by the time he was thirty. Interested in recapturing aspects of Spanish colonial heritage, Castillo painted *Manchay-puito*, an academically executed canvas based on one of the *Tradiciones* by Palma. During the 1880s and 1890s he lived in Buenos Aires and also visited Europe. It was on a short trip in 1909 to Madrid that he discovered the academic impressionism of Mariano Fortuny, a style he adopted and introduced into Peru. Two excellent examples are *The Funeral of Saint Rose*, painted in 1912, and the *Casa Colonial, Cuzco*. An innovator in Peruvian art and one of the precursors of anti-academic style in that country, Castillo was disappointed by the appointment of Daniel Hernández to the post of Director of the newly founded Escuela Nacional de Bellas Artes in 1919 and he attacked the school for its academic orientation. That same year he left Peru an embittered man.   TG

**Catherwood, Frederick** [England, 1799–1854]. Known primarily as an architect in his native Britain, Frederick Catherwood is remembered in the history of Mexican art as the illustrator of the book *Incidents of Travel in Central America, Chiapas and Yucatán*, published in the United States in 1841. J. L. Stephens, the North American archeologist, wrote the book, which was based on the two men's travels ten years before its publication.   JD

**Cavalcanti, Emiliano di** [Rio de Janeiro, Brazil, 1897–    ]. Emiliano di Cavalcanti had his first exhibition in 1916, when some of his caricatures were displayed in Rio's Salão dos Humoristas. The same year he enrolled in the Faculty of Law in Rio de Janeiro. After transferring to São Paulo, he soon abandoned his thoughts of a law career and dedicated himself to art. In São Paulo, Cavalcanti, the poet Guilherme de Almeida, and the novelist Oswaldo de Andrade formed the initial core of a group of interested young artists that sponsored exhibitions, recitals, and lectures concerning the new trends in modern art. Cavalcanti both helped to organize and participated in São Paulo's historic *Semana de Arte Moderna* in 1922, the exposition that brought modernism forcefully to a shocked Brazilian public. Since then he has been a tireless promoter of the new artistic principles expressed there, in Brazil as well as in Europe. In the past two decades Cavalcanti's paintings have been exhibited throughout major European cities, and in New York, Montevideo, and Buenos Aires. Cavalcanti is one of Brazil's foremost modern artists, a sensitive draughtsman and interpreter of the customs and life of his native land. He depicts with feeling and understanding the life of Brazil's Negroes – one of his favorite themes – capturing the gay colors of their clothing and the dance-like rhythms of their movement. Cavalcanti has been compared to another talented interpreter of the Brazilian scene, the novelist Jorge Amado, for the slight vein of irony that flavors his deep understanding of his country's life.   DD

**Challamel, Jules Robert** [Paris, 1813–?]. A French lithographer and painter, Challamel studied with Ingres and Rénard. He exhibited lithographs in the official Salons from 1835 to 1848.   CF

**Chambelland, Simone** [Born Paris, presently active in Chile]. Simone Chambelland has been living in Chile since 1939. During the past three years she has exhibited engravings in Lima, New York, Rome, and Geneva.   CF

**Charlot, Jean** [Paris, 1898–    ]. Jean Charlot went to Mexico to live with relatives in 1921. He quickly established himself in the pioneer group of artists who initiated the mural movement in the Escuela Nacional Preparatoria in the early 1920s. He and Ramón Alva de la Canal were the first to employ a true fresco technique. Charlot was also interested in graphic arts, and he helped revive interest in the work of José Guadalupe Posada, the late 19th-century popular wood engraver, by writing articles and helping to exhibit his work. He went on in this field, becoming a master of color lithography. Following a period as staff draughtsman of the Sterling archeological expedition to Yucatán, he made his home in the United States. There he had a varied and productive career, both as artist and writer, painting murals and teaching in many universities and art schools. His books and articles on 19th- and 20th-century Mexican art include a history of the Mexican Mural Renaissance, 1920–1925. He now lives and works in Hawaii. JD

**Charon, Louis-François** [Versailles, France, 1783 – after 1831]. Charon, a pupil in Paris of Chasteignier, became an accomplished steel engraver. His portrait of Bolívar was done in Paris following American designs. TG

**Cicarelli, Alejandro** [Naples, Italy, 1811–1879]. Cicarelli, trained at the Istituto Reale delle Belle Arti of Naples, came to Chile in 1848 after having served as private drawing instructor to Empress Maria Teresa of Brazil. In the following year, he was named Director of the Escuela (later Academia) de Pintura of Santiago de Chile, a post he held until 1869. For years the artistic resources of the school consisted of a series of steel engravings of the old masters that Cicarelli had brought with him. He is remembered today more for his pedagogical activity and as the master of the mid-century generation of Chilean artists than for his artistic output. He had been trained in the severely classical style of the early 19th century and remained in it. His portraits and studies from nature constitute his best work. CF

**Clark, Lygia** [Belo Horizonte, Brazil, 1920–    ]. Lygia Clark began her artistic studies with the landscape architect, Roberto Burle Marx. Later she studied for two years in Paris with Arpad Szennes, Dobrinsky, and Fernand Léger. Her first one-man exhibition, at the gallery of L'Institut Endoplastique in 1952, brought her to the attention of critics and fellow artists. In the same year she won the Prêmio Arte Abstrata in Petrópolis and the Prêmio Federico Schmidt in Rio de Janeiro. She was acclaimed the critics' choice as the "artistic revelation of the year," and won a major prize at the 4th Bienal of São Paulo (1957). Subsequent exhibitions of Lygia Clark's abstract reliefs and articulated sculptures earned for her numerous awards and renown as "an artist's artist." Tributes to her work have come from such diverse sources as the Filipino poet and sculptor David Medalla, the critic Mario Pedrosa, and Sandberg, former Director of the Stedelijk Museum in Amsterdam. In 1959 Lygia Clark co-founded the Brazilian Neoconcretist association "MAM," subsequently participating in numerous of the group's exhibitions. She represented Brazil at the Venice Biennale in 1960 and 1962 and, since 1962, has exhibited her work in Washington, D.C., New York, Rome, Paris, São Paulo, and London. The Signals London Exposition in 1965 presented nearly sixty pieces, tracing her artistic development over the past fifteen years, from her early reliefs and sculpture to recent architectural projects. DD

**Clausell, Joaquín** [Campeche, Mexico, 1866 – Lagunas de Zempoala, Mexico, 1935]. Joaquín Clausell spent his youth in his birthplace and moved to Mexico City in 1886. Perhaps Clausell really found himself in the 1890s when, while traveling in Europe, he discovered the Impressionist painters, and when, in 1896, he received his law degree. Clausell was motivated to paint through his friendship with his countryman, Dr. Atl (Gerardo Murillo). Thereafter, he devoted his life to painting and the practice of law. The new artist-lawyer traveled widely in Mexico, painting landscapes rich in color and vigorous in form. His works were perhaps best described by Dr. Atl as being "realistic, warm . . . [and] the most genuine expression of his own temperament, the perfectly natural spontaneous fruit of a passionate temperament and of a sharp and brilliant intelligence." DD

**Clavé, Pelegrín** [Barcelona, 1810–1880]. Pelegrín Clavé studied at the Accademia di San Luca in Rome, where he was schooled in the principles of 19th-century classicism. Ingres was in Rome at the time, and although Clavé may not have met him, his work clearly reflects the Frenchman's influence. The Mexican government contracted Clavé to help reorganize the Academia de San Carlos in 1846. There he became Director of Painting and exercised a considerable influence on Mexican painting for over twenty years. As there had been no meaningful activity at that institution since the outbreak of the Independence wars, his task was a formidable one. Nevertheless, Clavé was able to communicate his late neoclassical ideas and, at the same time, to paint some of his principal works. Several of his students – José Salomé Pina, Santiago Rebull, and Felipe S. Gutiérrez – were to add dimension and depth to his academic principles and produce works of quality. His unrelenting antagonist was the painter Juan Cordero, who deplored his importation of European standards. Clavé fell into disrepute in the 1860s. The official disapproval of Maximilian spurred him to leave, and he returned to Europe in 1868. Clavé's two main thematic interests were historical and allegorical subjects and portraiture.    JD

**Codesido, Julia** [Lima, 1892–    ]. It was not until she was nearly forty that the work of Julia Codesido won any sort of notice. It came in the form of one-man shows in Lima, Mexico City, New York, and Paris and in the acquisition of her works by several famous museums, among which were the San Francisco Museum of Art and the Musée de Jeu de Paume in Paris. International recognition was accompanied by recognition at home in 1933 in the form of a professorship in Lima's Escuela Nacional de Bellas Artes, where she had once studied. Unlike many of her younger contemporaries, however, Miss Codesido's style evolved from a largely thematic concern for her indigenous subject matter. Moving gradually toward abstraction, she still sought to convey the character and tradition of the Peruvian Indian. At the same time, however, she abjured the primitivism of the Indians' own art and the sometimes adopted primitivism of the indigenists.    CF

**Comisión Corográfica.** The Comisión Corográfica was organized early in 1850 under the administration of General José Hilario López to survey the geography of the Republic of Colombia in order to make its extremely diverse parts better known. It was concerned not only with physical geography but with political and human geography as well. It was organized by the geographer Agustín Codazzi, assisted by the writer Manuel Ancízar, the painter Carmelo Fernández, and the botanist José Jerónimo Triana. Others also took part in the work of the commission; in particular, two painters, Manuel María Paz who excelled as a cartographer, and the young Englishman, Henry Price. The work of the commission continued from 1850 to 1859, when its remarkable leader died. It served as a foundation of knowledge of the geography and customs of the country, and also of national art, especially of landscape.

Fernández was the most expert of the painters. Venezuelan by birth, he was trained in art in Caracas by the Frenchman Lessabe. His uncle, General José Antonio Páez, President of Venezuela, sent him to the United States to study. In 1827 he returned to Venezuela, where he began his collaboration with Codazzi on an atlas of Venezuela. He traveled in Europe and then returned to join the Comisión Corográfica. His later life was devoted to art in Caracas. He died in 1877.

Price, born in London in 1819, arrived in Bogotá in 1841 attached to a British business firm. A cultivated gentleman, he founded the Sociedad Filarmónica, the first in Colombia, and taught music. He also composed songs and painted. He worked on the Comisión during 1852, but his health failed, and he retired to the United States, where he died in Brooklyn in 1863.

He was replaced by Coronel M. M. Paz, born in Almaguer, Nariño, Colombia, in 1820. He fought in the civil wars. His interests in drawing and cartography led to his appointment as painter on the Comisión, which he served until it ended with Codazzi's death. He then became director of Bogotá's first art school, and had printed in Paris the *Atlas Geográfico de Colombia*. He died in 1902 in Bogotá.

The art work of the Comisión is preserved in 152 watercolor paintings in the *Album de la Comisión Corográfica*, now in the Biblioteca Nacional in Bogotá.    TG

**Cordero, Juan** [Teziutlán; Puebla, 1824 – Mexico, 1884]. Cordero studied at the Academia de San Carlos during the years before 1844, when that institution was in severe decline. He supported himself as an itinerant peddler during his years of study. In 1844 he went to Rome to study, where his first major work was *Columbus before the Catholic Kings*. In 1853 he returned to Mexico and exhibited at the Academia de San Carlos. This inaugurated a long public struggle with Clavé, the Spanish-born Director of the Academy, for Cordero considered himself the proper man for the post. Cordero's murals in the Church of Santa Teresa and the main dome of the Church of San Fernando (1857 and 1859, respectively) are precursors of the 20th-century mural movement. Cordero was also proficient as a historical painter and portraitist. His portrait of the young wife of General Santa Anna, Dolores Tosta, painted in 1855, is one of the major portraits of the period.    TG

**Costa, Lúcio** [Toulon, France, 1902–    ]. Costa studied at the Escola Nacional de Belas Artes in Rio de Janeiro, where he was a principal leader in the movement to establish modern principles in architecture. Now regarded as the father of modern Brazilian architecture, Costa was deeply affected both by Le Corbusier, during the latter's visit to Brazil in 1929, and by the youthful spirit of the Vargas Revolution of 1930. As Director of the Escola Nacional de Belas Artes, he acted as the moving force in Brazilian modern architecture by instilling in his students enthusiasm for new aesthetic concepts, and by fostering a spirit of rebellion against the old academicism. He has many works to his credit, from the building of the Ministry of Education and Health in Rio to the recent plan for Brazil's modern capital city, Brasília.    DD

**Cuneo Perinetti, José** [Montevideo, 1889–    ]. José Cuneo Perinetti began his studies at the Círculo de Bellas Artes in Montevideo. Since his early interest was both in relief sculpture and in painting, he studied with the sculptor Felipe Menini and with the painter Carlos María Herrera. Then, in 1907, he went to study in Turin, where his friendship with his drawing teacher, Anton Mucchi, induced him to become a painter. In 1909 Perinetti returned to Montevideo where, the following year, he exhibited thirty paintings. In 1911, and again in 1917, he visited Paris. He returned to Uruguay from his second trip to France with a new geometrical approach to landscape painting. There were later trips to Europe, in 1922, 1927–1930, and 1938. However, his intervals in Uruguay were given to an ever deeper and more personal evocation of the land. His important *Luna* (*Moon*) series of oil paintings date from the 1930s. About 1937 Perinetti began to use watercolor in renderings of powerful and poetic landscapes. He exhibited a series of these in Milan and Paris. Since that time he has continued his painting in Uruguay, frequently settling in rural areas such as Cerro Largo or Salto. TG

**Darondeau, Stanislas Henri Benoit** [Paris, 1807 – Brest, 1841]. Darondeau was trained in Paris as an engineer, becoming hydrographic engineer on the French corvette *La Bonite*, which circled the world in 1836–1837. This brought him to Montevideo, where he produced watercolor and pencil drawings, mainly of feminine costumes. He also painted landscapes, architectural views, and local people. DD

**Debret, Jean Baptiste** (**João Battista**) [Paris, 1768–1848]. Jean Baptiste Debret began his artistic studies in the Académie des Beaux-Arts in Paris. Although painting was his true passion, during his student days he found the time to study engineering. After Napoleon's fall, Debret, an ardent Bonapartist, was one of the principal members of the Lebreton Mission of 1816, which was invited by João VI to foster the education of young artists and the development of the arts in Brazil. Debret spent a productive sixteen years in Brazil, where he was instrumental in organizing the Académia de Belas Artes. He returned to Paris in 1831 and there published an account of his stay, *Voyage pittoresque et historique au Brésil*, which contains vivid pictorial descriptions of Brazil during the early years of the 19th century. In recognition of his work, Debret was made a member of the Instituto Histórico e Geográfico Brasileiro in 1839. Debret has left a number of important portraits and historical paintings, including *Retrato de D. João VI*, *Aclamação de D. Pedro I*, and *Sagração de D.*

*Pedro I*. His best-known works are the lithographs of Brazilian scenes illustrating the *Voyage*. Debret's significance for Brazil lay also in his pedagogic talents. This Frenchman, thought by Reis to be "positively the soul of the establishment of artistic instruction in Brazil," was responsible for training a whole generation of Brazilian artists. Among his most outstanding pupils at the Académia de Belas Artes were Agusto Muller, Manuel de Araújo Pôrto Alegre, and José Correia de Lima. DD

**Deira, Ernesto** [Buenos Aires, 1928–    ]. A lawyer, Ernesto Deira turned to art. He received a fellowship from the National Arts Fund in Buenos Aires and has since become one of the leading members of the current Argentine movement, *Nueva Figuración* (*New Figuration*). He has exhibited his drawings and very large paintings in lacquer and oil in major cities of the world, from Berlin to Saigon. TG

**de Lamonica, Roberto.** See: **Lamonica, Roberto de**

**de la Vega, Jorge Luis.** See: **Vega, Jorge Luis de la**

**del Carril, Delia.** See: **Carril, Delia del**

**Delhez, Víctor** [Belgium, 1901–    ]. Víctor Delhez came to Argentina in 1925. He was trained in wood engraving, an art that he continued in Argentina. The critic Massini Correas and other authorities divide his work into three periods: "Composiciones Musicales"; works inspired by Baudelaire and Dostoyevsky; and themes based on the Passion and Apocalypse. In 1933, he exhibited his Baudelaire series at the gallery of Amigos del Arte in Buenos Aires, revealing a new tendency toward poetic realism of Gothic character and intensity. The influence of North European Late Gothic art and ideas is clear in his *Danza Macabra* prints. Mixed in with these literary illustrations is a series of portrait prints, which Delhez continued to produce in all periods. He is recognized as one of the major printmakers working in South America. In the 1920s his abstract prints in linoleum played a part in the introduction of abstract art into Argentina. TG

**Della Valle, Angel** [Buenos Aires, 1852–?]. Angel Della Valle received his first training in art in Buenos Aires and completed his studies in Florence with Ciseri. Returning to Buenos Aires in 1883, he painted portraits – but his main interest was the life of the pampa. Although his style is that of the academic salons, there is a strong narrative element clearly visible in his most famous painting, *La Vuelta del Malón*. Della Valle was one of the most influential teachers of his generation and, upon his return from Europe, taught in the

169

school of the Sociedad Estímulo de Bellas Artes in Buenos Aires. TG

**de Sá, Simplício.** See: **Sá, Simplício de**

**Descalzi, Cayetano** [Italy; active after 1830]. Descalzi arrived in Buenos Aires before 1830. There he married the widowed mother of the artist Carlos Morel, the marriage ending in divorce in 1838. Specializing in portraiture, his best works were portraits of the dictator Juan Manuel Rosas. The lithographic print *Rosas el Grande* was made in Paris under Descalzi's supervision. TG

**de Simone.** See: **Simone, Alfredo de**

**D'Hastrel, Adolphe** [France, 1805 – France, 1870]. Adolphe D'Hastrel followed the military vocation of his family and enlisted in the French Naval Artillery in 1825. In 1839, as captain, he accompanied the French armada that blockaded the Río de la Plata as a retaliation against the Argentine dictator Rosas. Named commandant of Martín García Island, D'Hastrel was responsible for the defense of Montevideo during Rosas' attack on the Uruguayan capital in 1840. He returned to France in 1841 after a brief stay in Brazil, and retired from the armed forces in 1847, decorated with the Legion of Honor. D'Hastrel's military importance for Uruguay is equaled by his artistic achievement during his brief stay in that country. A sailor by trade, an artist by preference, he carried back to France a vast artistic baggage depicting the Uruguayan scene of the early 19th century. His watercolors, sketches, and lithographs are a faithful record of the life – urban and rural – of the country: gauchos, ranches, and scenes of Montevideo. D'Hastrel's watercolors reveal the precise touch of the miniaturist, faithful to detail, yet still able to capture with sweep and élan the character of the life they recorded. Many of his watercolors and lithographs were published in Paris in 1845–1850 in a series of albums devoted to the countries of South America. DD

**di Cavalcanti.** See: **Cavalcanti, Emiliano di**

**Dornheim, Johann Karl** [Gotha, Germany, 1760–?]. Dornheim worked in his native Gotha and in Leipzig as an engraver between 1780 and 1810. TG

**Doudtchitzky, Dinora** [Odessa, Ukraine, 1914–    ]. Dinora Doudtchitzky studied at the Academia Nacional and the Escuela de Bellas Artes in Buenos Aires before moving to Santiago in 1939. There she entered the Escuela de Bellas Artes of the Universidad de Chile. Later she became one of the original members of the Taller 99 associated with the Universidad Católica, where she is Assistant Professor of Engraving at present. She won first prize in the Official Salon of Santiago in 1961, and has been represented in the São Paulo Bienal. CF

**Doumic, N.** [Active 1844]. Nothing is known of Doumic as a personality. His only known work is the pen-and-wash drawing of a *Soldier of the Army of Oribe*, preserved in the Museo Histórico Nacional in Buenos Aires. It is signed N. Doumic, and dated 1844. TG

**Downey, Juan** [Santiago de Chile, 1940–    ]. Juan Downey studied architecture at the Universidad Católica de Chile and engraving at Nemesio Antúnez's Taller 99 in Santiago. In 1962 he went to Barcelona and then to Paris, where he worked under Sterling Hayter in the latter's Atelier 17. He has exhibited since 1958 in Santiago, Barcelona, Paris, Lisbon, Turin, and Havana, where he won the first prize in Cuba's 1964 Festival of Engraving. His works are abstract but executed with strong, controlled linear fervor that often has pictorial effect. He seems, as do many American artists, to be striving for a fusion between the latest techniques and goals of modern art and the forms and colors of pre-Columbian art, often with satiric effect. CF

**Dulin, J.D.** [France, ?–1919]. Dulin was trained as an artist in drawing and lithography. He arrived in Buenos Aires in the 1850s. He specialized in views of the city of Buenos Aires, doing the original drawings for lithographs printed either in Buenos Aires or in France. Only eight prints are known by Dulin, who lived most of his adult life in Argentina. TG

**Dutary, Alberto** [Panama, 1932–    ]. Alberto Dutary began painting at the age of twelve. He studied at the Escuela de Bellas Artes in Panama. In Spain between 1952 and 1959, he studied at the Academia de San Fernando and at the Escuela Nacional de Artes Gráficas. He is known as a draughtsman as well as a painter. His interest in representational draughtsmanship has revealed itself in his more recent paintings, which have turned from an earlier abstraction toward a more figurative style. He has had one-man shows in Spain, Italy, the United States, and several Latin American countries. A leader among the younger artists of Panama, Dutary has restlessly pushed into new areas of expression, rejecting clichés old and new in the effort to come to grips with contemporary reality. In this he represents a new spirit of independence and initiative that is generally evident in the work of his contemporaries in Panama and in that of other younger Latin American artists who have not yet won recognition. TG

**Egerton, Daniel Thomas** [England, ? – Tacubaya, Mexico, 1842]. Daniel Egerton was one of the founding members of the Society of British Artists during the 1820s. He came from England to Mexico in 1834, where he painted scenes that were later published in a book of lithographs in 1840, during a visit he made to England. Egerton and his wife returned to Mexico and settled in Tacubaya, where they were murdered in 1842 under mysterious circumstances. It was in Tacubaya that Egerton had painted his large oil, *Valley of Mexico*, with Mexico City in the background. He also painted landscapes in other parts of Mexico. DD

**Eielson, Jorge** [Lima, 1924–    ]. Eielson was awarded a grant to study art in Paris by the French Government in 1948. He also studied in Switzerland in 1951 and then in Rome. Eielson has received numerous awards including the Premio Nacional de Poesía in Peru (1945), Premio Nacional de Teatro in Peru (1949), and UNESCO's Journalism Grant (1952). His work has been shown at the Instituto de Arte Contemporáneo of Lima in 1948, in 1949 at the Galérie Collette Allendy in Paris, in the Carnegie International held at Pittsburgh in 1961, and in the 32nd Venice Biennale.

**Ender, Thomas** [St. Ulrich, Austria, 1793–1875]. Thomas Ender began the study of historical painting in his native city and, at the age of twelve, entered the Academy of Arts in St. Anna, where he studied for five years with Maurer. Ender soon turned to landscape painting, inspired by the countryside around Vienna, where he spent many joyful hours. In 1817 his connections with the royal court obtained for him the position of landscapist in the Austrian scientific commission destined for Brazil, a diverse group that included the naturalists Spix and Martius. Arriving in Rio de Janeiro the same year, Ender immediately began to depict, in sketches and watercolors, the rich diversity of the Brazilian *paisagem*. Unfortunately, Rio's climate did not agree with the young European, and after only ten months in Brazil, he was forced to return to Vienna. He died in his native land a wealthy and honored citizen. Though his stay in Brazil was brief, Ender left over six hundred sketches and watercolors expressing the spontaneity and joy he felt in that tropical land. His works, faithful to detail and varied in perspective, portrayed all aspects of the panorama of Brazilian life and constitute a valuable historical cross-section of Brazil's capital city, which was rapidly being transformed from a provincial town to a metropolitan center. Ender's works, hidden away in the Akademie der Bildenden Künste in Vienna, were little known in Brazil for over a century. They were brought to light when Siegfried Freiburg organized an exhibition containing some of Ender's sketches in Vienna in 1950. A few years later, Ender's works were exhibited in São Paulo, where they were received with appreciation. DD

**Escalante, Constantino** [Mexico City, 1836–1868]. Escalante, a lithographer and draughtsman, was one of the foremost political caricaturists of the Mexican reform period, an era that not only produced a generation of brilliant artists in this genre, but established a self-renewing Mexican tradition that has continued unbroken for over a century. He was associated with various Mexico City periodicals, particularly *La Orquesta*, *La Patria*, and *El Impolítico*, which owed much of their popularity to his drawing and his biting satire. Despite his premature death in a railroad accident on the outskirts of Mexico City, he became one of the greatest practitioners of an art which, in Chile, Argentina, Uruguay, and Brazil as well, reached a high point during the second half of the 19th century. DD

**Espinosa, José María** [Bogotá, Colombia, 1796–1883]. Espinosa, whose proudest boast was that he had been General Antonio Nariño's standard-bearer during the wars of Independence, is today best known for the portraits he did of the campaign leaders in those wars. Completely self-taught, he painted caricatures in watercolor while serving in the army. In 1819 he returned to Bogotá to dedicate himself completely to art, painting miniature and life-size works. A trip to Italy, promised by Bolívar, was never realized because of the Liberator's death in 1830. Espinosa also did genre sketches and great historical canvases of the battles of the wars of Independence. The battle scenes have little to recommend them, but the sketches, done in a nervous lineal style from life, are often excellent. CF

**Estrada, José María** [Guadalajara, Mexico, active c. 1830–1860]. José María Estrada studied under José María Uriarte and worked in Guadalajara, Jalisco. Little else is known of his life. For the most part he painted portraits of the mid-19th-century Jaliscan bourgeoisie, graceful young ladies, delicate children and carefully dressed men, whom he saw with a somewhat naïve eye and rendered with unerring discretion, elegance and intimacy. He also painted social and historical themes with religious and moral overtones. His work is among the most outstanding of the many Mexican and Latin American provincial portrait painters of the second third of the 19th century. DD

**Fader, Fernando** [Mendoza, Argentina, 1882 – Córdoba, Argentina, 1935]. Fernando Fader trained in Munich with the Impressionist, Frederick von Zügel. In 1904 he returned to his native city and continued painting landscapes in the manner of his master. Fader is considered the most important artist associated with the Nexus Impressionist painters, a group which he helped organize in Buenos Aires in 1907. Because most of its members had Italian training, this group opposed the stricter Impressionist style of Malharro. Eventually, most of their individual styles gravitated toward post-Impressionism. Fader, generally labeled an Impressionist, does not fit perfectly into this category. Although he was interested in light and painted a remarkable series of light studies of the same landscape at various hours from dawn to dusk (Juan B. Castagnino Museum, Córdoba), he emphasizes color for its own sake more than the Impressionists do. Fader's influence largely superseded that of Malharro's and was very strong in Argentina throughout the 1920s and 1930s.  TG

**Faz, Carlos** [Viña del Mar, Chile, 1931 – New Orleans, Louisiana, U.S.A., 1953]. A quiet, highly sensitive artist, Faz studied art at the Escuela de Bellas Artes in Viña del Mar in 1946–1947. Later he worked in Mexico with Diego Rivera. In the early 1950s he came to the United States on a scholarship and worked in Stanley Hayter's Atelier 17. He was found dead after a mysterious fall from his ship while en route to Europe from Mexico in 1953. Faz's paintings and engravings are figurative, expressionistic, and their prevalent interest in the social experience and circumstances of the poor has an unusual mystic interpretation as well as a tragic character. He painted a highly interesting series of murals in a private house in Tinguiririca, Chile.  CF

**Fernández Muro, José Antonio** [Spain, 1920–      ]. Fernández Muro came to Argentina in 1938. He returned to Europe in 1948, and lived for two years in Madrid and Paris. In 1957–1958, under UNESCO's sponsorship, he traveled in the United States and Europe to study museology. Since 1964 he has lived in New York with his artist-wife, Sarah Grilo. Fernández Muro's earliest work was in the Fauve tradition in which he painted still life and cityscapes. His "concretist" or "hard-edge" abstractionist painting of the 1950s tempered the usual severity of this style with subtle modulations of graded, rich color. In the 1960s he began to employ *frottage* or embossed rubbings in metalfoil of industrial products, manhole covers, and the like, which he composed into pictures overpainted with his usual glowing color. His long series of exhibitions began in 1944 at the Witcomb Gallery in Buenos Aires. Since then he has shown in international exhibitions in Paris and Amsterdam, and in the Venice Biennial of 1956. More recently he has shown in an increasing number of group as well as one-man shows in the United States. His art, grown steadily in scale and stature, is well on its way to international recognition.  TG

**Fierro, Pancho** [Rimac, Peru, 1803–1879]. What little is known about the life of the watercolorist Pancho Fierro is contained in a letter by the Peruvian author Ricardo Palma, written in 1885. Fierro's youth coincided with the period in which the Viceroyalty of Peru was undergoing the convulsions of independence. It was during this period that he began to paint his genre works and caricatures of Peruvian customs and society. In addition to his watercolors he is known to have painted some large murals in Lima, none of which has survived. In discussing Fierro's work, Palma compared it to some of Goya's cartoons of popular customs prepared for the tapestries of the Escorial and certain of the *caprichos*. It is possible that Fierro may have known Goya's work; certainly there are resemblances, particularly in some of the caricatures and in the custom of giving each drawing a title. In the painting of the bullfighter Juana Breña, the peculiarly fluid and graceful lines of the horse and bull remind one forcibly of another one of Spain's art treasures – the neolithic paintings of the Cave of Altamira. Palma records Fierro's death as occurring in July, 1879.  CF

**Figari, Pedro** [Montevideo, 1861 – Montevideo, 1938]. Pedro Figari earned his law degree in 1886 and soon acquired a reputation as a talented defense counsel. As a journalist, he founded the newspaper *El Diario*. He later occupied a seat in Uruguay's Chamber of Deputies and, in 1915, was named director of the Escuela de Artes y Oficios, in which he fostered reforms concerning industrial instruction. Figari wrote widely on many topics, from juridical matters to essays on education, aesthetics, and poetry. As a youth, he had studied painting with the Italian Godofredo Somavilla, but Figari's own style and unique vision were not revealed until 1921 when he moved to Buenos Aires, and devoted himself fully to art. After four years of intense activity he moved to Paris, where he remained for nine years and achieved his artistic maturity. Figari returned to Montevideo in 1933, and died there five years later, ending his extraordinary life as lawyer, painter, professor, journalist, parliamentarian, philosopher, and writer. His works have been exhibited in Montevideo, Buenos Aires, Paris, London, New York, Seville, Los Angeles, and other centers.  DD

**Figueroa, José Luis** [Jalisco, Mexico, active c. 1910–1940]. Figueroa worked in a studio in the Museo de Guadalajara in 1922. He painted in a remarkably strong and colorful expressionistic version of Art Nouveau style, with robustly humorous and satiric overtones. His works were left to the museum in which he worked, now the Museum of the State of Jalisco, when he began a series of travels in South America and the United States. In spite of his originality, his work is scarcely known outside Guadalajara. In the 1930s Figueroa became a teacher in the Misiones Culturales, an educational program inaugurated by the national government, in which he joined one of many missionary teams bringing art and education to isolated regions of the republic. TG

**Fisquet, Théodore** [Toulon, France, 1813 – Toulon, 1890]. Fisquet took part in the scientific voyage around the world made by the French corvette *La Bonite*, commanded by M. Valliant, in 1836–1837. Pictures executed by him and the other artists were lithographed to accompany a description of the voyage published in Paris in 1845. The painter spent the rest of his life in his native town. His most characteristic work consists of drawings and watercolors of people, customs, and landscapes observed on the voyage. CF

**Forner, Raquel** [Buenos Aires, 1902–    ]. Raquel Forner's interest in art was awakened at the age of twelve while visiting Spain with her parents. Entering the Academia Nacional de Bellas Artes in Buenos Aires, she was soon given the position of Professor of Drawing. In 1929 she went back to Europe and for two years studied in Paris with Othon Friesz. Upon her return to Buenos Aires in 1932, she helped found the Cursos Libres de Arte Plástico, where she continues to teach. In 1937 she won the Gold Medal of the International Exposition in Paris. Since then she has exhibited widely and successfully. Her many awards include the Grand Prize of Honor of the 45th National Salon in Buenos Aires (1955), an exhibition which she had boycotted during the Perón dictatorship. In 1959 five of her paintings were shown in the Venice Biennial. Her style has generally remained figurative, with strong emotive qualities that identify her with Expressionism. Her most recent paintings show a heavy impasto with jewel-like color spots, strongly patterned compositions and symbolist imagery. TG

**Forte, Vicente** [Lanús, Argentina, 1912–    ]. Vicente Forte studied with Emilio Pettoruti and later was a founding member of the Orion Group. He is a member of the Group of Twenty Painters and Sculptors. He has been exhibiting since 1946. Besides a number of one-man and group shows in Argentina, his work has been shown at the 1st São Paulo Bienal (1951), in New Delhi, and in the Netherlands. He has won several prizes, including a 1st prize in the Argentine National Watercolor, Pastel, and Print Salon (1951). In 1949–1950 he traveled in Europe, painting and studying independently. Recently he has also been teaching technical drawing. TG

**Fossa, Juan** [active c. 1830]. The wash drawing *Scene of the Civil War* is the only known work by this artist, who was active during the period of the Rosas dictatorship (1829–1852). TG

**Gallino, Cayetano** [Genoa, 1804–1884]. Cayetano Gallino began his artistic education in the Genoese Accademia Ligustica di Belle Arti in 1814. He later entered the workshop of Santo Tagliafichi. Forced to leave during the years of political turmoil preceding the Risorgimento, Gallino came to Montevideo in 1833, where he remained until 1848, when he returned to Italy. Like other foreign artists who visited South America in the early 19th century, Gallino was fascinated by the distinct character of its life and customs. He attempted to capture qualities of people and society through portraits of its outstanding public figures, military heroes, and society women. He romantically emphasized the finer points of his models, as in his *Placida Buxarero de Cibils* or *Luis Baena*. He allows few decorative accessories to detract from the psychological reality expressed. At times some detail of clothing is stressed to suggest a particular personal trait of the model. In addition to their quality as art Gallino's many oil portraits are of immense value as a record of Uruguayan social personality of the period in which he lived in that country. He was the first professional artist with whom the painter Juan Manuel Blanes had contact. DD

**Gamarra, José** [Uruguay, 1934–    ]. Gamarra studied at the Escuela Nacional de Bellas Artes in Montevideo. In 1959 he was awarded a scholarship by the Brazilian government to study in Rio de Janeiro. In 1960 he settled in São Paulo as a professor of painting at the Escola de Arte de la Fundação Armando Alvares Penteado; he moved to Paris in 1963 and now lives there. Gamarra has had individual shows in Buenos Aires, São Paulo, Santiago de Chile, and Montevideo, and has also taken part in the São Paulo Bienal, the Biennial of Tokyo, the 1963 Biennial of Young Artists in Paris, and the 1962 Bienal Americana in Córdoba. He has won major prizes in the latter two and also at Beca Itamaraty, Brazil, in 1959. CF

173

**Garay, Epifanio** [Bogotá, 1849 – Villeta, Colombia, 1903]. Garay studied in Paris at the Académie Julien on a government scholarship, working under Bouguereau, Constant, Bonnat, and Boulanger. Returning to Colombia, he became the prime motive force in the rebirth of Colombian painting in the latter half of the 19th century. He worked largely in oil, painting portraits and religious scenes, and did some church decorations. He was the chief figure in the establishment of the Colombian Escuela Nacional de Bellas Artes. He lived much of his life in that part of Colombia which now forms the Republic of Panama and therefore is considered Panamanian. CF

**García del Molino, Fernando** [Chile, 1813 – Buenos Aires, 1899]. García del Molino was brought to Argentina at the age of seven and considered himself an Argentine. He studied with Guth and Caccianiga at the University of Buenos Aires, where he specialized in miniature portraiture. He was a friend and occasional collaborator of Carlos Morel. He was both the portraitist and political adherent of Juan Manuel Rosas and, after the fall of Rosas, his career declined. TG

**Gasparini, Graziano** [Venice, Italy, 1924–    ]. Gasparini, a naturalized citizen of Venezuela, has specialized in the study of pre-Columbian and colonial architecture of the Americas and, at present, is both Professor of the History of Pre-Columbian and Colonial Architecture, and Professor of Basic Composition at the Universidad Central in Caracas. His work is figurative, but he is not so much interested in the forms themselves as in the relationships between them. His work is also marked by a bold use of color. An accomplished architectural photographer, he is also an internationally respected architectural historian. CF

**Gennis** [Switzerland, active in Chile c. 1825–1850]. Little is known about this Swiss artist except that he worked in Chile during the formative years of the Republic, in the second quarter of the 19th century. CF

**Gerzso, Gunther** [Mexico City, 1915–    ]. Gunther Gerzso studied first in Mexico and then in Europe, where he remained from 1925 to 1933. He decided to dedicate himself to painting at the urging of his friend, the Mexican artist Julio Castellanos. He was also influenced by Otto Butterlin. Gerzso held his first show in 1950 and since then has exhibited many times. There was a retrospective exhibition of his work at the Museo Nacional de Arte Moderno in Mexico City in 1963. He has worked extensively in scenography. DD

**Gil, Jerónimo Antonio** [Zamora, Spain, 1731 (or 1732)–1798]. Jerónimo Gil studied painting, drawing, and engraving in Spain. As the disciple of Tomás Prieto at the Academia de Bellas Artes de San Fernando in Madrid, Gil proved to be most talented at engraving. By 1778, his reputation was such that a Royal Commission entrusted him to establish an official school of engraving in New Spain (Mexico). In 1783, the school was incorporated into the Academia Real de San Carlos, of which Gil was made the first Director. In addition to his teaching and administrative duties at the Academia, Gil did many splendid medals for various institutions, the finest of which was of Charles III and presented to him in 1785. DD

**Gil de Castro, José** [Lima, ?–1841?]. José Gil de Castro, "El Mulato Gil," was the first and perhaps the most important international artist of the South American Independence era. Much of his work as a portraitist was painted in Chile and he is there considered one of the precursors of modern Chilean art. Born in the last decades of the Viceroyalty, he accompanied O'Higgins's Chilean Independence Army as a Captain of Militia and Attaché to the Engineer Corps. He probably lived in Chile from 1814 to 1822, where he became the "official" portraitist of Chilean society. After living and working in Argentina, he returned to his native Peru. Little is known about his early artistic training: he may have been apprenticed to a master of the old colonial school in Lima, or he may have been self-taught. Exclusively a portraitist, "El Mulato Gil" infused popular sentiment into his works and left a valuable record of the principal figures of Chilean history. CF

**Goeldi, Oswaldo** [Belém, Brazil, 1895 – São Paulo, 1961]. Goeldi, son of a Swiss naturalist, went with his family to Switzerland where he studied art in Zurich and Geneva. His first exhibit was held in the Wyss Gallery in Berne. In 1919, he returned to Brazil and began drawing and engraving, concentrating on woodcuts. He returned to Europe in 1930 where he exhibited in the Wertheim Gallery, Berlin, with Utrillo, Matisse, and others; later he exhibited again in Berne and Zurich. In the 1930s, he began to produce large woodcuts. His work has an Expressionist quality. He illustrated Poe's and Dostoyevsky's novels, using skeleton figures in the tradition of Ensor and Northern Renaissance prints. Goeldi is justifiably considered one of Latin America's major printmakers. TG

**Goitia, Francisco** [Patillos, State of Zacatecas, Mexico, 1886 – Xochimilco, Mexico, 1960]. Goitia went to Mexico City at the age of sixteen and, nine years later, entered the Escuela Nacional de Bellas Artes. From 1904 to 1912 he was in Europe, where his works attracted the attention of critics. On his return to Mexico, Goitia worked with the anthropologist Manuel Gamio, producing a series of pastels, oils, and charcoal drawings. One of his masterpieces is *Tata Jesucristo*, painted in 1927. Although his output was small, it is both arresting and profound in its penetration of Mexican indigenous character. DD

**Gómez Cornet, Ramón** [Santiago del Estero, Argentina, 1898–1964]. Ramón Gómez Cornet began his studies in the Academy in Córdoba, Argentina. He went to Paris where he studied at the Académie Ransom and later in the "Arts" studio in Barcelona. Since then, he has returned to Europe three times. The founder of the Museo Provincial de Santiago del Estero, Gómez Cornet's work was first shown in Argentina in 1921 at the Chandler Gallery in Buenos Aires. He has shown in the national salons between 1917 and 1946, and on several occasions in the United States, with a one-man show at the Wildenstein Gallery in New York in 1942. Gómez Cornet has received a number of prizes, including silver medals in 1937 at the International Exposition in Paris and at the Argentine Santa Fe Salon in 1950. TG

**González, Jaime** [Santiago de Chile, 1943– ]. González was trained at the Escuela de Arquitectura of the Universidad Católica de Chile; at present he is Professor of Painting and Drawing in that institution's Escuela de Arte. He has presented one-man shows in Rio de Janeiro and Buenos Aires, and took part in the 1st American Biennial at Córdoba (1962), as well as in other group shows. He has also brilliantly illustrated Vicente Huidobro's long poem *Altazor*. CF

**González, Juan Francisco** [Santiago de Chile, 1853–1933]. This leading American impressionist painter received his first artistic training at the Academia de la Pintura in Santiago under Ernesto Kirchbach and Juan Mochi while simultaneously pursuing a course in humanities at the Instituto Nacional. He traveled in Peru and Bolivia in 1870 and to Europe on three separate occasions. His most extensive journey was taken in 1897 when he visited Spain and North Africa. At this time he also exhibited his work in the Paris Salon. In 1887 he was named Professor of Drawing at the Liceo de Muchachos of Valparaíso, and in 1908 he received the same post at the Escuela de Bellas Artes in Santiago. Although González emphatically denied that he was an Impressionist, there can be no doubt that he belonged to this tradition in practice, if not in theory. His favorite subjects – flowers, portraits, and landscapes – dissolved form in the muted radiance of Chilean light and color. CF

**González Goyri, Roberto** [Guatemala City, 1924– ]. Roberto González Goyri studied at the Escuela de Bellas Artes in Guatemala and then in New York at the Art Students League and the Sculpture Center. Although he has also painted, his main interest has been sculpture. His work is conspicuous in Guatemala City in monumental bas-reliefs on government buildings and the recently erected monument to the national hero, Tecún Umán. He is represented in several important collections, including the Museum of Modern Art in New York. In 1964 he received the first prize in sculpture in the Esso competition for young artists from Central America. TG

**Gordon, Arturo** [Chile, 1883–1944]. Gordon worked under the Spaniard Fernando Alvarez de Sotomayor from 1908 to 1911. He is considered a member of the "Generation of 1913." His post-Romanticism is reminiscent of the Spaniard Nonell, but his bold rendering of everyday themes from Chilean popular life introduced a new approach to social truth while giving the nostalgic intimist spirit of the preceding generation a more tragic quality. CF

**Grandjean de Montigny, Auguste Henri Victor** [Paris, 1776 – Rio de Janeiro, Brazil, 1850]. Auguste Henri Victor Grandjean de Montigny displayed a penchant for drawing at an early age and entered the Paris École des Beaux-Arts, where he studied with the architects Percier and Fontaine. He won the grand prize for architecture in the Rome exposition of 1799. He continued his studies in Rome, where he designed gardens, and in 1803 drafted the restoration of the funeral monument of Cecilia Metela, wife of the dictator Sila. In 1816 he accompanied the Lebreton Mission of French artists to Brazil, where he received the title Professor of Architecture, the first such title to be given in Brazil. One of his major tasks was to design façades for the building that was to house the new Académia de Belas Artes in Rio de Janeiro, completed in 1826. Besides teaching architecture in the new Académia, he designed various temples and arches. In 1834 he designed the first large market for Rio. In 1838 he adapted the old Seminary of S. Joaquím for use as the Colégio Dom Pedro II. His design for the Biblioteca Nacional won a prize at the 2nd Exposição Geral in Brazil in 1841. He also designed a new imperial palace and collaborated on the plans for the Museu Nacional. Grandjean de Montigny's contribution to the architecture of Rio de Janeiro was enormous. He spent the greater part of his artistic career in the service of Brazil. DD

**Grashof, Otto** [Prenzlau, Prussia, 1812 – Cologne, Germany, 1876]. Grashof grew up in Cologne and was trained principally in the Düsseldorf Academy. Late in the 1830s he traveled to Russia, where he remained for six years painting at the Romanoff Court. During this time he met Liszt and painted a portrait of him. When he returned to Germany he found the political situation unsettled and continued his travels. In 1852 he sailed for Buenos Aires and spent the next six years in South America. Grashof evidently found the new environment stimulating, for he turned from portraits, until then his major interest, to the drawing and painting of local types and topography. In 1853 he spent four months in Montevideo and, at the end of that year, traveled through western Argentina in the company of Duke Wilhelm von Würtenberg. From this sojourn are known a series of drawings done in Rosario, Córdoba and Tucumán. Grashof spent two years in Brazil, where he painted, among others, two portraits of Dom Pedro II. In 1858 he returned to Germany where, because of blindness, he devoted himself to writing short stories and poetry instead of painting. TG

**Grassmann, Marcello** [São Paulo, 1925– ]. Grassmann, one of the most original contemporary draughtsmen of Latin America, invents monster-like fusions of men and animals, usually of military appearance, which have a High Renaissance quality in their drawing and a Medieval aspect in their macabre fantasy. A self-taught artist, he has received numerous awards, including a travel prize at the 1st National Salon of Modern Art in Rio de Janeiro (1954–1955), 1st prize for engraving at the 3rd São Paulo Bienal (1955), 1st prize for drawing at the 5th São Paulo Bienal (1959), and a special prize for sacred art at the Venice Biennial of 1958. His works may be found in numerous museums in Brazil, in the Dallas Museum of Fine Arts, and in the Pan American Union. In May of 1960 he held an extensive one-man show at the San Fedele Cultural Center in Milan. DD

**Grau, Enrique** [Cartagena, Colombia, 1920– ]. Grau studied at the Art Students League on a fellowship from the Colombian Government from 1940 to 1943. He has taught at the Escuela de Bellas Artes in Bogotá and received 1st Prize in Painting at the 10th Salon of Colombian Artists (1957). He has also presented work in the Venice Biennials of 1950 and 1958 and the 4th São Paulo Bienal (1957). Grau's career, from about 1948 to the present, has had three major phases. In the first (1948–1954) his art was figurative, lyrical, and impressionistic, full of nostalgia for the old-fashioned life of the 1920s. In 1954, a trip to Florence produced a radical change in his works: the human figure became dehumanized, dominated by geometry. Picasso's influence seemed obvious. After his return to Colombia in 1957, he broke his ties with Picasso and came under the influence of Alejandro Obregón. Lately, he has returned to the female figures of his pre-1954 work, but they are now more opulent and solid. The brilliant color of his earlier work has given way to a gamut of greys and lower-keyed hues. CF

**Grau, Ricardo** [Bordeaux, France, 1908– ]. Grau completed his art studies in France and Belgium under the tutelage of André Favory, André Lhote, Othon Friesz, and Fernand Léger. When World War II began Grau came to Peru, bringing with him this somewhat canonical version of the École de Paris. In so doing, he became one of the first representatives of modern painting in Latin America. A painter of true natural instinct, he was appointed a professor at the Universidad de San Marcos in Lima and, in 1943, was named Director of the Escuela de Bellas Artes where he effected the first stage of a new international outlook among Peruvian artists. His palette brightened considerably after 1940. In the 1950s he inclined toward pre-Columbian art and experimented with hard-edge planes heightened by bright colors. Recently his art has evolved toward non-figurative art in which he has returned to a more painterly technique. CF

**Greco, Alberto** [Buenos Aires, 1931– ]. Alberto Greco first studied in the Escuela Manuel Belgrano and later with Cecilia Marcovich and Tomás Maldonado. In 1954 he went to Europe for two years on a fellowship from the French government. In Paris he participated in the activities of avant-garde intellectual circles and had his first exhibition in 1955. At this point he was still torn between art and letters. After visiting several European countries, he returned to Argentina in 1956 to introduce *"el arte bruto,"* characterized by somber coloration, heavy impasto, collage additions, and a tragic sentiment. He is considered one of the pioneer exponents of Argentine informalism. In 1957 and 1958 he had successful one-man shows in Brazil. TG

**Grilo, Sarah** [Buenos Aires, 1921– ]. Sarah Grilo lived for a number of years in Madrid, where she taught herself to paint and where she had her first exhibition in 1949. On her return to Buenos Aires, she became in 1952 one of the original members of the Artistas Modernos group. During the decade of the 1950s she developed a distinctive style in the Constructivist tradition using flat color and semi-geometrical shapes.

Sarah Grilo was not a formal adherent of either Constructivism or Informalism, but she has contributed to both by her personal and very beautiful color, and by her unusual sensitivity to composition. San Martín speaks of her *"pathos expresivo."* In 1957 she exhibited in the Pan American Union in Washington, and has shown in a number of international group exhibitions. Her work since 1962 has turned toward a freer style, suggestive of walls with graffiti, dominated by a single color tone. She has lived in New York since 1964 with her husband, the Argentine painter José Antonio Fernández Muro.   TG

**Guayasamín, Oswaldo** [Quito, 1919–    ]. Guayasamín studied at the Escuela Nacional de Bellas Artes in Quito. Following his first one-man show, the U.S. State Department sponsored a traveling exhibit of his work in this country. Other honors have included a room devoted to his work at the 4th São Paulo Bienal (1957). The influence of the Mexican muralists, in particular of Orozco, is evident in Guayasamín's murals and larger paintings. His later work, still highly figurative, and concentrating on social as distinct from individual character and emotion, simplifies representational forms into broad planes and masses.   CF

**Guerrero, José Enrique** [Quito, 1905–    ]. After graduating from the Escuela de Bellas Artes in Quito, José Enrique Guerrero traveled to Paris, where he studied in the Académie Julien. In 1928 he worked for a short time at New York's National Academy of Design; the same year he won the Gold Medal of the City Council of Guayaquil; the previous year he had won the "Education" prize in Quito. After his early travels and successes he became professor of drawing in Quito's Colegio Nacional Mejía. In 1950, the Ecuadorian Congress, in recognition of his contribution to the artistic life of his nation, both as a practicing artist and as a teacher of art, voted him a grant to visit the United States. As other members of his generation, he has used the Ecuadorian scene in much of his work. His style, however, suggests an Expressionistic variant of Impressionism rather than the Neoclassical primitivism practiced by more orthodox indigenists.   CF

**Guignard, Alberto da Veiga** [Novo Friburgo, Brazil, 1896–    ]. Guignard began his artistic studies in the Königliche Akademie of Munich and continued them while traveling in Florence and Paris. He returned to Brazil in 1929 and won a bronze medal in the Salão Nacional of that year, the first of many honors he was to receive in following decades. He won a stipend in 1940 for travel in Brazil, and a gold medal (1942) and a medal of honor (1951) in national exhibitions. Since then, he has participated in exhibitions in Venice, Paris, Buenos Aires, and the United States. Guignard is a versatile, eclectic artist, painting and drawing landscapes as well as individual and group portraits. Guignard has moved from his earlier primitivistic approach to a more plastic treatment which, in his painting, presents wide, audacious, and often violent strokes of color. Recently he has simplified his technique and softened his palette in depicting the calm, monumental sobriety of the landscape of the state of Minas Gerais.   DD

**Gurvich, José** [Lithuania, 1927–    ]. José Gurvich arrived in Uruguay in 1939, and became a citizen shortly thereafter. He studied painting with Joaquín Torres García, entering his *taller* in 1945. In the two years between 1954 and 1956, he traveled in Europe and Israel, where he exhibited his drawings and ceramics. In Rome his work was displayed at the Galleria di San Marco. Gurvich works mainly in relief sculpture, a medium singularly well adapted to the Torres García principles he has espoused.   DD

**Guzmán de Rojas, Cecilio** [Potosí, Bolivia, 1900–    ]. Cecilio Guzmán de Rojas studied first in Cochabamba and then traveled and worked in France and Spain. While in Spain, he had an exhibition at the Barcelona Fair of 1929. Immediately upon his return to Bolivia he was named Inspector General of Fine Arts. In 1931 he became the director of the Escuela Nacional de Bellas Artes in La Paz, where he taught composition and theory of fine arts. As director he attempted to give a new direction to Bolivian art, away from a photographic romantic style to a "modern, simplified, rhythmic, Indo-American one." He was the founder of the Museo de Arte Representativo in Potosí as well as the illustrator of several books.   CF

**Hernández, Daniel** [Hurpay, Huancavelica, Peru, 1856 – Lima, 1932]. The family of Daniel Hernández settled in Lima in 1860. He revealed his artistic interests early and was taught by Leonardo Barbieri. In 1875 the Government of Peru gave him a scholarship to perfect his training in Europe. In Paris, he first visited Ignacio Merino, his fellow-countryman, who advised him to go to Rome, where he immediately went and remained for ten years. In 1885 he moved to Paris and became a member of the circle which included such fashionable masters as Fortuny, Pradilla, and Villegas. Hernández specialized in the feminine figure and portraits of women. *Señora Luisa de Mesones*, painted in 1883, reveals his ability to convey feminine personalities with great delicacy. In 1912, he visited Buenos Aires, where his work was shown with great success, and in 1913 he briefly returned to Rome. He was in Paris in

1917, but found the wartime atmosphere unconducive to art, and accepted the offer of the Peruvian Government to return to Lima to organize a school of fine arts. He was the first director of the Escuela de Bellas Artes in Lima.  TG

**Herrán, Saturnino** [Aguascalientes, Mexico, 1887–1918]. Herrán attended the Colegio de San Francisco Javier and the Instituto del Estado, where he studied with José Inés Tovilla Izaquirre, and Germán Gedovious. When he was fourteen, the death of his father led the family to move to Mexico City, where the artist entered the Escuela de Bellas Artes. In 1904, Herrán became the special disciple of his teacher, the Spanish artist Antonio Fabrés. In 1910 he presented his works in the Mexican Centenary Exposition and in 1913 in the Spanish Pavilion. Although Herrán died during his prime at the age of thirty-one, he left a poetic, subjective expression of the life of his country, emphasizing social themes. For example, *La Ofrenda* (1913), a depiction of Indians bringing an offering of flowers to the dead, expresses Herrán's aesthetic admiration and love for the Mexican people and their customs. His final years were extremely productive and, in 1914, he began his monumental piece, *Nuestros Dioses*, a series of decorative panels for the Teatro Nacional. This mural symbolized the fusion of indigenous and Hispanic peoples and cultures in the creation of modern Mexico.  DD

**Herrera Toro, Antonio** [Caracas, 1856–1914]. Herrera Toro began his artistic career as a decorator of churches and painter of religious works; later he took up portraiture and historical painting. In the latter genre, his best-known work was *Death of the Liberator*. He taught at the Academia de Bellas Artes of Caracas for a while. Toward the end of his life he began to concentrate on still-lifes, particularly flowers. His style was academic; his treatment reveals interest in anecdote rather than appreciation of theme.  CF

**Hlito, Alfredo** [Buenos Aires, 1923–      ]. Hlito studied in the Academia Nacional de Bellas Artes of Buenos Aires. He is a painter and graphic artist, and has also written considerably on the theory of art. As one of the founders of the Arte Concreto group, he especially came under the influence of the artist Max Bill. Up to 1945 there was an expressionist tendency in Hlito's art, but the recent work is of a mathematical-abstract nature in which he aims for the purest statement of two-dimensional shape and color relationships. In 1952 he was a member of the Artistas Modernos group, which included most of the abstractionists in Argentina.  TG

**Iberê Camargo, Sergio** [Rio Grande do Sul, Brazil, active since 1940]. Iberê Camargo studied at the Escola de Artes e Ofícios de Santa Maria and took courses in architectural techniques at the Instituto de Belas Artes of Pôrto Alegre, Rio Grande do Sul. In 1943 he and fellow artists organized the "Guignard Group" in Rio de Janeiro. In 1947 he was awarded a travel prize by the Salão de Arte Moderno of Rio de Janeiro and studied with De Chirico, Lhote, Petrucci, Achille, and Santa Rosa. He has taught engraving in Brazil and Uruguay and is currently teaching painting at the Instituto de Belas Artes in Rio de Janeiro. Many of his works are displayed in Brazilian and foreign museums and form parts of several private collections. Iberê Camargo has held individual exhibits at the Pan American Union in Washington, in Montevideo, and in many Brazilian state capitals. In 1961 he was awarded the "Best Brazilian Painter" prize at the Bienal of São Paulo.  DD

**Imaná Garrón, Gil** [Bolivia, active in the 1960s]. Imaná Garrón won 1st prize for painting at the municipal Salón in La Paz in 1961. He has presented several exhibits which featured scenes of local customs portrayed realistically and at the same time with tenderness. In his most recent efforts he has turned toward nonrepresentative art.  CF

**Irarrázabal, Ricardo** [Chile, 1942–      ]. This young artist studied in Santiago with André Racz and Claudio Di Girolamo. He then spent some time at the School of Fine Arts in Rome, the Académie Julien in Paris, and in Vallauris, France, working with ceramics until he became acquainted with John Duguid in London. Irarrázabal worked in the latter's painting workshop for five months. He has been exhibiting since 1956 and was represented at the 7th São Paulo Bienal in 1963. Thus far his work seems to be turning away from the search for psychic reality toward a more formal aesthetic. The subtle vibration of juxtaposed tonal bands in his work is perhaps reflective of mosaic technique on a grand scale.  CF

**Jaimes-Sánchez, Humberto** [San Cristóbal, Venezuela, 1930–      ]. Humberto Jaimes-Sánchez studied at the Escuela de Artes Plásticas in Caracas, where he now is a member of the faculty. He has had one-man shows in Washington, New York, and Caracas and has participated in many group shows in the United States and Europe, as well as in Latin America. His paintings have always been experimental, in the forefront of the avant-garde. His most recent work attempts to synthesize the figurative Pop-Art tendency with the visual punch of Retinal or Op Art.  TG

**Jimeno y Planes, Rafael** [Valencia, Spain, 1761 – Mexico, 1825]. Jimeno y Planes played a significant role in the introduction of Neoclassical art to Mexico at the turn of the 19th century. He had been strongly influenced by Tiepolo and Mengs in Europe, and it was their styles that he taught in his painting classes at the Academia de San Carlos in Mexico City. He had come to Mexico in 1794 as a professor of painting at the Academia and was named Director General in 1798. His style inspired a brief resurgence in the muralist art of Mexico, which lasted for a few years before the Romantic period. Among Jimeno's few extant works are portraits of two other Spanish Neoclassical artists who came to Mexico, Jerónimo Antonio Gil, the engraver and medalist, and Manuel Tolsá, the sculptor and architect.   JD

**Kingman Riofrío, Eduardo** [Loja, Ecuador, 1913–     ]. Eduardo Kingman received his original art training in the Escuela de Bellas Artes in Quito. He then moved to New York, where he studied with Camilo Egas. While there, he was selected to do the paintings for the Ecuadorian pavilion at the 1939 World's Fair. In 1940 he returned to Quito and founded the Caspicara Art Gallery, which he directed for a number of years. Immediately after World II he joined the staff of the San Francisco Museum of Art. He went back to Ecuador in 1947 to become Director of the Museo Nacional and of the National Artistic Patrimony. He has had individual exhibitions in a number of Latin American countries and in the United States. In 1936 he won the Mariano Aguilar Prize in Ecuador, his first major triumph. Since that time he has won a number of other important prizes. His work, comprising illustrations and woodcuts as well as paintings, is strongly indigenous in inspiration and reflects the influence of the Mexican muralists.   CF

**Kraft, Guillermo** [Brunswick, Germany, 1839 – Buenos Aires, 1893]. Kraft lived in Paris between the ages of fifteen and twenty-three. While there he learned lithography and printing. He moved to Argentina in 1862 and two years later founded the printing shop that bears his name. His name became well known because of his almanac, *Guía Kraft*, which first appeared in 1885. The shop produced many works of scientific and artistic value, such as the *Atlas de la República Argentina* (1886) and a magazine, *El Museo Histórico* (1892). One of the richest sources of Argentine caricature during the period was the satiric political weekly, *El Mosquito*, which Kraft began to publish upon his arrival in Buenos Aires.   TG

**Kratzenstein, Rodolfo** [active in Buenos Aires, 1822–1885]. Kratzenstein's active dates are marked by an 1822 lithographic view of Buenos Aires and a silk scarf with three lithographic views of the city dated 1885. Kratzenstein had a lithographic studio in Calle San Martín in Buenos Aires, where he produced prints of his own designs and those of other artists, specializing in portraits of national heroes: Rivadavia, San Martín, Urquiza, etc. He also did costumbrista prints, such as the print, *Gaucho*, after a painting by Grashof, and some views of the city of Buenos Aires. The 1850s seem to have been his period of greatest activity.   TG

**Lam, Wifredo** [Sagua la Grande, Cuba, 1902–     ]. Lam studied in Havana from 1921 to 1925, at which time he received a government scholarship to Spain. He lost the scholarship, however, refusing to paint the academic work expected of him. In 1938 he left Madrid with other refugees from Nationalist Spain and went to Paris, where he received aid from, and worked with, Picasso. With the Nazi invasion of France in World War II, Lam made his way back to Cuba, staying briefly in the United States en route. Early in his career, Lam painted objectively, showing a lyrical post-Impressionist interest in the subtleties of color and shape. He was soon influenced by Surrealism and produced compositions with irrational, biomorphic configurations of great delicacy. His style assumed full scale and stature in the early forties, following his contact with the Picasso of the post-Guernica period. In his art, Cubism and Surrealism are wedded and transformed into a powerful, still lyrical and perhaps essentially American vehicle of subconscious experience. In addition to his painting, he has also illustrated André Breton's *Fata Morgana* and Césaire's *Retour au pays natal*.   CF

**Lamonica, Roberto de** [Mato Grosso, Brazil, 1933–     ]. Roberto de Lamonica, one of the master contemporary engravers of the Western Hemisphere, studied art in São Paulo and completed an engraving course in the São Paulo Museu de Arte Moderna. He has held one-man exhibitions and has taken part in group exhibitions throughout the world.   DD

**La Placa, Alfredo** [Bolivia, 1929–     ]. La Placa, a self-taught painter, was one of the initiators of abstract painting in Bolivia. In 1960 he received the Grand Prize of the Municipality of La Paz; and in 1962 he participated in the Abstract Art Salon held in the same city. The artist works in Duco as well as in oil. His productions are marked by subtle distinctions of shade superimposed upon a background of predominantly one color, usually blue, red, or gray.   CF

**Lasansky, Mauricio** [Buenos Aires, 1914–    ]. Lasansky studied with Alfredo Guido at the Escuela Superior from 1933 to 1935. He was Director of the Escuela Libre de Bellas Artes in Córdoba, Argentina, from 1936 to 1939, and thereafter Director of the Taller Manualidades in Córdoba. In 1943 he came to New York City and spent two years on a Guggenheim Fellowship for research in black-and-white prints. In 1945 he was appointed Visiting Lecturer at the State University of Iowa to initiate a program in graphic arts. He has remained at Iowa, becoming a full Professor in 1948. In 1952 he became a naturalized citizen of the United States. Lasansky is represented in many collections, among them the U.S. National Gallery, the Museum of Modern Art, and the Rosenwald Collection. He has won many important prizes, including the 1st Prize, 17th International Exhibit of Prints, Seattle, 1944, and the Posada Prize, 1st Mexican Biennial, 1958. In 1953 he was again awarded a Guggenheim Fellowship. A large exhibition was organized by the Albright Art Gallery in Buffalo of the work of Lasansky and his pupils at Iowa. Lasansky has been a principal figure in the revival of printmaking in recent years, and one of the central figures in recent art of the Americas. TG

**Laso, Francisco** [Tacna, Peru, 1823 – Lima, 1869]. Laso first studied art with the Quiteño painter, Javier Cortés, who taught in Lima, and later with the academic painter Ignacio Merino. He completed his studies in Europe, and while in Italy he was strongly influenced by Veronese. On his return to Peru he produced important paintings of a national character, including *Indio alfarero* (*Indian Potter*), a notable prototype of later indigenist art. Perhaps his most famous work is *St. Rose of Lima*, now in the Municipal Palace.  TG

**Latorre, Guillermo** [Quito, 1896–    ]. Latorre devoted himself first to sketching and later turned to caricature. He was one of the founders of the satirical magazine *Caricatura*. In 1929 he first exhibited his watercolors and sketches outside his native country, in Panama. His early work shows the indigenist influence of Camilo Egas. At present Latorre is working and traveling in Spain.  CF

**Lauvergne, Barthélemy** [Toulon, 1805 – Carces, France 1871]. Lauvergne was both landscape painter and lithographer, exhibiting in the Paris Salons from 1828 until 1848. He also served as an administrative official in the French Navy until 1863. He visited Montevideo on the French corvette *La Bonite* in 1836. In 1842 he was commissioned by the Marine Ministry to paint a view of Algiers.  CF

**Leal, Fernando** [Mexico City, 1900–1965]. Leal, a pioneer of the folk mural, studied briefly in the Escuela de Bellas Artes. He found a freer, less narrowly academic atmosphere in the open-air Escuela de Pintura at Coyoacán, which was then under the direction of Alfredo Ramos Martínez. In his first mural, *La Fiesta del Señor de Chalma*, done at the Escuela Nacional Preparatoria in 1922–1923, Leal displayed a style that combined a classicist conception of form with an almost baroque sense of movement. The thematic base of his work is to be found in Mexican folklore. He has been faithful to this style and theme in the rest of his work. Two of his most important later murals are in the Anfiteatro Bolívar in Mexico City and in the San Luis Potosí railroad station. Early in his career Leal coöperated with Jean Charlot and Emilio Amero in reviving the graphic arts in Mexico. He was also a member of the ''30-30 Group'' that in 1928–1929 publicized the latest developments in art and expressed its opposition to stock academic ideas.  JD

**Lee, Wesley Duke** [São Paulo, Brazil, 1931–    ]. Lee studied drawing at the São Paulo Museum of Art, and graphic arts at the Parsons School of Design in New York. He participated in the 2nd Salon of Modern Art in São Paulo in 1952, and in the 1st Salon of Advertising of São Paulo. He worked in the advertising field for two years, returning to painting and drawing in 1957. In 1958 Lee traveled to France where he attended courses and visited many ateliers; and in 1960, after a trip to Sweden, he dedicated himself solely to painting and drawing. Lee's first one-man exhibit was held in 1961 at the Sistina Gallery in São Paulo. His works were exhibited in 1962 at the Michael Gallery in São Paulo, and in Europe in 1963. With a group of other artists, Lee started a movement called ''magic realism.'' In 1964, while a teacher of drawing at the College of Architecture, MacKenzie University, São Paulo, he turned to writing, and has produced a great many articles and pamphlets on art, as well as two volumes of poetry.  DD

**Leufert, Gerd** [Latvia, 1914–    ]. Before moving to Venezuela in 1950, Gerd Leufert studied and taught in a number of art and engraving schools, among them the Akademie der Kunst of Munich, New York's Pratt Institute, and the Art School of Iowa State University. Upon his arrival in Venezuela he was named Director of the Sección de Artes Gráficas in the Escuela de Artes Plásticas. Later he became professor of composition in the Facultad de Arquitectura y Urbanismo of the Universidad Central of Venezuela. He is at present Coordinador de Artes Plásticas for the Instituto Nacional de Cultura y

Bellas Artes. He has had one-man shows since 1954 in San Francisco, Los Angeles, Bogotá, Munich, and Caracas; his works are to be found in the Library of Congress, the Museum of Modern Art, New York, the Kunstmuseum in Basel, and the Chase Manhattan Bank collection. His work, which has evolved within the broad Constructivist tradition, freely applies quasi-geometrical principles of design and combines influence of both the U.S. hard-edge school and Venezuelan optical abstraction. In his earlier work he frequently used tonalities of one color on a black or white background, seeking to control light variations by means of texture and tone changes. Lately he has begun to experiment with a broader palette, juxtaposing contrasting colors to increase surface tension.   CF

**Lira, Pedro** [Santiago de Chile, 1845–1912]. Pedro Lira studied law at the Universidad de Chile and painting at the Academia de la Pintura under Alejandro Cicarelli. A trip to Paris in 1873 exposed him to the pictorial influence of Delacroix and to the more temperate romanticism of Elie Delaunay, with whom he worked. Other painters with whom he studied during his eleven years in Europe were Liminais, Lepage, and Jules Bastien. In 1885, a year after his return to Chile, he founded the Unión Artística and helped to organize the Museo de Bellas Artes in the Quinta Normal. He became a professor in the Escuela de Bellas Artes of Santiago and in 1892 was named director of that institution. Lira's artistic style evolved from romanticism through realism to naturalism and, finally, at the end of his life, to a tentative impressionism. He has been called the first Chilean painter with a perfect technical command of the oil medium, a command that he preferred to exercise in paintings of the human figure and in portraits. However, painting was not his only field of endeavor; he translated Hippolyte Taine's *La philosophie de l'art* and wrote a *Diccionario biográfico de pintores*.   CF

**Lisboa, Antônio Francisco,** called O Aleijadinho [Minas Gerais, Brazil, 1738–1814]. O Aleijadinho, who received his primary education from his father, a Portuguese artisan and sculptor, was the key figure in Brazilian 18th-century religious architecture. He designed and worked on numerous churches and church sites of the interior, both as architect and sculptor, achieving a brilliantly successful version of Portuguese-Baroque style within the 18th-century ambiance of the gold-mining towns of Minas Gerais. Among his numerous architectural works are the Church of S. Francisco de Assis in Ouro Prêto and the Sanctuary of Nosso Senhor Bom Jesus de Matazinhos in Congonhas do Campo. His sculpture includes the famous stone prophets and Via Crucis groups in painted wood in Congonhas do Campo. In addition to his work as architect and sculptor, O Aleijadinho became a legendary popular figure. He lived in voluntary "exile" with peasants in the *sertão*. Suffering acutely from leprosy, he had to be carried by litter from church to church, and toward the end of his life his limbs were in such an advanced state of decay that his tools had to be strapped to his wrists. Before his death he was as well known as a folk hero as an artist.   DD

**López, Cándido** [Buenos Aires, 1840–1902]. López is supposed to have studied with Cayetano Descalzi (although the latter may have left Argentina in 1845) and with Baldassare Verazzi, an Italian painter. He was in the town of San Nicolás de los Arroyos in 1865 when the Triple Alliance (Argentina, Uruguay, Brazil) declared war against Paraguay. Joining a local infantry battalion, he fought in the battle of Curupatí where he lost his right hand. This loss did not deter him from his determination to be a painter, and he learned to paint with his left hand. Devoting himself to subjects from the Paraguayan war, López specialized in grand panoramas of battles and in bird's-eye perspectives. Twenty-nine oil paintings on these subjects are preserved in the Museo Histórico Nacional de Buenos Aires. They were shown for the first time in 1885 at the Gymnastic and Fencing Club in an exhibition sponsored by that club and the Centro Industrial Argentino.   TG

**Lovera, Juan** [Caracas, 1778–1841]. While still in his teens, Lovera studied with Antonio José Landaeta, a painter in the colonial tradition. By 1799 he had his own workshop, where he did many portraits and, contrary to the usual custom of late colonial painters, very little religious work. Alexander von Humboldt, the German scientist and explorer, was one of his subjects in later years. Lovera was present at the uprising of April 19, 1810, and at the signing of Independence on July 5, 1811, in which Venezuela freed herself from Spanish rule. He subsequently recorded these occasions in two paintings which are among the foremost works of art celebrating Independence in the Western Hemisphere. When the Spanish invaded Caracas in 1814, he fled with the rebel army and did not return to the capital until after 1820. He apparently played a fairly prominent role in the cultural and social life of the young republic. In 1831 he was one of the subscribing members of the Sociedad Filarmónica. From his almost fifty years of artistic production, only some fifty or sixty works are known to have survived. From these his artistic evolution seems to fall into three periods. In his early work he followed the colonial tradition, paying close attention to detail. Between 1825 and 1830, probably the period of his best work, he used a more variegated palette. In his later work, his treatment of figures became broader and more sober, but always with a free, original, and highly expressive use of line. Some influence of José Gil de Castro, the Peruvian Independence painter, has been noticed in work of this period, but Lovera remained individualistic. He is counted among the first Latin American native painters of the early 19th century. CF

**Luque, Angel** [Córdoba, Spain, 1927–      ]. Angel Luque, a self-taught painter and engraver, did his early work in Madrid, where he formed part of an extra-academic group called Artistas de Hoy. Since 1955, he has been working in Venezuela with an informalist group. He had his first one-man show in Madrid just before he went to Venezuela. He has been winning awards since 1955, most notably Venezuela's Premio Nacional de Grabados in 1962. His abstract expressionist style has become more lyrical in recent work both in assemblage and in combinations of bright, flatly applied color. CF

**Lynch, Alberto** [Lima, 1851–?]. Alberto Lynch studied art at the Ecole des Beaux-Arts in Paris with Gabriel Ferrier. While in Paris he received several prizes: a third-class medal in 1890, a first-class medal in 1892, and a gold medal in 1900 at the Exposition Universelle. Lynch was made a Chevalier of the Légion d'Honneur in 1901. His works have been exhibited in Paris, New York, and Sydney. TG

**Mabe, Manabu** [Kumamoto, Japan, 1924–      ]. Mabe came to Brazil as a child of ten. A member of the immediate postwar generation of Brazilian painters, his artistic success in the '50s was rapid and brilliant. Today he is considered one of the outstanding artists of Latin America. He has won the following prizes: 1st Prize in the 5th São Paulo Bienal (1959); the Fiat Prize in the 30th Venice Biennial (1960); 1st Prize in the 1st Inter-American Biennial of Art in Córdoba, Argentina (1962); and 1st Prize in the 2d Biennial of Young Artists in Paris (1961). He has had exhibitions throughout Latin America, Europe, and the United States, where his work is also included in several museum collections. DD

**Macció, Rómulo** [Buenos Aires, 1931–      ]. Macció was an apprentice at the age of fourteen in a publicity agency and later worked in graphic design and theatrical decor. A self-taught painter, Macció first exhibited his paintings in 1956 and since that time has had many successful exhibitions. He has shown his work in Paris, London, Rio de Janeiro, New

York (in the Guggenheim International Exhibition of 1964), Washington, Caracas, and his native city of Buenos Aires. He has won several prizes, the most important being the 1st International Prize in the 1963 exhibition of the Instituto Torcuato Di Tella in Buenos Aires. He lives in Paris. TG

**Magariños, Víctor** [Argentina, 1924–      ]. Magariños studied in the Escuela Nacional de Bellas Artes in Buenos Aires. In 1950 he received a French Government scholarship for study in Paris. On his return to Argentina, he had a one-man show in the Instituto de Arte Moderno. The exhibit, which comprised geometric abstractions, was considered an important new departure in Argentine painting at the time. His work continues within the broad limits of the Constructivist tradition, elaborating intuitively conceived abstract designs into carefully simplified quasi-geometric schemes of subtle balance and tension, and strong visual impact. TG

**Maldonado, Tomás** [Buenos Aires, 1922–      ]. Maldonado, who is both a painter and graphic artist, studied in the Academia de Bellas Artes in Buenos Aires. In 1944 he was a collaborator in the publication of the magazine *Arturo*, to which he contributed graphic art as well as literary material. Through this magazine he helped to initiate the abstract art movement in Argentina. He also assisted in the publication of a magazine for the Asociación de Arte Concreto-Invención. In the 1950s he was a member of the group Artistas Modernos. For some time Maldonado has taught in the Hochschule für Gestaltung in Ulm, Germany, which is directed by Max Bill. Bill's philosophy of art has been influential in eastern South America and is particularly congenial to Maldonado. TG

**Malfatti, Anita** [São Paulo, Brazil, 1896–      ]. Anita Malfatti began her formal studies in art at Mackenzie College, São Paulo, continued them in Dresden, and completed them at the Royal Academy of Berlin. Her travels in Europe and her work under Bruger, Lowis Corinth, and Bischoff Culn opened her eyes to the currents of modern painting. She found additional inspiration during her stay in the United States, where she attended the Art Students League and the Independent School of the Arts in New York, studying with Homer Boss of the "Fifteen Group." Under these influences, Malfatti incorporated into her early style the tenets of both Cubism and Expressionism. In 1917, the year following her return to Brazil, she presented the first large-scale one-man exhibition of modern art in São Paulo. Anita Malfatti gained the approval of the Modernist poet-novelist Mário de Andrade and, in 1922, joined with him and other young avant-garde artists in presenting São Paulo's Modern Art Week. She is one of the pioneer figures of modern art in Brazil.  DD

**Malharro, Martín A.** [Argentina, 1865–1911]. Malharro studied at the Sociedad Estímulo de Bellas Artes and was a disciple of Francisco Romero. Despite little public success or encouragement, he dedicated himself to his art, devoting his early years to a study of the light and landscape of his native region. His work finally won a following and he was subsidized for travel to Europe, where he adopted Impressionism and carried it back to Argentina. Far ahead of the public for many years, he remained a solitary exponent of the style. In 1902 Malharro presented the first exhibition of Impressionist painting in Argentina in the Galería Witcomb, Buenos Aires. A second such exhibition was held in the same gallery in 1908. He remained faithful to a fairly strict Impressionist style, although the more influential Impressionist manner in Argentina was that of Fader and the Nexus group who, by comparison, were technically less advanced at the time. However, his work eventually led to a coloristic post-Impressionist style. Malharro is now esteemed as one of the true precursors of modern art in Argentina.  TG

**Manosalvas, Juan** [Quito, 1840–1906]. Manosalvas received his first lessons from his aunt, Angela de la Madre de Dios Manosalvas, who became a Carmelite nun. He entered the studio of Leandro Venegas and, subsequently, at the age of twelve, the Sociedad Artística Miguel de Santiago. In 1871 he received a scholarship from the government of García Moreno to study at the Accademia di San Luca in Rome, where he took private lessons from Alessandro Marini. It was during this trip that he met the Spanish artist Mariano Fortuny, from whom he learned watercolor technique. Upon his return to Quito in 1873 his studio became a gathering place for artists. He shared his European knowledge with the younger Joaquín Pinto, who learned watercolor from him. He was offered posts in Mexico, Colombia, and Bolivia. Instead, he became director of the Academia de Bellas Artes in Quito, a post he held until the closing of that institution following the assassination of García Moreno. In 1904 he became a member of the faculty of the newly founded Escuela de Bellas Artes. He specialized in small studies of Quiteño life.  CF, TG

**Mariaca Arguedas, Antonio** [Bolivia, 1929– ]. Mariaca Arguedas studied in Spain with Vásquez Díaz and Pancho Cossío before returning to his native Bolivia. There he has been a significant figure in art since 1953, when he won his first major award. His early work was figurative. Lately he has turned to abstraction after a transition period during which he painted "schematic portraits." His present work is nonobjective, yet expressive of a "certain spirit of meditation and nostalgia."  CF

**Mark, Edward Walhouse** [Málaga, Spain, 1817 – Norwood, England, 1895]. Mark, the son of an English foreign service officer, adopted his father's profession, arriving as British Vice-Consul in Santa Marta, Nueva Granada (Colombia), in 1843. After three years he was transferred to Bogotá. There, as Vice-Consul, he was an active, successful diplomat and, out of personal interest, traveled throughout the country. In the course of his travels he painted watercolors of every facet of Colombian life: human types in great variety, landscapes and architecture, plants, flowers, insects, and local occupations. He painted with an expert assurance that gives his work a value far beyond the documentary. During the later years of his stay in Columbia Mark undoubtedly became acquainted with Léon Gauthier, the French painter who arrived in Bogotá to show his work and to make similar reportorial paintings. He may also have known members of the Colombian Comisión Corográfica, whose work he anticipated. In 1856 Mark was transferred to Baltimore, and two years later to Marseilles. He retired from the foreign service in 1888.  TG

**Martens, Conrad** [London, 1801 – Australia, 1871]. Conrad Martens was born in London in 1801, where he studied painting and watercolor with the English artist Copley Fielding. When his father died Martens decided to go to Uruguay, arriving in Montevideo in 1833. Shortly after his arrival, the famous HMS *Beagle*, on its voyage around the world and with the young naturalist Charles Darwin aboard, put into port at Montevideo. Martens secured passage on the ship in 1834 and worked in company with Darwin. He abandoned the expedition in Valparaíso, continuing by himself to Tahiti, and eventually to Australia, where he remained until his death in 1871. Like the Frenchman, D'Hastrel, Martens left a number of costumbrista sketches and watercolors depicting the Uruguayan scene: views of the city of Montevideo, country life, gauchos. His engraving *Vista de Montevideo* was published by Darwin in his journal of the *Beagle*'s voyage.  DD

**Martínez, Ricardo** [Mexico, 1918– ]. Coming from a family of artists, Martínez subordinated his early inclination toward painting in order to take a law degree. His association with artists and poets during his studies at the University of Mexico, however, soon led him to devote his full energies to painting. His first important exhibition was held in Guadalajara in 1942 and his first one-man show in Mexico City in 1947. In the summer of 1948 he was invited to teach at the Colorado Springs Fine Arts Center and the following summer at San Diego College. Martínez has done sets and costumes for the Hanya Holm ballet, *Xochipili*, and for Shaw's *Saint Joan*, both produced in Mexico City. He has illustrated books, including *Epigramas americanos* by Enrique Díez-Canedo.  DD

**Martins, Aldemir** [Ingàzeira, Ceará, Brazil, 1922–      ]. Aldemir Martins' semiabstract characterizations of the folklore and the natural phenomena of the coastal regions and interior of Brazil have contributed to the international image of the popular life and environment of his vast country. A muralist as well as graphic artist and painter, his works have been shown publicly since 1942, and since have found a place in many museums and private collections in Europe and the United States, as well as in Latin America. He has won numerous prizes, including 3rd prize at the "Salon of the 19" in São Paulo (1949); the "Olivia Guedes Penteado" prize at the 1st São Paulo Bienal (1951); the "Nadir Figueredo" prize at the 2nd São Paulo Bienal (1953); the Gold Medal at the 4th Bahia Salon; the Gold Medal at the 5th National Salon of Modern Art (1956); the "Trip Around Brazil" prize at the 7th São Paulo Salon of Modern Art; and the "Trip Abroad" prize at the 8th National Salon of Modern Art. He has held both individual and collective exhibits in cities throughout the world.  DD

**Matta Echaurren, Sebastian Antonio** [Santiago, 1912–      ]. One of the most original as well as internationally respected modern artists of Latin American origin, Matta first studied architecture, receiving his degree from the Universidad Católica de Chile in 1931. Three years later he went to Paris to work with Le Corbusier. In Paris he met the Surrealists and began to devote himself to painting. In 1935, on a trip to Madrid, he worked with García Lorca (who sponsored his first exhibition), Pablo Neruda, and another Spanish poet, Rafael Alberti. Back in Paris in 1936 and 1937, he gave up all pretense of working on architecture and joined the group of artists around Joan Miró, Max Ernst, and André Breton. In New York from 1938 to 1948, he worked primarily with Marcel Duchamp and Yves Tanguy. He lived in Rome from 1949 to 1954, and then moved to Paris, and is now a French citizen. Matta's early work is surrealist, but it is a "metaphysical" nonfigurative surrealism. The violently expressionist feeling of his earlier work, possibly induced by his reactions to World War II, was replaced around 1948 by a somewhat more relaxed and deli-

cate tone. Matta had a retrospective one-man show at the Museum of Modern Art in New York in 1957. At that time he stated that he had begun to face the problem of representing "nonanthropomorphic man."  CF

**Mérida, Carlos** [Quetzaltenango, Guatemala, 1891–      ]. Carlos Mérida is one of the pioneer figures of 20th-century Latin American painting. In his youth in Guatemala City he became acquainted with the artist Carlos Valenti and, with Valenti, went to Europe for a period of four years. Mérida became a friend of Modigliani and partly through his influence became deeply involved in the interests of the Parisian avant-garde. Upon his return to Guatemala he sought to incorporate the rich artistic heritage of his native country into the modern idiom that he had learned abroad; this has been his lifelong aim. He settled in Mexico City, where he participated actively in the movements of the 1920s and '30s, and where he continues to work today. His paintings have an architectonic quality derived from their ultimately Cubist ancestors, and for this reason they adapt well to the requirements of the mural. Mérida has designed and executed a number of important murals in painting, cement, and mosaic, a recent series of mosaic murals in the new Municipal Palace of Guatemala City being among his finest.  TG

**Meza, Guillermo** [Ixtapalapa, Mexico, 1917–      ]. Meza, of Tlaxcaltecan Indian origin, worked as an apprentice in his father's tailor shop, studying nights at an art school for laborers. In 1937 his teacher took him to Morelia as an assistant, thereby giving him an opportunity to paint in earnest. Going to Mexico City in 1938, he held various odd jobs until he showed his paintings to Diego Rivera, who received them enthusiastically. Sponsored by Inés Amor, Meza began to concentrate all of his energies on art. He had his first one-man show at the Galería de Arte Mexicano in 1940 and several others in following years. He has also had an exhibition in Boston. Meza's early work as painter and draughtsman achieved a new and stunning formulation of irrational experience in ancient Indian tradition, which he redefined in both a surrealist and classical spirit employing distortion and metamorphosis with dramatic effect. The same interest in supernatural forces, both godlike and demonic, which he sees beneath all surface appearance, continues in his present work, although the outward form departs less from the observed landscapes and still-life themes he takes for subject matter.  DD

**Michelena, Arturo** [Valencia, Venezuela, 1863–1898]. Michelena showed a remarkable gift for sketching as a child. At the age of thirteen he illustrated Francisco de Salas Pérez's *Ratos perdidos* (*Leisure Hours*), a series of anecdotes from everyday life in the costumbrista tradition. In 1885 Michelena received a scholarship for study with Jean-Paul Laurens, dean of French academic art, in Paris. The latter's academicism made use of themes based on such fashionable intellectual interests of the time as Naturalism and Parnassianism. After receiving a prize at the Salon Officiel of Paris for his *El Niño enfermo* (*Sick Child*), Michelena returned to Venezuela in 1889. Michelena's palette, possibly influenced by the tropical Venezuelan light, became noticeably more luminous in his later historical paintings. Within his academic style he posed and solved a series of pictorial problems in composition, rhythm and chiaroscuro before his death from tuberculosis at the age of thirty-five.   CF

**Monsanto, Antonio Edmundo** [Caracas, 1890–1947]. Monsanto studied at the Escuela de Bellas Artes in Caracas with Herrera Toro. In 1913 his interest in Cézanne's interpretation of landscape led him to join the School of Caracas when this group was formed in opposition to the current academic style. Later the artist taught in the Escuela de Artes Plásticas, and eventually directed it from 1936 until his death. As a teacher he set new standards for artists of the post-war generation and is respected by many as one of the forerunners of Venezuelan modernism.   CF

**Montenegro, Roberto** [Guadalajara, Mexico, 1885–      ]. Roberto Montenegro has played an important role in 20th-century Mexican art, having contributed to it not only with his own mural and oil painting, but through his active interest in preserving and promoting the popular arts of his country. He studied at the Academia de Bellas Artes in Mexico City in 1905. He won a scholarship in 1906, and lived for most of the next thirteen years in Europe. Four of these years he spent in Majorca, where he painted several murals in public buildings. The earliest important influence on Montenegro was the work of Aubrey Beardsley. Although his point of view broadened considerably during his long stay in Europe, a current of Art-Nouveau fantasy runs through much of his later production. His work has been varied in genre and technique. Upon his return to Mexico he joined the muralist movement and injected a strong folk sentiment into such works as *La Fiesta de la Santa Cruz* (*The Feast of the Holy Cross*) (1922–1923) in the ex-convent of San Pedro and Pablo, Mexico City. He has also worked as a portraitist.   JD

**Monvoisin, Raymond Quinsac** [Bordeaux, France, 1790–1870]. Monvoisin studied art in Bordeaux with Lacour and in Paris with Guérin at the École des Beaux-Arts. At the age of thirty-two Monvoisin won the school's highest honor, the Grand Prix de Rome, an award that enabled him to study in Italy from 1821 to 1826. After a period of official favor, he fell out with the Directeur-Général des Musées at the time of Louis-Philippe and decided to seek more propitious surroundings in South America. He arrived in Chile in 1845. He spent sixteen years in voluntary exile there and in Peru and Argentina before returning to France by way of Brazil. He helped to found a school of painting in Peru; and an art gallery in Chile bears his name. Monvoisin's style, a not-so-severe post-Davidian classicism in his European work, became much more romantic in content and in spirit during his stay in Latin America.   CF

**Morales, Armando** [Granada, Nicaragua, 1927–      ]. Armando Morales began his study of art in 1950 at the Escuela de Bellas Artes in Managua, Nicaragua. He began exhibiting in 1953. In 1954 he won the 1st prize for Latin America at the 5th Bienal of São Paulo. His paintings are freely composed abstractions of broad, flat shapes, somber in color, often painted with a smooth, heavy impasto, and of unusual formal subtlety. Morales received a Guggenheim Fellowship and studied in the United States at the Pratt Graphic Art Center. His works are owned by the Museum of Modern Art in New York, the Museum of Contemporary Art of the University of São Paulo, and other museums and private collections in Latin America and the United States.   TG

**Morel, Carlos** [Buenos Aires, 1813–1894]. Morel studied drawing at the University of Buenos Aires with the Swiss artist Josef Guth and the Italian Paolo Caccianiga. He graduated in 1831 at the age of eighteen, and signed his first lithograph seven years later. Morel's major accomplishments in art were limited to a ten-year period, from about 1835 to 1845. A significant early costumbrista artist, he completed his most important lithographs, entitled *Usos y Costumbres del Río de la Plata* (*Habits and Customs of the River Plate*), in 1844. His oil portraits, battle pictures, and scenes from gaucho life combine sensitive perception with lusty realism, and warrant his consideration as one of the foremost native American artists of the early 19th century. When Morel was thirty-two years old, he and his brother-in-law Julián Dupuy, were arrested by troops of the tyrant Rosas. They were taken to Santos Lugares, where Dupuy was beheaded. Just as Morel was about to suffer the same fate, it was discovered that he was the wrong man. He was released but never recovered from the shock, and remained insane the rest of his life. Although he lived to be eighty-one years old, Morel never did another piece of significant art.  TG

**Mota, Agostinho José da** [Rio de Janeiro, Brazil, 1824–1878]. Agostinho José da Mota entered the Académia de Belas Artes at the age of thirteen. In 1850 he won the Prêmio de Viagem in Brazil's Exposição Geral, which allowed him to study and travel in Europe. After studying in Rome with the French painter Benonville, da Mota was awarded a gold medal for work shown in the Exposição Geral de Belas Artes in Rio in 1852. On his return to Brazil he succeeded Augusto Muller in the chair of Landscape Painting at the Académia de Belas Artes, where he taught until his death. Da Mota is perhaps best remembered for his paintings of Brazilian fruits and flowers. These he depicted with authenticity, simplicity, and sincerity. He is also considered one of the good Brazilian landscapists of his time. His portraits show da Mota as a sensitive observer of the subtleties of physical and psychological character.  DD

**Moulin, Hipólito** [Argentina, active in the 1830s]. Describing himself as a soldier with his home in France, Moulin entered Argentina from Montevideo on January 1, 1831. Evidently an amateur at art, by 1833 he was collaborating with Bacle, a well-known lithographer in Buenos Aires. During the next two years much of the finest work produced by the Bacle studios was done by Moulin, including the second folder of Bacle's *Trajes y Costumbres (Dresses and Customs)*, portraits of the dictator Rosas, and many of the illustrations for *Museo Americano, Libro de todo el Mundo (American Museum, Book of the World)*. The arrest and imprisonment of Bacle by Rosas and finally Bacle's death may have been factors in Moulin's departure from Argentina about 1838.  TG

**Müller-Lewit, Mario** [Quito, 1940–    ]. Mario Müller received his first training at the Windsor Mountain School in Lenox, Massachusetts, in 1954. From 1954 to 1958 he worked in the private school of Lloyd Wulf in Quito and then continued his studies in Mexico City College. Between 1959 and 1962 he made several trips abroad, spending time in Germany and Greece. He has been living in Quito since 1962. He has had several exhibitions since his first, which was held in 1960 in Düsseldorf, Germany.  CF

**Nebel, Karl** [Altona, Germany, 1805 – Paris, 1855]. An accomplished lithographer, Nebel contributed to the romantic rediscovery of the Mexican past. He came to Mexico in 1829,

three years after Claudio Linati established the first lithograph workshop in that country. He remained five years working on a book of fifty lithographs, published in Paris in 1836 and in Mexico City in 1840. This elaborate publication was titled *Viaje pintoresco y arqueológico sobre la parte más interesante de la República Mexicana en los años transcurridos desde 1829 hasta 1834*. Nebel's expertly executed lithographs depicted pre-Columbian buildings, contemporary Mexican city life, and popular customs. Very little is known of Nebel's artistic education or his activities outside of Mexico. He did publish ten lithographs and a map in *The War Between the United States and Mexico*, which appeared in New York in 1851.  JD

**Noreña, Miguel** [Mexico, 1843– ? ]. A disciple of the Catalonian sculptor Manuel Vilar at the Academia de San Carlos, Noreña's major work is the statue of *Cuauhtémoc* on the monument to the last Aztec emperor, which stands on the Paseo de la Reforma in Mexico City. He also executed a seated bronze statue of *Benito Juárez*, a Mexican president during the 19th-century Reform period.  DD

**Obregón, Alejandro** [Barranquilla, Colombia, 1920–    ]. The brilliant light of his native town, a major Atlantic port, has been a predominant influence in Obregón's painting. His work, which is consistently figurative on a cubist base, returns repeatedly to a carefully chosen vocabulary of forms and symbols. In his earlier work these appear variously as arrows, cocks, fishes, doves, and eagles. After 1959 he entered a period in which he painted condors, both alone and in combination with other natural objects such as the sea and volcanoes. In 1962 he received the National Grand Prize at the Salón Nacional of Colombia for his oil, *Violación*, a painting that reflects the violence endemic in Colombian life at the time of the Bogotá uprising in 1948.  CF

**O'Gorman, Juan** [Mexico, 1905–    ]. Juan O'Gorman, the son of the painter Crawford O'Gorman, developed an interest in sketching and painting very early in his life. In 1927 he received a degree in architecture, and subsequently participated in the movement of modern architecture in Mexico. His professional interest in architecture did not prevent him from continuing his early interest in painting. His first enthusiasm in this genre was for popular art, which he depicted with a refined technique, firm lines, and a lyrical sense of color. The three major themes of his paintings have been landscape, allegory, and portraits. O'Gorman is generally recognized as one of Mexico's best landscapists, although his work avoids naturalistic representation and tends toward a more interpretative, inventive, often fantastic portrayal of the Mexican country-side. His allegory, *Monumento Fúnebre al Capitalismo (Funeral Monument to Capitalism)* (1943) creates a fantastic landscape and a demonic structure of industrialism, clearly reflecting the rise of modern industry in Mexico and the artist's concern for its inhuman implications. O'Gorman has executed various successful portraits of Mexican ladies, one of his most applauded attempts being the *Retrato (Portrait)* of 1942, which is a balanced and refined interpretation of a seated woman. His fantastic landscape *Recuerdo de los Remedios (Memory of Los Remedios)* (1943), done in a near surrealistic manner, suggests the remembrance of things past, distorted by memory and imagination. O'Gorman turned to murals in the 1940s, executing work in the city of Pátzcuaro. In 1952 the Instituto Nacional de Bellas Artes exhibited his work.   DD

**Orozco, José Clemente** [Zapotlán, Jalisco, Mexico, 1883 – Mexico City, 1949]. Orozco spent his formative years in Mexico City, where his family moved in 1890. He took night classes at the Academia de Bellas Artes and, after some work at the University's Escuela Preparatoria and the Escuela de Agricultura de San Jacinto, he enrolled as a regular student at the Academia. The major artistic influences of his student years were his rigid academic training in perspective and anatomy, the engravings of the cartoonist Posada, and the teachings of Dr. Atl, a fervent admirer of Michelangelo. Orozco did not study in Europe, but when he finally got there in 1932, he spent his time seeing the works of the masters he and Atl respected. He returned to the Western Hemisphere as firmly determined as ever to continue creating a new American art that would not be a mere imitation of either European or pre-Columbian models. Orozco's early work consisted mainly of oils and political cartoons of the Revolution. In 1922 he entered a second period, creating his first mural in an early form of the style that was to distinguish him among the great artists of the 20th century. He was abroad from 1927 to 1934, most of the time in the United States. In this fertile period he executed the Pomona and Dartmouth College murals, giving full expression to his sense of movement and tension. Upon his return to Mexico, Orozco entered into his period of full maturity. The numerous murals and oils he created then showed him to be the master of a rich and varied technique, striking to the eye and always expressive of basic themes of process and conflict. At Mexico City, at Guadalajara, and at Jiquilpan, he has left vast works that are considered by many to be among the best examples of modern American art.   JD

**Ortúzar, Carlos** [Chile, 1935–    ]. Ortúzar received his training at the Escuela de Bellas Artes of the Universidad de Chile. He has participated in the Biennials of Paris, Córdoba (Argentina), and São Paulo. His work is more symbolic than abstract, incorporating figurative elements similar to Indo-American emblems. The impasto on many of his works is built up so heavily in sober, muted colors that they appear more like bas-reliefs than oils.   CF

**Ostrower, Fayga** [Poland, 1920–    ]. Having moved to Brazil while very young, Fayga Ostrower is a Brazilian citizen. An accomplished artist, she has had showings in the most important art centers of the world and has won national and international prizes such as "Best Brazilian Engraver" at the 4th São Paulo Bienal (1957) and the International Grand Prize for Engraving at the 29th Biennial of Venice (1958). Miss Ostrower has visited the United States as a Fulbright Scholar and, at the invitation of the John Hay Whitney Foundation, is lecturing at the University of Atlanta, Georgia, while on leave from her post as Professor of Theory of Composition and Critical Analysis at Rio de Janeiro's Museu de Arte Moderna.   DD

**Otero, Alejandro** [El Manteco, Bolívar, Venezuela, 1921–    ]. Otero received his early training in Caracas at the Escuela de Artes Plásticas, where he later was Profesor de Vitrales (1943–1945). The following seven years were spent primarily in Paris, and resulted in his one-man show at the Pan American Union in Washington, D.C. in 1948. A year later, he helped found *Revista los Disidentes* in Paris, which protested against the academicizing tendencies of modern art. In 1952, Otero returned to his country, where he helped reform the Escuela de Artes Plásticas, and where he became Coördinator of the Museo de Bellas Artes. In 1960, he returned to Paris once again. Otero's early work was figurative, with an almost obsessive concentration on such objects as skulls and coffee pots. Around 1949 his work became more abstract, as it eliminated color, subject, and form and reduced them to white on white. Gradually elements of color and form were reintroduced, first with straight lines. His works resemble certain of Kandinsky's Improvisations. In the early 1950s, he began to do "color rhythms," color forms organized by superimposed patterns of verticals. His latest work consists of collages, accomplished against a solid background. He attempts to set up a tension between the reality of the object and its function in the work of art. Otero has also collaborated in architectural work, most notably in the murals for the acoustical shell in the Facultad de Ingeniería of the Universidad Central, Caracas.   CF

**Pacheco Pereyra, Armando** [Rio de Janeiro, Brazil, 1910–      ]. Pacheco received his early training at the Liceu de Artes e Oficios in Rio de Janeiro in 1930–1931, and later studied privately with Oswaldo Teixeira, and with Augusto Bracet and Rodolfo Chanbeland at the Escola de Belas Artes of Rio. In 1943 he was awarded a fellowship by the Brazilian Government for travel within the country, and from 1947 to 1951 he studied in the United States. Since that time he has been one of the most important figures in Bolivian art representing contemporary cosmopolitan artistic tendencies.   CF

**Palacios, Luisa** [Caracas, 1923–      ]. Luisa Palacios studied painting at the Escuela de Artes Plásticas in her native city under Abel Vallmitjana. She has won her greatest success, however, with her engravings, which she began to produce five years ago.   CF

**Pallière, Juan León** [Rio de Janeiro, Brazil, 1823 – Paris, 1887]. Pallière was the son of a French painter, and his maternal grandfather was the famous architect and painter, Grandjean de Montigny. His father took him to Paris at the age of seven where he was apprenticed to a follower of the Neoclassic style. In 1848, he returned to Rio de Janeiro and studied at the Academia. The next year he won a scholarship to study in Rome. After five years, he returned to Latin America, this time to Buenos Aires, where he painted mainly in the costumbrista tradition for eleven years. He made one trip to Chile in 1858, which was documented in his *Diario de Viaje por América del Sud*. Pallière returned to Europe in 1861 to exhibit in Paris. He settled there permanently in 1866. However, he continued to paint and sketch Argentine subjects. Today his watercolors and sketches, rather than his oils, are of special interest.   TG

**Pancetti, José Gianini** [São Paulo, Brazil, 1903–      ]. The son of Italian immigrants, José Pancetti went to Italy at the age of eleven. After several years in school he joined the Italian Merchant Marine for a period and then returned to Brazil. Pancetti describes his becoming an artist as follows: "I enlisted in our Navy at the age of 19. I never stayed too long in one place. A constant uneasiness dominated me. One day, for some unexplainable reason, I experienced a strong desire to paint all I felt and saw. So strong was the urge that since that time I have not put down the brushes." Pancetti's urge to paint led him to formal study at the Escola de Belas Artes. In the following decades he won many medals and awards. Pancetti has always been a sailor by preference, and from his works emanate the sounds, colors, and smells of the beaches along the coast of Brazil from Bahía to São Paulo. Some of his most important works depict the deserted beaches of northeastern Brazil, especially the banks of the Abaeté lagoon and the beach of Itapoã. Solitude and serenity characterize his scenes.   DD

**Pardo, Mercedes** [Caracas, 1922–      ]. Mercedes Pardo studied in the Escuela de Artes Plásticas in Caracas. She then spent a long period abroad, first in Santiago de Chile from 1945 to 1949, then in Paris from 1949 to 1952. In 1953 she returned to Caracas and in 1958 became Director of the Educational Section of the Museo de Bellas Artes. She held her first one-man show in Caracas in 1947. Her work has undergone a marked evolution. She started with quasi-geometrical forms under the influence of Klee, then passed through an almost calligraphic stage of black on white. Her present style is freely abstract.   CF

**Paredes, Diógenes** [Quito, 1910–      ]. Paredes studied painting at the Escuela de Bellas Artes of the Universidad Central of Ecuador. In 1947 he received a grant from the French Government following a successful Paris exhibition. He has traveled extensively in Europe and in the Americas, both before and after becoming Professor of Decorative Painting at the Escuela de Bellas Artes in Quito.   CF

**Pellegrini, Carlos Enrique** [Chambéry, Savoy, 1800 – Argentina, 1875]. Carlos Enrique Pellegrini studied in his home city, then in Turin, and finally in Paris, where he was trained as an engineer. In 1827, he was hired as an engineer by the Argentine Government. Arriving in Montevideo, he remained there several months because of the British blockade of Buenos Aires. When he reached Buenos Aires in 1828 his post had disappeared, and in order to earn his living, Pellegrini began painting portraits. He was commissioned by the dictator, Juan Manuel Rosas, to paint portraits of two of his generals. He drew numerous portraits of other distinguished Argentines, which were lithographed by Bacle. This talented artist was also a poet, editor, publisher of magazines, builder, historian, and municipal engineer. He excelled in architectural views, but perhaps his greatest talent lay in portraiture. Between 1830 and 1837, he painted eight hundred portraits. His name was not to be forgotten after his death as one of his children became President of the Republic for two years, when President Juárez Celmán was ousted from office in 1890.   TG

**Petres, Fray Domingo de** [Petrés, Valencia, Spain, 1759 – Bogotá, 1811]. Petrés received his early training with his father, a mason, and at the age of nineteen he became a lay brother in the Order of Capuchins. He was then sent to the Academia de Bellas Artes of Murcia, where he worked under the religious sculptor Francisco Salcillo. He arrived in Bogotá in 1792, and there spent the rest of his life. His first work was to repair and enlarge many of the churches damaged in the earthquake of 1785. In addition to designing the Cathedral of Bogotá and other churches, he worked on public buildings, among them the first observatory in Latin America, a bridge, additions to the Bogotá mint, and a water system for part of the city. His architectural style is Spanish Neoclassical, but more intimate than that which prevailed in Spain. CF

**Pettoruti, Emilio** [La Plata, Argentina, 1892– ]. After an unusually short period of study, Emilio Pettoruti was granted a scholarship for European study by the Province of Buenos Aires in 1913. He went to Europe, remaining there for twelve years, supported by his family and his own efforts. He took part in the Futurist movement in Milan and in Paris, and was acquainted with the Cubists, especially Juan Gris, who influenced him most of all. In 1923 he exhibited at Der Sturm Gallery in Berlin, showing thirty-five works. In 1924, he returned to Argentina, where he exhibited to a shocked public the first Cubist painting seen in Buenos Aires. It was not until 1941 that Pettoruti received even a modest prize in an Argentine show. Even as late as 1949, his work was publicly described as ''degenerate'' at the inauguration of the National Salon, in which Pettoruti was represented. It was mainly signs of recognition by foreign museums, such as his invitation to the First Guggenheim International in 1957 as the South American representative, that brought Pettoruti acceptance at home. His work was also shown in many European museums: Rome (1953), Paris (1958), and London (1960). In 1962 he was given a retrospective exhibition in the Museo Nacional de Bellas Artes in Buenos Aires, *Homenaje Nacional a 50 años de labor artística*. Of his generation, he is almost alone in remaining completely faithful to the avant-garde style that he first espoused. He is generally recognized as the major exponent of Cubist art in Latin America. TG

**Pinto, Joaquín** [Quito, 1842–1906]. The son of a Portuguese father and an Ecuadorian mother, Joaquín Pinto gave evidence of his artistic leanings from childhood. He studied in the workshops of Ramón Vargas, Rafaél Venegas, and Nicolás Cabrera in Quito. In other aspects of his education he is said to have been self-taught, learning, among other things, Latin, Greek, Hebrew, French, and German. Although he never left Ecua-

dor, he benefited from the experiences of his friends who did. Thus he learned watercolor from Juan Manosalvas, who had developed the technique in Europe. Pinto taught first in the Escuela de Bellas Artes in Quito and later in the Academia de Dibujo y Pintura of Cuenca. He is both one of the last interpreters of religious art according to the pictorial tradition of the colonial school of Quito and one of the first painters to record the Ecuadorian Indian and his costumes and customs through direct observation. His watercolors of Ecuadorian landscapes date from the latter part of his life, toward the end of the century. CF

**Pissarro, Camille** [St. Thomas, West Indies, 1830 – Paris, 1903]. Before going to France in the company of the Danish painter, George Melbye, Camille Pissarro spent some time in Venezuela. From this period survives a series of pencil sketches of local costumes, scenes, and landscapes in the Museo de Bellas Artes of Caracas. CF

**Piza, Arthur Luiz** [São Paulo, 1928– ]. Arthur Luiz Piza studied drawing with A. Gomide and engraving with Johnny Friedländer. He has taken part in the majority of the São Paulo Bienals; in the 5th International Biennial of Color Lithography in Cincinnati; the 2d Engraving Biennial at Ljubljana (1957); the 1st Triennial at Grechen, Switzerland (1958); the Paris Salons de Mai (1953, 1956, and 1958) and in Brazilian exhibits in cities in many parts of the world. He lives in Paris. DD

**Poleo, Héctor** [Caracas, 1918– ]. Poleo received his early training in the Escuela de Artes Plásticas in Caracas. He has spent some time in Mexico and in Europe. He has exhibited in Caracas since 1937. His early work shows a Mantegnesque sculptural and linear emphasis as well as a taste for the archaic qualities of Italian Quattrocento art in general. After his trip to Mexico, his work became much more subdued in color, showing massive landscapes inhabited by small and helpless human creatures. In his later works, which have been influenced in turn by surrealism and abstract expressionism, this sense of desolation with implications of protest has remained. CF

**Polesello, Rogelio** [Argentina, 1939– ]. Rogelio Polesello is one of the most successful of the newest generation of Argentine painters. He studied in the Escuela de Bellas Artes in Buenos Aires. Since 1959 he has won prizes including the Losada Prize, an honorable mention in the De Ridder competition, and 1st Prize in the 1965 Esso Interamerican Competition, Washington, D.C. He has had one-man exhibitions in

Buenos Aires, Washington, Lima, and Bogotá, and has participated in many group shows. His most recent work is in a colorful retinal style with suggestions of science-fiction in imagery and psychological overtones.  TG

**Portinari, Cándido** [Brodowski, São Paulo, Brazil, 1903 – Rio de Janeiro, 1961]. Candido Portinari left his birthplace as a youth to study in the Escola de Belas Artes in Rio de Janeiro. He entered his first painting in the Salão of 1922, after receiving instruction from Rodolfo Amoêdo and João Baptista da Costa. During the following six years the young artist won several awards, including the Prêmio de Viagem of 1928, which allowed him to study in France, Italy, England, and Spain. Upon his return from Europe, Portinari renounced his earlier academic style to become one of Brazil's most ardent Modernists, expressing his sense of nationalism and consciousness of social problems in works distinctly Brazilian in theme. In sharing the desire of many Modernists for a reincorporation of art and society, Portinari turned mainly to social art, a commitment that found expression in mural as well as easel painting. He painted important murals in the Ministério da Educação e Saúde and the Estação de Rádio Tupi, Rio de Janeiro; the Library of Congress, Washington, D.C.; the Pampulha Church in Belo Horizonte; and the United Nations. Portinari's inspiration flows from all facets of the Brazilian scene – the variegated life on São Paulo's large plantations, the customs of Brazil's Indians, cowboys, Negroes, and fishermen, the production of coffee and cacao, and the primitive and often tragic life of the people of the interior.  DD

**Pôrto Alegre, Manuel de Araújo** [Rio Grande do Sul, Brazil, 1806 – Portugal, 1879]. Manuel de Araújo Pôrto Alegre began his education with his stepfather at the age of five. He showed talent for drawing and the natural sciences in his childhood and spent long hours collecting, examining, and sketching objects of nature, which he kept in a small museum of his own making. Becoming a pupil of Jean Baptiste Debret, a member of the Lebreton Mission of French artists who established the Academia de Belas Artes in Rio de Janeiro, Pôrto Alegre studied painting, sculpture, and architecture at the Academia in Rio. In 1831 he went to Europe with Debret on a trip subsidized by José Bonifácio and Evaristo da Veiga, two of Brazil's leading public figures. He studied in Paris for four years with Baron Gros and Emery, spent two years in Italy, and after touring Europe returned to Brazil in 1837, where he was named Professor of Painting at the Academia. From 1854 to 1857 Pôrto Alegre served as Director of the Academia; from

1859 to 1867 he was Brazil's ambassador to Prussia, transferring in 1867 to Portugal, where he died twelve years later, having been honored in 1874 by Pedro II with the title of Baron of Pôrto Alegre. Pôrto Alegre's versatility as an artist, poet, writer, and diplomat brought him into the mainstream of the cultural, intellectual, and political currents of his time. His interest in the history of art led him to be one of the first chroniclers of Brazilian painting, and he wrote profusely on the subject. He left a number of historical paintings, one of the most widely appreciated being his *Coroação de D. Pedro II* (*Coronation of D. Pedro II*).  DD

**Portocarrero, René** [Havana, 1912–    ]. At the age of twelve, Portocarrero studied at the Academia Villate and San Alejandro in Havana. Largely self-taught, Portocarrero became a professor in the Estudio Libre de Pintura y Escultura in 1938 and taught drawing in 1943 in the Havana penitentiary. Portocarrero has traveled in Europe, the United States, and the Antilles, and has exhibited his murals, ceramics, and paintings on three continents. Among the prizes he has won is the Premio Internacional "SANBRA" in the 7th Bienal of São Paulo. He lives and works in Cuba.  DD

**Posada, José Guadalupe** [Aguascalientes, Mexico, 1852 – Mexico City, 1913]. This famed wood and zinc engraver, one of the great figures of 19th- and early 20th-century Mexican art, learned sketching and lithography under Trinidad Pedroza in Aguascalientes. Later he collaborated with his teacher on a journal, *El Jicote*. Its biting political criticism so aroused local officials that Posada had to move to León, where he continued to work with Pedroza. In 1887 Posada established his workshop in Mexico City where he joined with his friend, the printer Antonio Vanegas Arroyo, to publish his long series of popular prints on social and political subjects satirizing personalities, customs, and events of the Porfirian era. Posada's prolific *œuvre* played on two major themes: portrayal of the circumstances and personalities of everyday Mexican popular life; and a nether world peopled with skulls and skeletons. He left a double legacy: a comprehensive satiric chronicle of his times and a brilliant art style that has inspired every succeeding generation of Mexican artists, including the leaders of the mural movement of the '20s and '30s.  DD

**Potyguara, Lazzarotto; called Poty** [Curitiba, Paraná, Brazil, 1924–    ]. Poty studied in Brazil with Carlos Oswald and in France at the Ecole des Beaux-Arts on a French Government scholarship. He was awarded the Gold Medal at the Salão Nacional de Belas Artes. He has held several individual exhibits in Rio de Janeiro, and has participated in many group exhibits abroad. DD

**Pozo, José del** [Seville, Spain, c. 1757 – Lima, 1821]. Pozo was born the son of the Director of the Academia Real de la Pintura in Seville. He joined the Spanish expedition of Alejandro Malaspina as a painter and produced some botanical studies and landscapes. His lack of diligence and insolent manner caused the expedition's leader to put him ashore in Lima with orders that he be sent back to Spain. However, Pozo remained in Lima, where he founded an art school. He produced portraits, landscapes, and religious works, and designed the decorations for the interiors of a chapel in Santo Domingo, and the Tribunal del Consulado. He remained in Lima for thirty-one years. Today many of his works are found in Peruvian private collections. TG

**Pradier, Charles Simon** [Geneva, Switzerland, 1783 – Paris, 1847]. Charles Simon Pradier, the elder brother of the French sculptor James Pradier, was sent to study in Paris as a youth. His talent for engraving led him to the atelier of the engraver and painter, Auguste Boucher. After a few years of apprenticeship, Pradier entered his works in the Paris Salons of 1812 and 1814. In 1816 he was invited to join the Lebreton Mission of French artists to Brazil as engraver. Pradier returned to Europe in 1818 to complete engraved reproductions of two of Debret's oils – the portrait of Dom João VI, and the embarkation of the Empress Dona Leopoldina – since Brazil did not have the necessary equipment to make engravings at the time. Pradier never returned to Brazil, primarily because of the intrigues of Henrique José da Silva, the Portuguese artist who plotted to undermine the prestige and important posts accorded the French artists of the Lebreton Mission. He continued working in Paris as painter and engraver. Perhaps Pradier's major work is the engraved reproduction of Ingres' *Tu Marcellus eris.* DD

**Pucciarelli, Mario A.** [Buenos Aires, 1928– ]. Mario Pucciarelli studied with Vicente Forte and other Argentine artists. He received an honorary degree from the Ministry of Education, a degree reserved for outstanding artists who did not study at the Escuela Nacional de Bellas Artes. In 1955–1956 he visited London and in 1959 he was chosen to represent his country in the Biennial of Young Artists at Paris. In 1960 he received the Guggenheim International Award and the Instituto Torcuato Di Tella Prize. In 1961 he showed five paintings in the Venice Biennial. Since then he has lived in Rome. TG

**Pueyrredón, Prilidiano** [Buenos Aires, 1823–1870]. Pueyrredón received his early education in Buenos Aires. In 1835 his famous father, one of the first heads of the Argentine state, but not in sympathy with the government at the time, moved the family to Paris, where they remained for six years. In 1841 the family settled in Rio de Janeiro, then an important cultural center, and Pueyrredón may have studied art in the academy there. From 1844 to 1849 he was back in France studying architecture and engineering, but still practicing his art. Shortly after the family returned to their estates in Argentina at the end of 1849, the elder Pueyrredón died. It was also at this time that Pueyrredón painted his most famous picture, the full-length portrait of Manuela Rosas, the daughter of the dictator. In March of the following year, Pueyrredón and his mother moved back to Europe. He returned to Buenos Aires in 1854 as an architect and designed most of the major buildings in that city during a ten-year period. He painted little during these years, though he began again to show his work about 1860. From that time on, he worked steadily, painting both portraits and scenes from daily life in Argentina. Most of his best painting was done during the last ten years of his life, though he continued to work on architecture. Pueyrredón is a major figure, both as an architect in the Neoclassic style and as a naturalistic painter. He is better known as a painter and is the first of the important Argentine artists. His work is severely painstaking in execution, restrained in color and drawing, and yet, particularly in the genre scenes, projects the warmth, the bigness, and the expansive mood of the Argentine pampa. TG

**Quinquela Martín, Benito** [Buenos Aires, 1890– ]. Benito Quinquela Martín is the renowned portrayer of the Boca, the river front and harbor of Buenos Aires, to which he has devoted his life. A self-taught painter, he began showing his work in 1918. His paintings of docks and cranes, hard-working stevedores, smoke-pouring chimneys, and the bright-hued bustle of Boca harbor traffic have since entered museums the world over. In 1936 he became interested in wall painting, particularly in a colored concrete technique invented by Constantino Yuste, with whom he collaborated. He produced a series of murals in the buildings of several national institutions and waterfront organizations in Buenos Aires, including the River Plate Athletic Club. He has worked as well in ceramic sculpture, but a more important contribution is the series of sixty etchings done after 1939 on all aspects of waterfront life. TG

**Quiroa, Marco Augusto** [Chicacas, Guatemala, 1937–    ]. Marco Augusto Quiroa studied at the Escuela Nacional de Artes Plásticas in Guatemala and afterward received a scholarship to study in Mexico. The pre-Columbian traditions of Guatemala have exerted a continuing influence on his work. He has had one-man exhibitions in Mexico, Guatemala, and Washington, D.C., and he has participated in biennials in Mexico and Paris. He won an important prize in El Salvador in 1961. TG

**Ramírez Rosales, Manuel** [Chile, 1804–1877]. Although he has been called the first Chilean painter, little is known about Ramírez Rosales' life except that he studied in France with Théodore Rousseau of the Barbizon School. His paintings are completely romantic in spirit and form. He used muted colors, but with strong chiaroscuro effects. He showed an inclination to paint picturesque scenes with sentiment. His landscapes, which form the most characteristic part of his work, are executed in minute detail. CF

**Ramírez Vázquez, Pedro** [Mexico, active now]. Among the notable buildings on which Ramírez Vázquez has collaborated are the Museo Histórico-Didáctico de Chapultepec and the Museo Nacional de Antropología. He has served as the head of the Comité Administrador del Programa Federal de Construcción de Escuelas, whose plan is to construct one thousand urban classrooms and two thousand rural classrooms per year. JD

**Ramírez Villamizar, Eduardo** [Pamplona, Colombia, 1923–    ]. Ramírez Villamizar studied painting at the Escuela de Arquitectura of the Universidad Nacional of Colombia and at the Escuela de Bellas Artes in Bogotá. He was later appointed Professor of Painting and Sculpture at the Escuela de Cerámica. Ramírez is considered to be the originator of abstract art in Colombia. His early work was strongly expressionistic, showing the influence of Rouault. About 1950 he began to experiment with "forms in themselves," organizing geometrical shapes and equilibrated planes in many abstract compositions. In the late '50s he began to put these forms into motion, making greater use of the curve, and reduced his palette to black and white. In 1959 he turned to abstract reliefs in plaster or wood done completely in white on white with black accents. CF

**Ramos Martínez, Alfredo** [Monterrey, Mexico, 1875 – Los Angeles, California, 1946]. Ramos Martínez first studied with Rebull in the Academia de San Carlos. The years from 1896 to 1910 he spent in Paris, where he was influenced by the Impressionists. On his return to Mexico, Ramos Martínez associ-

ated himself with a group of young painters devoted to the promotion of a new Mexican art. He was named director of the Academia Nacional de Bellas Artes in 1911. Two years later he established the first Escuela de Pintura al Aire Libre, in Santa Anita. He founded twenty-six other open-air schools of painting in his lifetime. Major figures of the 20th-century Mexican Renaissance studied in these schools, which were free of restrictive academicism. He painted a series of murals at Scripps College in Claremont, California. DD

**Rayo, Omar** [Roldanillo, Department of Valle, Colombia, 1928–    ]. Rayo began his artistic career at the age of nineteen as an illustrator and caricaturist in Bogotá, but later he turned to painting. Since 1954, he has had one-man shows in various Latin American cities. From 1959 to 1961 he studied graphic art in Mexico City on a fellowship from the Organization of American States. He came to the United States in 1961 for a one-man show at the Pan American Union. Now working in a pop spirit, Rayo makes intaglio prints, using neither ink nor type, that humorously stylize everyday objects. CF

**Reidy, Alfonso Eduardo** [Paris, 1909–1964]. Alfonso Eduardo Reidy was taken as a youth by his father to Brazil where he studied architecture at the Escola Nacional de Belas Artes in Rio de Janeiro, and, after graduation in 1929, became a municipal architect. At that time Reidy already had advanced ideas for a new architecture. Strongly influenced by Le Corbusier, Gropius, and Mies Van der Rohe, he soon related modern architectural currents to the Brazilian environment, creating a style of his own. He was invited to join Lúcio Costa's group of "future catalysts of Brazilian architecture and urbanism." The activity of this circle, which included the brilliant architects, Niemeyer and Moreira, led ultimately to the planning of Brasília. Before his sudden death, Reidy was Director of the Department of Urbanism in the Federal District and professor in the Faculdade Nacional de Arquitetura of the Universidade do Brasil, where he held the chair of Theory and Practice of Urbanism. He also was a member of the group that designed the Ministério da Educação e Saúde. Among Reidy's most impressive works are the Pedregulho buildings and the Museu de Arte Moderna in Rio de Janeiro. He also planned the Boa Vontade Inn (1931–1932); the Marechal Hermes Theater (1950–1951); residential groups at Jacarepaguá (1950–1952), Tijuca (1953–1955); and Itaiparká (1959–1960); the experimental secondary school Paraguay-Brazil in Paraguay; the office of the World Health Organization in Geneva (1959); and the National Museum of Kuwait (1960). DD

**Renart, Emilio J.** [Mendoza, Argentina, 1925–    ]. Renart was trained as an illustrator, printmaker, and painter. He has been exhibiting since 1953. He has gradually turned from printmaking to painting and, in 1958, had a one-man show of his paintings in the Asociación Estímulo de Bellas Artes in Buenos Aires. His most recent work is a very personal kind of sculpture which he calls "integralismo." These are abstract forms with strong organic connotations, entitled *Bio-Cosmos*. They are made and numbered in series. They are in the recent sculptural trend that calls for the use of color, modern industrial materials, and ideas of modern science.   TG

**Rendón, Manuel** [Paris, 1894–    ]. The son of a distinguished writer, physician, diplomat, and judge at the World Court in The Hague, Manuel Rendón was educated in Paris, where he held his first exhibition in 1916. He continued to live and paint there until 1937, when he went to live in Cuenca, the mountain city in the southeast of Ecuador. Since 1947, he has divided his time between Paris and Ecuador.   CF

**Reschreiter, Rudolf** [Germany; active in Ecuador late 19th century]. Reschreiter was a landscape painter schooled in the naturalistic tradition of the German academies. He settled in Ecuador for a period sometime between 1870 and 1900 and devoted himself to portraying the grandeur of the Andean volcanoes. He took as an assistant the Ecuadorian painter Rafael Troya, who became one of Ecuador's finest late 19th-century landscapists.   TG

**Reverón, Armando** [Caracas, 1889–1954]. Reverón began his studies at the age of fifteen in the Academia de Bellas Artes in Caracas. In 1911, he went to Barcelona to study in the Escuela de Artes y Oficios y Bellas Artes. Two years later, he associated himself with the anti-academic School of Caracas before returning to Madrid, where he studied under Antonio Muñoz Degrain and Manuel Marín at the Academia de San Fernando. The most constant influence on Reverón's work was his friend and fellow member of the School of Caracas, Antonio Edmundo Monsanto. Other artists who influenced his work were the Rumanian Samys Mützner, a Russian Art Nouveau decorator, Nicolas Ferdinandov, and Emilio Boggio, the Venezuelan impressionist. In 1921, the artist isolated himself in his little house in Macuto, near Caracas, and began to evolve an "impressionism" of his own. The work he did between 1924 and 1946 can be divided into two periods: white and sepia. He made use of the bare canvas for background in his later works, and explored the "space between objects, light as an object, and light at the expense of the object." He had his first one-

man show in 1933 in Caracas and, later, another in Paris. Increasingly withdrawn from life and absorbed in his work, he suffered a nervous breakdown in 1945 and spent several months in a sanatorium. In the remaining years before his death, Reverón executed some of his most powerful works. He is one of the outstanding figures of early Modernism in Venezuela and one of the greatest Latin American impressionists.   CF

**Rivas Mercado, Antonio** [Active in the early 20th century]. Antonio Rivas Mercado studied architecture in Paris and in Great Britain, returning to Mexico in 1879. He became Director of the Escuela de Bellas Artes in Mexico City in 1903, toward the end of the period of academic classicism. Rivas Mercado's grand style is preserved in Mexico City in the *Monumento a la Independencia* on the Paseo de la Reforma. A Winged Victory stands at the top of the tall column, and the base is peopled by allegorical and historical figures. Rivas Mercado is also remembered for the Teatro Juárez in Guanajuato.   JD

**Rivera, Diego** [Guanajuato, Mexico, 1886 – Mexico City, 1957]. Diego Rivera is one of the great figures of the Mexican 20th-century artistic revival. At the age of ten, he enrolled in the Academia de San Carlos in Mexico City, which was then directed by the last of the 19th-century eclectic classicists. Although an independent, Rivera was influenced by the classical ideas of form of his teacher, the landscapist, José María Velasco. After his first show, in 1907, he received a scholarship to study in Europe and there worked under the Spanish realist, Eduardo Chicharro. On this trip, he also traveled in France, Belgium, Holland, England, and Italy. In Europe a second time, from 1911 to 1921, Rivera experimented successfully with various styles including Cézannesque post-Impressionism and Cubism. In 1920, while in Paris, Rivera and Siqueiros discussed the need for a new Mexican national art that would express the "life of the people." His inclination toward such an art was reinforced by a visit to Italy where he became engrossed in Byzantine mosaics and Renaissance mural painting. Rivera returned to his homeland at the end of the military revolution.

From 1922 to the end of his life, Rivera devoted much of his time to mural painting in Mexico and the United States. His themes present the history and contemporary life of his nation and of the world, largely according to personal interpretations of Marxism. He developed a comprehensive and systematic iconography based upon the social and political interests, as he saw them, of the working classes, first of Mexico, and later of the world at large. The first mural (1922), an encaustic painting for the Anfiteatro Bolívar, was an interpretation of creation. Very soon afterwards his interest in Indian tradition and his Marxist theories of history and value became more prominent. Although notably a muralist, in mosaic as well as fresco and encaustic, Rivera also produced many portraits, landscapes, figure studies, and paintings, drawings and prints of a wide range of subjects drawn from Mexican Indian and popular life. Rivera's art laid the artistic foundation of a modern redefinition of Mexican national character. Its influence, which has been felt throughout the Western Hemisphere, has probably been greater than that of any other single Latin American artist of the 20th century.   JD

**Rivera, Juan de Dios** [Cuzco, Peru, 1770 – Buenos Aires, 1824]. Rivera was employed in the Mint in Potosi as a seal and die cutter. In 1787, he and his brother Luciano traveled to Buenos Aires, where he worked as a silversmith, printmaker, and seal designer and cutter. Among his works is the medal, struck in Buenos Aires, that commemorates the accession of Carlos IV of Spain. In 1808 he printed the *Lámina de Oruro*, a copper engraving commemorating the defeat of the British at Buenos Aires. In 1810 he engraved the arms of the city and in 1813 the arms of the Argentine nation, by order of the Constituent Assembly. He was an artisan who worked in the style of the Neoclassic commemorative print.   TG

**Rojas, Cristóbal** [Wá, Venezuela, 1858–1890]. Like his compatriot, Arturo Michelena, Rojas received a pension in 1883 from the dictator, Guzmán Blanco, to study in Paris with the academician, Jean-Paul Laurens. Rojas attempted to assert his own personality while using Jean-Paul Laurens' style, moving from a classical historical style through one that tended toward naturalism. He was influenced by the chiaroscuro tradition of 17th-century Spain and by the social consciousness of Daumier. In the last two years of his life, his art became impressionistic. He died of tuberculosis before he could create the "official" historical art for which he had been trained.   CF

**Ruelas, Julio** [Zacatecas, Mexico, 1870 – Paris, 1907]. The Ruelas family moved to Mexico City when Julio was five years old. There he attended the Colegio Militar. He studied art in the old Academia, later renamed Escuela Nacional de Bellas Artes. From 1891 to 1895 he studied at the University of Karlsrühe with Mayerbeer and in Germany with Arnold Böcklin. When he returned to Mexico in 1898, he exhibited with other young artists. He joined a group of poets and artists and with them founded the *Revista Moderna*, to which he

contributed sketches. In 1904, he was able to return to Europe on a stipend from the Mexican Government. He settled in Paris where he studied with Cazon and worked brilliantly as an engraver and illustrator until his death in 1907. His works, in the Art Nouveau tradition, show an anguished spirit and strong eroticism. He was both a romantic and a precursor of new trends in Mexican art.   DD

**Rugendas, Johann Moritz** [Augsburg, Bavaria, 1802 – Weilheim, Württemberg, 1858]. Johann Moritz Rugendas was trained first by his father, director of the Augsburg Academy of Art, but was most interested in the art of engraving practiced by his uncle. He studied in the Augsburg Academy and then in Munich. At eighteen, eager to see the world, he joined the expedition of Baron Georg Heinrich Langsdorff to Brazil in the 1820s. He was captivated by the new lands, but found working for the Baron uncongenial and soon went off on his own. In 1823 he returned to Europe with a collection of drawings and paintings. He formed an enduring friendship with Alexander von Humboldt. Rugendas' *Voyage Pittoresque au Brésil*, illustrated with a hundred of his lithographs, was published in Paris in 1834. With Humboldt's aid and encouragement, the artist traveled again to America with the idea of a great volume of artistic views of the recently opened lands of Latin America. In 1831 he arrived in Mexico, where he remained until 1834. During these three years he is supposed to have produced 1700 works of art in drawing, watercolor, and oil, many of them still in Mexican national collections. In 1833 he became involved in an attempted revolution and was imprisoned and expelled from the country. He sailed for Chile, where he remained for twelve years, except for short trips to the Argentine pampa (1837–1838) and Peru and Bolivia (1842–1844). These were productive years: drawings and watercolors of Araucanian Indian life and of all aspects of Latin American life served as the basis for important oils. His style is almost a definition of the Romantic style, full of contrasts of light and color and dashing in action, concentrating on the exotic life around him.

In 1845 he sailed from Valparaíso for Buenos Aires and Montevideo, where he produced many drawings and watercolors of military figures and scenes. Two years later he arrived in Rio de Janeiro by way of the Uruguay river, and after a short time there sailed for Europe. He was unable to find support for the publication of his American work either in Paris or in Augsburg, although he did receive royal patronage in his homeland. The Bavarian State acquired 3,072 works, mostly drawings. His last years were spent in Europe in illness and discouragement, and with longings for America. TG

**Ruiz, Antonio** [Mexico City, 1897–    ]. Antonio Ruiz studied in the Escuela Nacional de Bellas Artes, where he later was active in teaching. From 1926 to 1929 he worked on film scenarios in California, after which he returned to Mexico and dedicated himself to painting. During this period, he also developed original ideas for theater decoration and worked on children's theater. Many of his oil paintings deal with popular scenes. The early work of Ruiz tended toward decorative simplification; he later moved toward richer colors and finer lines. More recently Ruiz has worked with more imaginative themes that reflect elements of surrealism. Working with fresh color on a small scale, his jewel-like compositions have elevated aspects of Mexican popular life to a new poetic plane. DD

**Sá, Simplício de** [Lisbon, ?–1839]. De Sá began his studies of art with Debret in Brazil at the Imperial Academia. He so distinguished himself during his course of study that he was named professor of design for the sons of Dom Pedro I and Painter of the Imperial Court. His canvases are marked by a firmness and surety and by its material density, the latter a quality unusual in that epoch.

**Sabatier, León Jean-Baptiste** [Paris, ?–1887]. An illustrator, lithographer, and architectural draughtsman, Sabatier studied in Paris with Baron Taylor and Bertins. He later collaborated with Taylor to illustrate *Voyages pittoresques et romantiques dans l'ancienne France*. Sabatier exhibited regularly in the Salons from 1827 to 1879 and was Vice-President of the Association des Artistes, Peintres et Sculpteurs. Other works for which he executed lithographs were Johann Moritz Rugendas' *Voyage pittoresque en Brésil* and Girauld de Prangy's *Souvenirs de Grenade et de l'Alhambra*. CF

**Sabogal, José** [Cajabamba, Peru, 1888–1956]. Sabogal, the father of Peruvian indigenist art of the between-war period, traveled to Europe in 1909 and spent three years in Spain, France, and North Africa. From 1912 to 1918 he studied in the Escuela de Bellas Artes of Buenos Aires. In 1920 he was named professor in Lima's Escuela de Bellas Artes, a post he held until 1933, when he was appointed director. A trip to Mexico in 1922 brought him into close contact with José Clemente Orozco and Diego Rivera. In 1934 he illustrated Carleton Beals' *Fire on the Andes*, a work about the rising APRA Party. In 1943 Sabogal was dismissed from his post as director of the Escuela de Bellas Artes, ostensibly because of a "disagreement" with a high official but very likely because of his indigenist political views. Rejecting academic painting from the start, Sabogal found his first inspiration in the tortured expressionism of the Basque, Ignacio Zuloaga. However, his trip to Mexico converted him to the indigenism exemplified by the Mexican muralists, and he became the leading exponent in Peru of that school. Balancing brightly colored masses in extremely simple structural formats, his pictures portrayed Peruvian landscapes, Indians, and customs. Later he showed a predilection for the costumes of the Peruvian Indians. In the late 1920s, he experimented with new techniques in woodcut and toward the end of his life he elaborated a style of painting in adobe, based on popular ceramics. CF

**Sáez, Carlos Federico** [Mercedes, Uruguay, 1878 – Montevideo, 1900]. Sáez displayed an intuitive grasp of the arts at an early age and began painting and drawing while still a child. When he was thirteen, his family moved to Montevideo, where he received his first lessons from Juan Franzi. Two years later the celebrated Uruguayan painter, Juan Manuel Blanes, expressed admiration for the youth's talents and advised him to go to Europe to study. At the age of fifteen, Sáez went to Rome where he entered the Academy of Fine Arts and frequented the workshops of Marcelino Santamaria, Sedano, Francisco Pradilla, and others, though he did not come under the influence of any one school. After remaining in Europe for seven years, Sáez returned to Montevideo gravely ill. Just before his death he won First Prize for Painting in the Concurso de Affiches in the exposition organized by the Ateneo de Montevideo under the direction of Figari. Despite his short life, Sáez left a vast number of paintings. His mastery of sketching gives many an appearance of drawing, their color notwithstanding. DD

**Salas, Rafael** [Quito, 1830–1906]. Salas, the son of Antonio Salas, was the most important member of this large family of artists. He learned drawing and painting from his father and perfected his technique in Europe on a scholarship awarded him in 1854 by the government of General José María Urbina. Salas was one of the first professors of the Academia de Bellas Artes founded by President García Moreno. Since the Academia disappeared when the President died, Salas turned his own studio into a school where he taught his own children and numerous other students. He introduced landscape painting to Ecuador and was the genre's most important representative in the 19th century. He received a gold medal from the city of Guayaquil in 1888 and the Ecuadorian Congress awarded him a lifetime pension in 1902. In 1904 he became one of the first professors in the Escuela de Bellas Artes.  CF

**Samaniego, Manuel** [Quito, c. 1767–1824]. Samaniego continued the pictorial traditions of the colonial period in Ecuador. He began to paint as an adolescent. By the age of thirty he had directed the construction and decoration of the *retablo mayor* of the church of Santa Clara in Quito. His specialty was religious painting. His stature as an artist has been considered to rest mainly on his draughtsmanship. The somewhat limited range of his palette can be attributed to the lack of good oils in early 19th-century Ecuador. A colorful figure with libertine ways uninhibited by a strong religious belief, Samaniego painted few portraits. He avoided them, he said, because "in my portraits, even the pigs look as though they had taken the vow."  CF

**Santa María, Andrés de** [Colombia, 1860 – Brussels, 1945]. At the age of two Santa María was taken first to England, and then to France, where he grew up. He studied art in France under Fernando Humbert, Enriques Gerver, Ignacio Zuloaga, Prince Eugene of Sweden, and in Spain with Santiago Ruiseñol. In 1893, he returned to Colombia to become director of the Escuela de Bellas Artes, a post he held for seven years. Disillusioned by the lack of public comprehension of his work, he returned to Europe, settling in Brussels, where he lived for the remainder of his life. Santa María was a prolific painter, working in a variety of media, with a wide range of subjects. His work, especially that done in Colombia, is Impressionist. In later years, his style approached German Expressionism in the bold and deliberate imbalance of his composition, his strong color, and kinetic brushwork.  CF

**Santos Chávez, José** [Canihual, Arauco, Chile, 1934–    ]. Born in the far south of Chile, Santos Chávez received his early artistic training at the Sociedad de Bellas Artes in Concepción. Later he worked at the Taller 99 associated with the Universidad Católica. He has exhibited in Santiago de Chile, Rio de Janeiro, Havana, and at the 1st American Biennial for Engraving in Santiago.  CF

**Segall, Lasar** [Vilna, Lithuania, 1891 – Brazil, 1957]. Lasar Segall went to Germany as a youth, where he attended the Berlin Akademie der Künste from 1906 to 1909. After receiving the Libermann Prize in 1910, he left Berlin for Dresden and worked at the academy there as a student-teacher. Segall slowly began to express himself in a freer manner, often depicting in his work the tribulations of Europe's Jews. After holding his first one-man exhibition, Segall lived in Holland,

and visited Brazil for the first time from there. His exhibitions in São Paulo and Campinas in 1913 were the first expositions of modern art in Brazil, and served as a prelude to the Modern movement that erupted in 1922. During and after the First World War, Segall lived in Dresden, where he took part in exhibitions of the Expressionist movement and published a book of five etchings, *Souvenirs of Vilna*, and two books illustrated with lithographs, *Bubu* and *Die Säufte*. In 1923 Segall returned to Brazil, and there became a citizen. He entered actively into Brazilian artistic circles and was soon ranked, with Portinari and Di Cavalcanti, among the outstanding modern painters in the country. After a series of European exhibitions Segall returned to São Paulo in 1930, where he helped found the Sociedade de Arte Moderna of São Paulo. In 1935 he began work on the subjects for which he is best known: the rustic landscapes of Campos de Jordão, bordello scenes, the *Portraits of Lucy*, and *Pogrom*, *War*, *Concentration Camp*, *Exodus*, and *The Emigrants' Camp*, portrayals of the masses of persecuted humanity in an expressive style dominated by line and a poignant, detailed figuration. In 1944, he published *Mangue*, drawings revealing the poverty and suffering of Rio de Janeiro's slums in an atmosphere of fantasy and deliberate naïveté. From 1949 until his death he was engaged in the series of the *Wandering Women* and of the *Forests*. In 1951 Segall showed in two important exhibitions of his work in São Paulo, one of which was incorporated into the 1st Bienal of São Paulo (1951).  DD

**Serpa, Ivan** [Rio de Janeiro, 1923–    ]. Ivan Serpa studied with Axel Lescochek. Among contemporary Brazilian artists, he is one of the most versatile, successfully exploring the possibilities of various postwar stylistic movements, especially Concretism and Informalism, and becoming a leading exponent in each. He first exhibited in 1947 at the National Fine Arts Salon. Other showings followed: "Teatro de Bôlso" (1953); Washington, D.C., (1954); Museu de Arte Moderna, Rio de Janeiro (1961); Tenreiro Gallery, Rio de Janeiro, (1963); Barcinski Gallery, Rio de Janeiro (1964). He has taken part in all São Paulo Bienals, receiving several prizes. In 1957 he won the National Fine Arts Salon's "Trip Abroad" Prize. He has also shown in the Venice and Barcelona biennials and various exhibitions in Europe, U.S.A., and Japan. He currently teaches courses in painting to children and adults at the Museu de Arte Moderna in Rio de Janeiro.  DD

**Sheridan, Enrique** [Buenos Aires, c. 1835–1860]. Sheridan was born of English parents on their Argentine sheep ranch.

After the death of his parents he was raised by his elder sister, Elizabeth, who took him to England because of his delicate health. There he was educated in Liverpool. His work at this time includes scenes of Scotland and Switzerland. In 1857 he returned to Argentina. He formed a friendship with León Pallière, with whom he collaborated on a number of costumbrista and landscape paintings. They showed their work together with great success in 1859. Sheridan was also active as a teacher of art.   TG

**Silva, Henrique José da** [Lisbon, 1772 – Rio de Janeiro, Brazil, 1834]. Henrique José da Silva studied in Lisbon with Pedro Alexandrino de Carvalho. He went to Rio de Janeiro with the intention of copying a painting. He remained there to work at the new Academia de Belas Artes. In 1820, through the intervention of his patron, the Visconde de São Lourenço, Silva was named Professor of Painting and Director of the Academia. Silva has been described as a jealous, querulous egotist, intensely resentful of the French artists of the Lebreton Mission, who enjoyed the prestige and respect of the court in Rio. It has been claimed that he hindered the functioning of the Academia in his fierce opposition to the administrative suggestions of Debret and Taunay. He opposed Debret's suggestion of holding annual exhibitions, but yielded in 1829. When Silva died, he was succeeded as director by Félix Emile Taunay, the first member of the Lebreton Mission to serve in that capacity. Henrique José da Silva left only a few paintings, among them a portrait of Senator João Antônio Rodriguez de Carvalho, and a religious work, *Virgin and Child*. His portrait of Emperor Dom Pedro I is considered one of his better works.   DD

**Simone, Alfredo de** [Latarico, Italy, 1898 – Montevideo, 1950]. Alfredo de Simone went to Uruguay at the age of three. He became a citizen in 1924. A grant from the Círculo de Bellas Artes allowed him to pursue his artistic studies under the painters, Guillermo Laborde, Vincente Puig, and Carmelo de Arzadum. A painter who developed a personal variant of the Impressionist tradition, he used divided brushwork with abrupt strokes of heavy pigment. His works are found in collections throughout Uruguay, including the Museo Nacional de Bellas Artes and the Museo Municipal "Juan Manuel Blanes." In 1929 the Salón de Otoño awarded him the Casa La Giralda Prize. He won a silver medal at the Exposición Ibero-Americana of Seville (1930). At the Salón Centenario he won the 3rd prize for painting with his oil, *Mis vecinas* (*My Neighbors*). He exhibited in the Salones de la Escuela del Taller de Artes Plásticas and the Salón de Independientes from 1933 to 1937. He won awards at the Salón Nacional in 1938, and later at the Salón Municipal.   DD

**Sinclair Ballesteros, Alfredo** [Panama, 1916–      ]. Sinclair studied in Panama with Humberto Isvaldi, one of the precursors of modern art in Panama. He completed his studies in Buenos Aires, where he won several honors. He had his first one-man show in Buenos Aires in 1950. Sinclair has developed from figurative art into abstraction and recently back toward a figurative style. His recent series "Ciudad sin luces" ("City without lights") takes its theme from the broad-eaved tenement houses in the dock areas of Panama City built to house workers on the Panama Canal. He has exhibited in Buenos Aires, Washington, at the biennials in Mexico, São Paulo, and Spain, as well as in San José, San Salvador, and Panama.   TG

**Siqueiros.** See: **Alfaro Siqueiros**

**Sívori, Eduardo** [Buenos Aires, 1847–1918]. Born of Italian parents, Eduardo Sívori was inspired to become an artist when he toured Italian museums in 1874. Upon his return to Buenos Aires, he studied drawing with Francisco Romero. In 1880 Sívori won a gold medal in the Salón Continental. Before that, he had won an honorable mention with a pencil drawing in a Paris exhibition. In 1882 he traveled again to Europe, studying there with J. P. Laurens until 1888. In Argentina he served as a member of the Comisión Nacional de Bellas Artes and as Professor and Director of the Academia.   TG

**Soto, Jesús** [Ciudad Bolívar, Venezuela, 1923–      ]. Soto attended the Escuela de Artes Plásticas in Caracas from 1942 to 1947. For the next three years, he was Director of the Escuela de Belles Artes in Maracaibo. Since 1950, he has lived alternatively in Paris and Venezuela. He had a one-man show in New York, and his work appeared in the Venice Biennials of 1958 and 1960. From the early 1950s on, his most characteristic works have been in the constructivist tradition. In 1955 his concern for "movement in space and the tensions it generates" led him to experiment with the superposition of plexiglass sheets on background panels. Several years later, he began to experiment with the suspension of wire shapes in front of panels accented in red, blue, and green. In his most recent work he has begun to incorporate found objects, thus setting up a further play between the reality of the object and the reality of the painting.   CF

**Spilimbergo, Lino Eneas** [Buenos Aires, 1896–1964]. Lino Eneas Spilimbergo studied at the Academia Nacional de Bellas Artes in Buenos Aires. He worked in Italy and France between 1925 and 1928, returning to exhibit extensively in Argentina,

197

where he won many prizes. During his lifetime his work also appeared in shows in New York, Pittsburgh, San Francisco, Paris, and Venice. His strong, sculpturesque style emphasizes plastic solidity and hence may be considered to be in the modern classical tradition that led from Cézanne to the Cubism of Picasso and Braque. Spilimbergo was a teacher and the Director of the Instituto Superior de Artes de la Universidad Nacional de Tucumán. Eight years before his death, he was named a member of the Academia Nacional de Bellas Artes. TG

**Squirru, Carlos** [Buenos Aires, 1934– ]. Carlos Squirru has lived and worked in the United States and in Europe. In 1957 he studied at the Art Students League in New York with Robert Beverly Hale. The following year he traveled and studied in Europe. On his return to Argentina he held his first important one-man show in the Bonino Gallery in Buenos Aires. He has also participated in a number of group shows. In 1962 he was awarded a fellowship by the Pratt Institute in New York for the study of engraving and lithography. Squirru now lives in Buenos Aires where his most recent work has combined figurative interest and assemblage with social and psychological overtones. TG

**Subercaseaux, Ramón** [Santiago de Chile, 1854–1936]. Ramón Subercaseaux's father was a millionaire merchant, and his mother was the daughter of the political figure, Francisco Ramón Vicuña. He studied art in Chile under the classicist, Ernesto Kirchbach, and in Paris under Dagnan Bouveret. In later years he was influenced both by his friend, John Singer Sargent – whom he painted – and by Boldini. Art was his avocation; his profession was diplomacy. He was entrusted with the delicate task of re-establishing relations with the Papacy in 1891; from 1897 to 1903, he was Chilean Minister to Italy and Germany. He returned to Chile to participate in domestic politics, eventually holding the portfolio of foreign affairs in several of the ephemeral cabinets of "the parliamentary régime." In 1917 he became President of the Permanent Commission of Fine Arts; and from 1924 to 1930 he once again represented Chile at the Vatican. His literary efforts include *La Enseñanza de las bellas artes* and *El Genio de Roma*. In his art Subercaseaux reacted against both Impressionism and the prevailing academic style, achieving a personal style in which he rendered the subtleties of light, volume, and mass, usually in out-of-door subjects, with great sensitivity. He balanced these elements in compositions of firm structure, which in certain canvases, such as the *Docks of Valparaiso* in the Museo Nacional de Bellas Artes, approached abstraction. CF

**Swett, Jorge** [Guayaquil, Ecuador; active since the 1940s]. This painter and mosaicist received his degree in Law and Social Science from the Universidad Central del Ecuador. He has received prizes for his paintings and he has also published a book of short stories entitled *La montaña y los recuerdos* (*Mountain and Memories*). He decorated the exterior of Guayaquil Airport with mosaic murals of effective semiabstract design. He lives in Guayaquil. CF

**Szyszlo, Fernando de** [Lima, Peru, 1925– ]. Fernando de Szyszlo studied at the Escuela de Artes Plásticas of the Universidad Católica in Lima, where he is now a member of the faculty. He later studied in France and Italy. Widely regarded as one of Latin America's most important contemporary painters, he exhibited in the 4th and 5th São Paulo Bienals, in the 23d Venice Biennial, at the Carnegie Museum, and in the Guggenheim Museum's International Exhibition (1964). He has had one-man shows in galleries in Paris, Florence, New York, Buenos Aires, and Caracas. De Szyszlo has been a visiting professor at Cornell University and is currently a visiting lecturer at Yale. He has also written on contemporary painting in Latin America. TG

**Tamayo, Rufino** [Oaxaca, Mexico, 1899– ]. Tamayo moved to Mexico City with his family when he was eight years old. At eighteen he began his studies at the Escuela de Bellas Artes, and then painted independently until his first shows, which were held in Mexico City in 1926 and in New York in 1927. Tamayo did not respond to the representational style of the Mexican muralists who were his contemporaries. He chose to follow an individual path, painting still-lifes, portraits, and a few themes symbolic of national revolutionary ideals, in his early period. He found artistic roots both in the pre-Columbian ambient of his native Oaxaca and in the European styles of the Cubist and post-Impressionist schools. His art reached maturity in the early 1940s in a style that successfully fused modern European with ancient and contemporary Mexican traditions. He paints explosive abstract forms in a muted range of blues, reds, and earth colors, elements that he combines in canvases of brooding ancestral vision and modern psychological impact. Although his work for a time may have seemed partly a reaction against muralism, Tamayo has in the last decade executed several powerful and original works of his own in that medium. One of his most significant contributions to Latin American as well Mexican art is his honest and wholly integrated cosmopolitanism. JD

**Tarsila.** See: **do Amaral, Tarsila**

**Tatis, José Gabriel** [Cartagena, 1813–?]. Tatis belonged to an old family which had traditional interests in art and the military. He followed both traditions, attaining the rank of colonel in the army and leaving a long series of miniature portraits of distinguished Colombians of his time.   TG

**Taunay, Auguste Marie** [Paris, 1768 – Rio de Janeiro, Brazil, 1824]. Auguste Marie Taunay, who was left an orphan, found a protector in his elder brother, Nicholas Antoine. He studied sculpture with Moitte, and soon won a stipend for travel to Rome. Political circumstances, however, prevented his departure. His work in Paris involved the decoration of the grand staircase in the Palace of the Louvre and various sculptures that were exhibited in the Salon of 1808. Auguste Marie accompanied his brother and a number of other French artists in the Lebreton Mission to Brazil in 1816. He was named Professor of Sculpture at the newly established Academia de Belas Artes and trained a number of outstanding pupils, including João Joaquim Alão, who succeeded Taunay as Professor of Sculpture on the latter's death. Auguste Marie Taunay executed numerous works during his stay in Brazil. His statue, *Minerva Protecting the Bust of the Monarch with Her Shield*, was one of the many pieces executed for the festival commemorating the acclamation of Dom João VI in 1816. He also realized a bust of the Portuguese epic poet, Camões, and a number of statues, allegories, and bas-reliefs for the façade of the Academia where he taught.   DD

**Taunay, Félix Emile** [France, 1795–1881]. Félix Emile Taunay accompanied his father, Nicolas Antoine, on the Lebreton Mission to Brazil in 1816. He studied landscape painting with his father at the Academia de Belas Artes in Rio de Janeiro, where he assumed the chair of Landscape Painting upon his father's return to France in 1821. The younger Taunay's talents included a remarkable administrative capability which he exercised as the third director of the Academia. The annual General Exhibition introduced in 1840 was an innovation during his long stay at the Academia. Although Félix Emile did not attain his father's mastery, he left a number of important Brazilian landscapes.   DD

**Taunay, Nicolas Antoine** [Paris, 1755 – Paris, 1830]. Nicolas Antoine Taunay's early interest in the arts led him to Lepicié's workshop in Paris at the age of thirteen. He later studied under the historical painters, Brenet and Casanova. At the age of twenty-one, he exhibited his first works in the Prussian Youth Exposition. In 1784 his second exhibition won him the title of *agrée* of the Royal Academy of Painting in Paris and brought him a pension from the Academy of Rome. In 1795 he was made a founding member of the Institut de France. A close friend of the Empress Josephine, Taunay enjoyed a privileged position in the French court until the Emperor's downfall. Thus, he welcomed an invitation, in 1816, to join the Lebreton Mission to Brazil commissioned by the Portuguese king, Dom João VI. Taunay, considered the most eminent member of the French artistic mission, remained in Brazil for five years, helping establish the Academia de Belas Artes, in which he held the chair of Landscape Painting. In 1821 he returned to Paris, where he died nine years later. Like many other foreign visitors to Brazil, Taunay was deeply impressed with that country's striking natural beauty. Working in the Neoclassic style of the French Academy, he showed his sensitivity to the local scene in such oil landscapes as his *Carioca Marketplace* (1816) and *Saint Anthony's Hill* (1816).   DD

**Testa, Clorindo** [Naples, Italy, 1923–      ]. Clorindo Testa went to Argentina with his parents when he was a year old. He was trained as an architect at the University of Buenos Aires. He traveled to Spain and Italy in 1949, and began to paint about 1950, having his first exhibition at the Van Riel Gallery in Buenos Aires in 1952. Since that time, he has exhibited widely: at São Paulo in the 1961 Bienal, in New York at the Guggenheim International and at the Time-Life Building, and at the Musée de l'Art Moderne in Paris. He received the first prize in the International Exhibition at Punta del Este, Uruguay, in 1959, and the first prize of the Instituto Torcuato Di Tella in Buenos Aires in 1961.   TG

**Tolsá, Manuel** [Valencia, Spain, 1757–1816]. Manuel Tolsá was one of the most distinguished figures of the late 18th-century Neoclassicism in New Spain (Mexico). An architect and sculptor, he went to Mexico in 1792 when the Spanish crown founded the Academia Real de San Carlos de Nueva España. There he was a pioneer of the new style and taught such artists as Pedro Patiño Ixtolinque (1774–1835), a sculptor of Indian descent. Tolsá produced brilliant works in Mexico, including the Palacio de Minería in Mexico City and the cupola of the Cathedral. He also executed the imposing equestrian statue of Carlos IV of Spain in that city.   JD

**Toral, Mario** [Santiago de Chile, 1934–      ]. Mario Toral's training was largely outside of Chile, first in the Escuela de Bellas Artes of Montevideo, later in the Ecole Supérieur National des Beaux Arts of Paris. He returned to Chile to become Professor of Painting at the Universidad Católica there. He has held one-man shows in Santiago, São Paulo, and Frankfurt, and received prizes in Paris (1961), Santiago de Chile (1962), and Ljubljana, Yugoslavia (1963). Besides working with pastels and prints, he has illustrated several books of poetry, most notably Pablo Neruda's *Macchu Picchu*.  CF

**Torres García, Joaquín** [Montevideo, 1874–1949]. Joaquín Torres García received his first lessons in painting and drawing from Vindardelli in 1889 in Mataró, Spain. A year later he entered Barcelona's Academia de Bellas Artes, studying under Antonio Caba. He also attended the Academia Baixa. In Barcelona, Torres García formed part of the Circle of St. Lluch, and converted his home *Mon repos* into a social and intellectual gathering place for poets, artists, and writers. After having studied the Impressionists, Torres García was attracted to the mural painting and aesthetics of Puvis de Chavannes, decorating in this style the churches of San Agustín and San Jorge, the Sala del Ayuntamiento, the Salón de San Jorge de la Diputación of Barcelona and, at the request of the architect Gaudí, the stained-glass windows of the Cathedral of Palma de Mallorca. In 1910 he painted the decorative tapestries for Uruguay's exhibit at the Brussels International Exposition. From 1919 to 1921 Torres García worked in Paris and New York. In Europe in 1921 he dedicated himself to creating mechanical toys in a Constructivist style. From 1925 to 1932 Torres García had one of his most productive periods, realizing some fifteen hundred works before returning to Uruguay in 1932. There he established his workshop and taught his students his theory, "Constructivism." To affirm, defend, and inculcate his theories, he worked, taught, and wrote tirelessly until his death. He delivered over five hundred lectures, published several books, and revealed himself as a philosopher, critic, theorist, and creator of an aesthetic doctrine. Torres García's genius as an artist was perhaps equaled by his skill as a teacher. He was instrumental in the formation of many of Uruguay's younger artists.  DD

**Torres Mendes, Ramón** [Colombia, 1809–1885]. Although largely self-taught, Torres Mendes did serve an apprenticeship in his youth to a firm of English lithographers. Later he painted over one hundred miniatures before turning to larger oil portraits and genre paintings. The latter were largely in watercolor. In 1846 he was named Secretary of the newly founded Academia de Dibujo y Pintura.  CF

**Tovar y Tovar, Martín** [Caracas, 1828 – Paris, 1902]. Tovar y Tovar was the first Venezuelan specifically trained to record pictorially the great moments of his nation's history. He first studied sketching with Carmelo Fernández, a painter of the Comisión Corográfica, then worked under José Nuceta Sardí in Caracas. Later he was sent to France and to Spain, where he studied with the Madrazos, returning to Venezuela in 1855. Ten years later he established an art and photographic studio in Caracas. In 1874, he received a commission from the government to portray leaders of the Wars of Independence and to paint the decisive battles of those wars. A strict academician, Tovar y Tovar synthesized the lineal art of David and the colorism of such Spanish romantics as Vicente López and Federico de Madrazo. His historical works are noted for their equilibrium of composition and Olympian dignity. He also did a certain amount of genre work in pencil, as well as a number of portraits of members of mid-to-late 19th-century Venezuelan society. He is one of the outstanding Latin American portraitists of his century.  CF

**Tresguerras, Francisco Eduardo** [Celaya, Mexico, 1759–1833]. Architect, painter, and engraver, Tresguerras spent most of his life in his birthplace. He went to Mexico City with the idea of entering a religious order, but he changed his mind and studied art at the Academia de San Carlos. However, he learned less from the Academia than from books on Renaissance and Neoclassical masters. Although he immersed himself in the study of the Neoclassical style, his paintings and drawings seem to lie somewhat outside European tradition. Mexican critics consider him one of the first authentically American architects. He produced his major work, the *Iglesia del Carmen* in Celaya, from 1802 to 1807.  DD

**Troya, Rafael** [Ibarra, Ecuador, 1845–1921]. Rafael Troya was a member of the generation that in the latter half of the 19th century introduced new themes and European ideas into Ecuadorian art. He studied with Luis Cadena, and worked under Rudolf Reschreiter, the German painter living in Ecuador. By 1872 Troya had chosen the major subject of his life work, the varied and powerful Ecuadorian landscape; he traveled extensively, making sketches, and in 1890 he declined an invitation to go to Bogotá, settling permanently in Ibarra. From this time on Troya devoted himself to the mountains, fields, and river of his home city. Troya's landscapes established a new principle in Ecuadorian art. This was, in the artist's own words, "Do not destroy the form of Nature." His work is preserved in the Cathedral of Ibarra and in private collections in Quito.  JD

**Trujillo, Guillermo** [Horconcitos, Panama, 1927–    ]. Guillermo Trujillo was trained as an architect at the Universidad de Panamá but obtained a fellowship from the Instituto de

Cultura Hispánica to study painting in Madrid at the Academia de San Fernando. He is known as a painter, draughtsman, and muralist, with five murals executed in Panama. He has exhibited in Caracas, Washington, and Madrid, as well as in Panama, and has participated in several of the major biennial shows, receiving an honorable mention in the São Paulo Bienal in 1959. He is also a university professor in Panama. His work was recently included in the Inter-American competition in Washington, D.C.   TG

**Turner, Charles** [Woodstock, England, 1773–1857]. In 1795 Turner entered the Royal Academy and studied engraving. He specialized in portrait prints such as his famous mezzotint of Bolívar, which he published in 1827 in London. Bolívar had sent the full-length portrait of himself by Gil de Castro to a friend in London. This work, now in the National Congress building in Caracas, was Turner's model. Turner's print became the best-known likeness of Bolívar in Europe.   TG

**Ugarte Eléspuru, Juan Manuel** [Lima, 1911–      ]. Juan Manuel Ugarte Eléspuru began his studies in Europe and completed them in Buenos Aires in the Escuela Superior de Bellas Artes. He held his first one-man show in Santiago de Chile in 1938. He has had numerous one-man shows in Lima, and has participated in many group shows. He has been active as an oil painter, mural painter, lecturer, writer, critic, and a cultural leader. In Lima, his murals are found in the Unidad Escolar Mercedes Cabello, the Ministerio de Educación, and on the exterior of the insurance building "El Universal." He has served with distinction as Director of the Escuela Nacional de Bellas Artes in Lima since 1957. He has also served as a member of the international jury of the 2d Mexican Biennial Exhibition in 1960, and as commissioner for the Peruvian selection for the 6th Bienal at São Paulo.   TG

**Urteaga, Mario** [Cajamarca, Peru, 1875–1959]. Urteaga, a self-taught artist, occupies a position in Peruvian art similar to that of the Douanier Rousseau in France. His work was relatively unknown until the late 1930s. He won first prize at the Salon of Viña del Mar, Chile, in 1937, and gave a one-man show in Lima in 1938. Urteaga painted scenes from the everyday life of the Peruvian Indian with incisive draughtsmanship and fresh color that not only preserved the charm of his subjects but penetrated to their strength and dignity.   CF

**Valencia, César** [Quito, 1918–      ]. Although influenced in his early work by his brother, Jaime Valencia, currently Director of the Escuela de Bellas Artes of Quito, Valencia is essentially self-taught. In 1947 he went to Argentina, to devote full time to art, where his interests moved from caricature to tempera and oil painting. After his one-man exhibition in Buenos Aires' Museo Municipal de Arte Moderno in 1963, he moved to the United States, where he now lives.   CF

**Vargas Rosas, Luis** [Chile, 1897–      ]. Vargas Rosas was one of the leading members of the Groupe Montparnasse, active in Chile between 1923 and 1930. This group espoused the Modernism of the Ecole de Paris, in particular its Cubist and Futurist phases and its interest in subjective expression. Vargas Rosas epitomized this early aspiration toward a renewal of Chilean art along advanced European lines, leaning toward a Futuristic interpretation of nature in his personal style. Vargas Rosas is presently Director of the Museo Nacional de Bellas Artes in Santiago.   TG

**Vasarely, Victor** [Pecs, Hungary, 1908–      ]. In Budapest, Vasarely changed his studies from medicine to art. In 1928–1929 he attended the Dessau Bauhaus where he studied with Moholy-Nagy. Since 1930 he has lived in France where he has been a member of the Galerie Denise René group, in Paris, since its foundation in 1944. In Venezuela, Vasarely executed two murals for the Ciudad Universitaria designed by Carlos Raúl Villanueva. Vasarely has become particularly well-known as one of the foremost exponents of geometrical abstraction. He won the grand prize of the 8th Bienal of São Paulo (1965).   CF

**Vega, Jorge Luis de la** [Buenos Aires, 1930–      ]. Jorge de la Vega trained as an architect at the University of Buenos Aires, where he now teaches. A self-taught painter, he began exhibiting his work in 1946 and, since that time, has had a long series of successful shows. In 1962, he was awarded a scholarship by the Spanish Fund for the Arts, which enabled him to spend a year in Europe. He returned to Buenos Aires, where he is one of the principal exponents of the *Nueva Figuración*, an informal, psychologically oriented, vigorously figurative style.   TG

**Velasco, José María** [Tematzalcingo, Mexico, 1840 – Mexico City, 1912]. José María Velasco entered the Academia de San Carlos in 1858, where he studied landscape painting with Eugenio Landesio. Ten years later he was named Professor of Perspective in the Academia. After an initial unsuccessful attempt at photography, Velasco turned to lithography, and in the early 1870s, published his *Flora of the Environs of Mexico*. In 1874 he moved with his family to the Villa Guadalupe, on the northern outskirts of the capital, where he remained for the greater part of his life, painting the unsurpassed spectacle of the Valley of Mexico from that and other elevated vantage points. The years between 1870 and 1877 were Velasco's most productive. His landscapes of the time emphasized the crags, cliffs, and mountain peaks, vegetation, and, significantly, the human inhabitants of this magnificent area which was the capital of the Aztec Empire and whose natural beauty staggered the Spanish conquerors. He reached a high point in 1875 with his painting *The Valley of Mexico*, a large canvas depicting the vastness of the Valley in a harmony of light and color. When his old master Landesio saw this oil, he remarked: "Nothing better can be done after this." In 1876 the painting won a prize at the Philadelphia Centenary. In the period 1877–1889, Velasco broadened the scope of his landscape themes, introducing new historical and archeological themes inspired by his travels to southern Mexico. He left for Europe in 1889 to attend the Universal Exposition in Paris, in which he presented 78 paintings and served as head of the Mexican mission. After traveling through England, Germany, Italy, and Spain, Velasco's homesickness brought him back to Mexico and his classes at the Academia, where he continued teaching until his death.  DD

**Victorica, Miguel Carlos** [Buenos Aires, 1884–1955]. Born of a well-to-do family, Miguel Carlos Victorica began to paint as a child of eight. In 1901, he entered the Academia de la Sociedad Estímulo de Bellas Artes, remaining there until 1906, with Sívori as one of his teachers. In 1911, Victorica obtained a government stipend to study in Europe, where he remained until 1918. He spent time copying in the Louvre, and traveled in Spain, Italy, and Switzerland. A painter in a late Impressionist, Nabi-Fauve tendency, he sent two canvases, *El Collar de Venecia*, and *Madariaga* to the Salón Nacional in Argentina in 1917. Today both of these works belong to the Museo Nacional de Bellas Artes in Buenos Aires. He painted figures, interiors, and still-lifes. He lived and exhibited frequently in Buenos Aires.  TG

**Vidal, Emeric Essex** [Bredford, Middlesex, England, 1791 – Brighton, England, 1861]. Vidal's father, a Frenchman, had a career in the British Navy, into which his three sons followed him. Emeric Essex, the youngest, began his avocation of painting watercolors as a young officer during the War of 1812. From 1816 to 1818 young Vidal was paymaster aboard the *Hyacinth*, which was stationed in Brazilian waters. During this time he visited Uruguay and Argentina, where he be-

came the earliest portrayer of life in that new republic and was the first of the costumbrista painters. Upon his return to England in 1818, he repainted for publication twenty-five of these South American works and prepared a text to accompany them. The book, *Picturesque Illustrations of Buenos Ayres and Montevideo*, appeared in 1820. He made two later voyages to South America but drew and painted little. These visits were to the Island of St. Helena in 1820–1821, and to Buenos Aires and Montevideo in 1828-1829.  TG

**Vilches, Eduardo** [Concepción, Chile, 1932–    ]. Vilches first studied art at the Escuela de Bellas Artes at the Universidad de Chile. From 1958 to 1960 he worked under Nemesio Antúnez at the Taller 99 in Santiago. The following year he received a scholarship to study graphic arts at Yale University. Vilches has participated in a number of international shows, including the 3d Biennial of Engraving in Tokyo, the International Exhibition of Engraving, Ljubljana, Yugoslavia (1963), and the 8th São Paulo Bienal (1965). He is presently Professor of Drawing and Coloring at the Escuela de Bellas Artes, Universidad Católica, Santiago.  CF

**Villacis, Aníbal** [Ambato, Ecuador, 1927–    ]. Villacis began painting at a very early age and at sixteen was the art teacher in the elementary and high schools of his hometown. At twenty-one he won a fellowship for study in Europe. He spent a year in Paris, and two years in Spain (1953–1956). He later lived in Caracas for a year, visited Colombia, Brazil, and the United States by invitation of the several national governments. He has won many prizes and exhibited in the Pan American Union, Washington, D.C., in 1962.  TG

**Villanueva, Carlos Raúl** [Croyden, England, 1900–    ]. Carlos Villanueva received the most important part of his architectural training at the Ecole des Beaux-Arts in Paris. Since his return to Venezuela, he has played an extremely active role in professional architectural circles. He helped to found the Facultad de Arquitectura y Urbanismo of the Universidad Central of Venezuela, and the Sociedad Venezolana de Arquitectos. At present, he serves as Counselor to the Workman's Bank Government Housing Agency and Director of the National Commission of Urbanism. Villanueva's most important work is probably his design for the Ciudad Universitaria in Caracas, a project that took more than fifteen years to complete. Several of the individual buildings, most notably the theater and the partially covered courtyard, were also designed by him. Perhaps the most interesting part of Villanueva's design for the Universidad Central is the success he has had in integrating art and architecture. Enlisting the aid of other outstanding artists, such as Alejandro Otero, Alexander Calder, and Vasarely, he has created a "new architectural-sculptural-pictorial organism in which no element is of minor importance." CF

**Vinatea Reynoso, Jorge** [1900–1931]. Born at the turn of the century, Jorge Vinatea Reynoso was one of the foremost members of the Indigenist movement that dominated Peruvian art in the 1920s and 1930s. Under the instruction of Daniel Hernández, the first Director of the Escuela de Bellas Artes in Lima, Vinatea Reynoso developed a sound technique. This was to distinguish him among the indigenists, many of whom were inclined to pursue their theme without sufficient technical skill. Vinatea's own thematic ideas were influenced by the leading indigenist, José Sabogal. Vinatea's paintings of Indian life are marked by a weaving distribution of figures, rather than the central perspective and generally simple structure favored by other indigenists. The critic Juan W. Acha has discerned a tapestry-like continuity in his works. Vinatea Reynoso favored monochromes until the last two years of his life, when he attempted to enliven his colors. He died in 1931, leaving an *œuvre* of intrinsic artistic interest which avoided chichés. JD

**Visconti, Elyseu d'Angelo** [Salerno, Italy, 1867 – Brazil, 1944]. Visconti's parents moved from Salerno to Rio de Janeiro before their child was a year old. In 1884 he entered the Liceu de Artes e Oficios, and one year later, after displaying an early talent for painting, began studying at the Academia de Belas Artes under the direction of José María de Madeiros, Henrique Bernadelli, and Rodolfo Amoêdo. In 1888 he won a gold medal for painting in Brazil, in 1892, a silver medal at the Chicago Exposition, and that same year was awarded a stipend for travel in Europe. Visconti attended the Ecole des Beaux-Arts in Paris, exhibiting his work in Paris Salons over a period of seven years and traveling in Italy and Spain. He was strongly influenced by the Italian Renaissance masters during this period, as reflected in his Italianate *S. Sebastian's Reward* (1898), and *The Nymphs* (1898). The latter two won for him a silver medal at the Paris Universal Exposition in 1900, after which he returned to Brazil and exhibited over sixty pieces of his work in Rio de Janeiro. In 1905 he executed the decorations for Rio's Teatro Municipal.

After various Atlantic crossings, and a gold medal from the St. Louis Exposition of 1906, Visconti settled down in Brazil following the First World War. After 1924 Visconti turned to highly nationalistic themes expressing Brazilian Regionalism in a series of landscapes dominated by vivacious luminous coloring. Visconti lived a variegated artistic life. He progressed through a variety of styles, from his early Naturalism through Divisionism and Realism to Impressionism; from a predominance of line through an equilibrium of color and drawing to an overwhelming use of light and color. DD

**Viteri, Oswaldo** [Ambato, Ecuador, 1931– ]. After attending secondary school in his native city, Viteri studied architecture at the Universidad Central del Ecuador in Quito, where he now teaches as Professor of Architecture. CF

**Whiting, Daniel Powers** [Troy, New York, 1808 – Washington, D.C., 1892]. A graduate of West Point, Whiting was promoted in 1847 from Infantry Captain to Major because of his gallantry in the Battle of Cerro Gordo in the Mexican War. While in Mexico he did sketches of scenes from the war which were published in 1849, in a book of lithographs entitled *The Army Portfolio*. DD

**Williams, Amancio** [Buenos Aires, 1913– ]. Amancio Williams studied architecture at the University of Buenos Aires. His best-known building is the house in Mar del Plata built in 1945–1947 for Alberto Williams, a severe rectangle floating on a bridge over a stream. Williams, a prolific and imaginative designer, has had but few of his projects come to fruition. Nevertheless, he is justly considered one of the major modern architects of Argentina and Latin America. TG

**Wisse, Sebastian** [Active in the 1840s]. Wisse, a French engineer and architect was called to Ecuador in 1839 to be a professor in the Universidad Central. He became a personal friend of President García Moreno, who gave him the task of constructing the highway from Quito to Guayaquil. One of a group of foreign architects brought to Ecuador "for the beautification of Quito," Wisse also designed García Moreno's private house in Quito, now the Ministry of Education. CF

**Wulf, Lloyd** [Nehawka, Nebraska, U.S.A., active Ecuador 1940–1964]. Lloyd Wulf studied at the University of Nebraska and the School of Fine Arts in San Francisco. After teaching primary school and working for the Works Project Administration in the 1930s, he went to Ecuador in 1941 on a Rosenberg Fellowship. There he founded his own school of painting. He has won prizes regularly since the 1950s in Ecuador and although he recently left that country he is respected by members of a younger generation of Ecuadorian artists. CF

# Bibliography

Acha V., Juan W. *Peru* ("Art in Latin America Today" Series). Washington, D.C.: Pan American Union, 1961.

*Anuário do Museu Imperial*. Petrópolis: Ministério da Educação e Cultura (n.d.).

Argul, José Pedro. *Pintura y escultura del Uruguay*. Montevideo: Publicación de la Revista del Instituto Histórico y Geográfia del Uruguay, 1958.

*Arte de América y España, Catálogo General*. Madrid: Instituto de Cultura Hispánica, 1963.

*Art mexicain du précolombien à nos jours*. 2 vols. Paris: Les Presses Artistiques, 1952.

*Artes Plásticas*. Havana: Consejo Nacional de Cultura (n.d.).

Bardi, P.M. *The Arts in Brazil*. Milan: Edizione del Milione, 1956.

———. *Lasar Segall*. Milan: Edizione del Milione, 1959.

———. *The Tropical Gardens of Burle Marx*. Amsterdam-Rio de Janeiro: Colibris, 1964.

*Bienal de São Paulo. Catalogues of I-VII* (1951–65). São Paulo: Museu de Arte Moderna.

Boulton, Alfredo. *Los Retratos de Bolívar*. 2nd ed. Caracas: Editorial Arte, 1964.

Cardoza y Aragón, Luis. *José Guadalupe Posada*. Mexico: Universidad Nacional Autónoma de México, 1963.

*Carreño*. Havana: Instituto Nacional de Cultura, 1957.

Carril, Bonifacio del. *Monumenta Iconographica*. Buenos Aires: Emecé Editores, 1964.

Carrillo Gil, Alvar. *Obras de José Clemente Orozco en la colección Carrillo Gil*. Mexico: 1953.

Catlin, Stanton L. *Art moderne mexicain*. Paris: Braun et Cie., 1951.

Bénézit, E. *Dictionnaire critique et documentaire des peintres, sculpteurs, dessinateurs et graveurs*. 2nd ed. 8 vols. Paris: Gründ, 1948–1955.

*Catálogo*. São Paulo: Museu de Arte de São Paulo, 1963.

*Catálogo del Museo Histórico Nacional*. 2 vols. Buenos Aires: Museo Histórico Nacional, 1957.

Chacón, T., Mario. *Pintores del siglo XIX*. La Paz: Dirección Nacional de Informaciones de la Presidencia de la República, 1963.

Charlot, Jean. *The Mexican Mural Renaissance*, 1920–1925. New Haven and London: Yale University Press, 1963.

*Crítica de Arte*. Ano 1, No. 1. Rio de Janeiro: December 1961–March 1962.

Damaz, Paul F. *Art in Latin American Architecture*. New York: Reinhold, 1963.

*De Blanes a nuestros días*. Punta del Este: Comision Nacional de Bellas Artes, 1961.

De Souza, Wladimir Alvez and Flávio de Aquino. *Arte brasileira*. Rio de Janeiro: Enciclopedia Delta-Larousse (c. 1960).

*Diego Rivera: 50 años de su labor artística*. Mexico: Instituto Nacional de Bellas Artes, 1949.

*El Museo de Bellas Artes*, 1880–1930. Santiago de Chile: Universidad de Chile, 1930.

*Exposição: Aspectos do Rio*. Rio de Janeiro: Ministério da Educação e Cultura y Museu Nacional de Belas Artes, 1963.

*Exposição da Missão artistica francesa de 1816*. Rio de Janeiro: Museu Nacional de Belas Artes y Ministério da Educação e Saude, 1940.

*Exposição de arte do século XX*. Araraquara: Museu de Arte Contemporanea da Universidade de São Paulo, 1963.

*Exposição: Le Breton e a Missão artistica francesa de 1816*. Rio de Janeiro: Museu Nacional de Belas Artes, 1960.

*Exposição: Pintura Contemporánea do Mexico*. Rio de Janeiro: Secretaria de Relaciones Exteriones, 1965.

*Exposição retrospectiva de Elyseu D'Angelo Visconti*. Rio de Janeiro: Museu Nacional de Belas Artes, 1949.

*Exposición retrospectiva de Armando Reverón*. Caracas: Museo de Bellas Artes, 1955.

Escobar, Luis Antonio. *Guía arquitectónica de Bogotá*. Bogotá: Asociación de Profesionales Especializados en los Estados

Unidos de América, 1964.

Farias, Ixca. *Biografía de pintores Jaliscienses* 1882–1940. Guadalajara, Jalisco: Ricardo Delgado, 1939.

Fernández, Justino. *Arte moderno y contemporáneo de México*. Mexico: Imprenta Universitaria, 1952.

Ferrez, Gilberto. *O Velho Rio de Janeiro através das gravuras de Thomas Ender*. São Paulo: Edições Melhoramentos (n.d.).

*Forte, 20 oleos*. São Paulo and Rio de Janeiro: Ministério de Educacion y Justicia de la República Argentina, 1961.

Gassiot-Talabot, Gérald. "A. E. Reidy," *Cimaise*, IX (March–April 1962).

Giraldo Jaramillo, Gabriel. *La Pintura en Colombia*. Mexico and Buenos Aires: Fondo de Cultura Económica, 1942.

Giuria, Juan. *La Arquitectura en el Uruguay*. Montevideo: Imp. Universal, 1958.

Gómez Sicre, José. *4 Artists of the Americas*. Washington, D.C.: Pan American Union, 1957.

Graham, Maria. *Journal of a Residence in Chile*. London: Longman, Hurst, Rees, Orme, Brown, and Green, and John Murphy, 1824.

Grieder, Terence. "Argentina's New Figurative Art," *Art Journal*, XXIX (1964).

———, and Charles Berry. *Bibliography of Latin American Philosophy and Art since Independence* (mimeographed). Austin: University of Texas, Institute of Latin American Studies, 1964.

Gullar, Ferreira. *Lygia Clark*. Rio de Janeiro: Imprensa Nacional, 1958.

*Gunther Gerzso*. Mexico: Instituto Nacional de Bellas Artes, 1965.

*Homenaje a Cuzco: 11 Pintores*. Cuzco. Instituto Americano de Arte, 1965.

Hitchcock, Henry-Russell. *Latin American Architecture since 1945*. New York: Museum of Modern Art, 1955.

*Iconografía de Montevideo*. Montevideo: Concejo Departamental de Montevideo, 1955.

Hope, Henry R. *Encyclopedia of World Art*. Vol. III. New York: McGraw-Hill, 1959.

James, David. *Monvoisin*. Buenos Aires: Emecé, 1949.

*Joaquín Torres García*. Buenos Aires: Centro de Artes Visuales, Instituto Torcuato Di Tella, 1964.

Jochamowitz, Alberto. *Pintores y pinturas*. Lima: Torres Aguirre, 1949.

Kirstein, Lincoln. *The Latin American Collection of the Museum of Modern Art*. New York: Museum of Modern Art, 1943.

Lake, Carlton, and Robert Maillard, eds. *Dictionary of Modern Painting*. 2nd ed. (rev.). New York: Tudor (n.d.).

Lago, Tomás. *Rugendas, pintor romántico de Chile*. Santiago de Chile: Universidad de Chile, 1960.

Machado, Aníbal M. *Goeldi*. Rio de Janeiro: Ministério da Educação Cultura (n.d.).

Martínez, Ignacio. *Pintura mural, siglo XX*. Mexico: Alfredo Leal Cortés, 1960.

*Masterworks of Mexican Art*. Los Angeles: Los Angeles County Museum of Art, 1965.

Mérida, Carlos. *Modern Mexican Artists*. Mexico: Frances Toor Studios, 1937.

Merli, Joan. *Raquel Forner*. Buenos Aires: Poseidon, 1952.

Merlino, Adrian. *Diccionario de artistas plásticas de la Argentina*. Buenos Aires, 1954.

*Mexican Art*. Ann Arbor: University of Michigan, 1958.

*Mexican Art Today*. Philadelphia: Philadelphia Museum of Art, 1943.

*Morales*. New York: Galeria Bonino, 1965.

Morley, Grace L. McCann. *An Introduction to Contemporary Peruvian Painting*. San Francisco: San Francisco Museum of Art, 1942.

Mujica Láinez, Manuel. *Argentina* ("Art in Latin America Today" Series). Washington, D.C.: Pan American Union, 1961.

———. *Victorica*, 1884–1955. Buenos Aires: Ediciones Bonino, 1955.

*Museo Nacional de Historia, Castle of Chapultepec*. Mexico: Instituto Nacional de Antropología e Historia, 1957 and 1963.

Nebel, Carlos. *Viaje pintoresco y arqueológico sobre la parte más interesante de la República Mexicana*. Mexico: Manuel Porrua, 1963.

Nelken, Margarita. *Carlos Mérida*. Mexico: Universidad Nacional Autónoma de México, 1961.

Neuvillate, Alfonso de. *Francisco Goitia*. Mexico: Universidad Nacional Autónoma de México, 1964.

*New Art of Argentina*. Buenos Aires: Instituto Torcuato di Tella, 1964.

*O Rio na caricatura*. Rio de Janeiro: Biblioteca Nacional, 1965.

*150 años de arte argentino*. Buenos Aires: Republic of Argentina, 1961.

Otta, Francisco. *Guía de la pintura moderna*. Santiago de Chile: Editorial Universitaria, 1959.

Pagano, José León. *Fernando García del Molino*. Buenos Aires: Secretaria de Educación, Subsecretaria de Cultura, 1948.

————. *Historia del arte argentino*. Buenos Aires: L'Amateur, 1944.

Payró, Julio E. 23 *Pintores de la Argentina*, 1810–1900. Buenos Aires: Editorial Universitaria de Buenos Aires, 1962.

*Permanent Collection of Contemporary Art of Latin America*. Washington, D.C.: Pan American Union, 1960.

Petrés, Fr. Domingo de. *Homenaje al arquitecto Capuchino Fray Domingo de Petrés en el segundo centenario de su nacimiento, 1759 – 9 de Junio – 1959*. Puente del Común, Colombia: Ediciones Seminario Serafico Misional Capuchino, 1959.

Pevsner, Nikolaus. *Academies of Art Past and Present*. Cambridge: Cambridge University Press, 1940.

*Pinacoteca do Museu Imperial*. Petrópolis: Ministério da Educação e Cultura, 1956.

*Pintores y viajeros francesces en la iconografía uruguaya de los siglos XVIII y XIX*. Montevideo: Sociedad Arrigos de Francia, 1961.

*Pintura venezolana*, 1661 – 1961. Caracas: Museo de Bellas Artes, 1960.

Plenn, Jaime, and Virginia Plenn. *A Guide to Modern Mexican Murals*. Ixtapalapa: Ediciones Tolteca, S.A., 1963.

*Premio Nacional e International Instituto Torcuato di Tella 1964*. Buenos Aires: Instituto Torcuato di Tella, 1964.

*Rafael Coronel*. Mexico: Instituto Nacional de Bellas Artes, 1965.

Reis, Júnior, José Maria dos, *Historia da pintura no Brasil*. São Paulo: Editõra "Leia," 1944.

*René Portocarrero*. Mexico: Museo de Arte Moderno, 1965.

Rios, Juan E. *La Pintura contemporánea en el Perú*.

Romera, Antonio R. *Historia de la pintura chilena*. Santiago de Chile: Zig-Zag, 1960.

Rugendas, João Mauricio. *Viagem pitoresca através do Brasil*. São Paulo: Libraria Martins, 1940.

Sabogal, José. *Pancho Fierro*. Lima.

*Salão Nacional de Arte Moderna* (Catalogue). Rio de Janeiro: Ministério da Educação e Cultura, 1965.

San Martín, María Luisa. *Pintura Argentina Contemporánea*. Buenos Aires: Editorial La Mandrágora, 1961.

Schiaffino, Eduardo. *La pintura y la escultura en Argentina*, 1783–1894. Buenos Aires: 1933.

*2ª Bienal Americana de Arte*. Córdoba: Universidad Nacional de Córdoba, 1964.

*South American Art Today*. Dallas: Dallas Museum of Fine Arts, 1959.

Seuphor, Michél, ed. *Dictionary of Abstract Painting*. New York: Paris Book Center, 1958.

Stewart, Virginia. 45 *Contemporary Mexican Artists*. Stanford: Stanford University Press, 1951.

Sujo, Clara Diament de. *Venezuela* ("Art in Latin America Today" Series). Washington, D.C.: Pan American Union, 1962.

Szyszlo, Fernando de. "Contemporary Latin American Painting," *College Art Journal*, XIX (1959–1960), 134-145.

Taunay, Alfonso de E. *A Missão artística de 1816*. Rio de Janeiro: Ministério da Educação e Cultura, 1956.

Thieme, Ulrich, and Felix Becker. *Allgemeines Lexikon der bildenden Künstler von der Antike bis zur Gegenwart*, 37 vols. Leipzig: Wilhelm Engelman, 1907–1950.

Thoby-Marcelin, Philippe. *Haiti* ("Art in Latin America Today" Series). Washington, D.C.: Pan American Union, 1959.

Traba, Marta. *Colombia* ("Art in Latin America Today" Series). Washington, D.C.: Pan American Union, 1959.

————(text), and Hernán Díaz (photos). *Seis Artistas contemporáneos colombianos*. Bogotá: Alberto Barco (c. 1963).

Tupynambá, Yara. *Tres Séculos e meio de pintura no Brasil*. Belo Horizonte: Universidade de Minas Gerais, 1961.

*Twenty Centuries of Mexican Art*. Mexico and New York: The Museum of Modern Art and the Instituto de Antropología e Histórica de México, 1940.

Ugarte Eléspuru, Juan Manuel. *Anuario del año académico*. Lima: Departmento de Publicaciones de la E.N.B.A.F., 1962.

————. *Escuela Nacional de Bellas Artes del Perú*. Lima: Departamento de Publicaciones de la E.N.B.A.F., 1963.

————. *Perú en la VI Bienal de San Pablo*. Lima: Santiago Valverde, 1961.

*Um século da pintura brasileira*. Rio de Janeiro: Ministério da Educação e Saúde, Museu Nacional de Belas Artes (c. 1950).

Uribe Arce, Armando. *La Humanidad de Roser Bru*. Santiago de Chile: Embajada del Brasil, 1963.

Vargas, José María. O.P. *El Arte ecuatoriano*. Quito: Conferencia Interamericana, 1960.

————. *Historia del arte ecuatoriano*. Quito: Editorial Santo Domingo, 1963.

————. *Los Maestros del arte ecuatoriano*. Quito: Imprenta Municipal, 1955.

*Visión de la pintura chilena: Agenda*. Santiago de Chile: Compañía de Acero del Pacífico, 1963 and 1964.

Zingg, David Drew. "The Wind of Change: South America's lively new generation of artists," *Show*, III (November 1962), 60-66.

# Acknowledgments

The sponsors of the project wish to thank the following national, state, municipal, institutional, and professional officials; members of National Committees and Commissions and their Executive Secretaries; and Yale University alumni and other representatives in Latin America who individually and collectively in all provinces of administration have provided the interorganizational collaboration that has made possible the various national participations in the exhibition:

## Argentina

Excmo. Sr. Dr. Miguel Angel Zavala Ortiz, *Minister of Foreign Affairs and Worship*

Excmo. Sr. Dr. Norberto M. Barrenechea, *Ambassador to the United States*

Excmo. Sr. Dr. Alconada Aramburú, *Minister of Education and Justice*

Excmo. Sr. Dr. Anselmo Marini, *Governor of the Province of Buenos Aires*

Excmo. Sr. Dr. Justo Paez Molina, *Governor of the Province of Córdoba*

Excmo. Sr. Dr. Antonio de La Torre, *Under-Secretary of Education for Culture*

Sra. Silvia Ambrosini, *National Museum of Fine Arts*

Dr. Carlos Barreiro Ortiz, *Cultural Advisor, General Direction of Cultural Diffusion, Ministry of Foreign Affairs*

Sr. Jorge Beltrán, *Director, Emilio A. Caraffa Provincial Museum of Fine Arts, Córdoba*

Sr. Guillermo Buitrago, *Director, Eduardo Sivori Museum of Plastic Arts, City of Buenos Aires*

Mr. Stanley R. Burke, Jr.

Capitán de Navío Humberto F. Burzio, *Director, National Historical Museum, Buenos Aires*

Sra. Ruth Fraga, *First Secretary, Cultural Officer, Argentine Embassy, Washington, D.C.*

Sr. Jorge Roberto Hayzus

Dr. Juan J. Mathé, *Former First Secretary, Director of Cultural Affairs, Argentine Embassy, Washington, D.C.*

Dr. Angel O. Nessi, *Director, Museum of Plastic Arts of the Province of Buenos Aires, La Plata*

Sr. Arquitecto Samuel F. Oliver, *Director of National Museums and the National Library*

Sr. Secretario de Embajada Julio Ortiz del Moral, *General Direction of Cultural Relations, Ministry of Foreign Affairs*

Sr. Hugo Parpagnoli, *Director, Museum of Modern Art, City of Buenos Aires*

Sr. Samuel Paz, *Assistant Director, Instituto Torcuato di Tella, Buenos Aires*

Srta. Ruth Perea Muñoz

Dr. Francisco Rabanal, *Intendant of the Municipality of Buenos Aires*

Dr. John T. Reid, *Cultural Affairs Officer, United States Embassy, Buenos Aires*

Dr. Jorge Romero Brest, *Director, Centro de Artes Visuales, Instituto Torcuato di Tella, Buenos Aires*

Sr. Arquitecto Pedro Sinopoli, *Director, Juan B. Castagnino Municipal Museum of Fine Arts, Rosario*

Dr. Manuel A. Soto, *Secretary of Culture of the Municipality of Buenos Aires*

Dr. Jorge Soto Aceval, *Director of the National Academy of Fine Arts*

## Bolivia

Excmo. Sr. Col. Joaquín Zenteno Anaya, *Minister of Foreign Affairs*

Excmo. Sr. Col. Hugo Banzer Suárez, *Minister of Education*

Excmo. Sr. Col. Julio Sanjínes Goitia, *Ambassador to the United States*

Mr. Michael P. Boerner, *Cultural Affairs Officer, United States Embassy, La Paz*

Sr. Antonio Mariaca, *Director, National Museum of Art*

Arq. Teresa Gisbert de Mesa, *Vocal of the Bolivian National Artistic Patrimony*

Arq. José de Mesa F., *Dean of the Department of Architecture, Universidad Mayor de San Andrés*

Sr. Armando Pacheco, *Vocal of the National Council of Art*


## Brazil

Excmo. Sr. Dr. Vasco T. Leitão da Cunha, *Minister of Foreign Affairs*

Excmo. Sr. Gen. Juracy Magalhães, *Ambassador to the United States*

Excmo. Sr. Dr. Flávio Suplicy de Lacerda, *Minister of Education and Culture*

Excmo. Sr. Ambassador Everaldo Deyrell de Lima, *Chief, Department of Culture and Information, Ministry of Foreign Affairs*

Excmo. Sr. Conselheiro Vasco Mariz, *Chief of the Division of Cultural Diffusion, Ministry of Foreign Affairs*

Excmo. Sr. Dr. Rodrigo Mello Franco de Andrade, *Director of Service of the National Artistic and Historic Patrimony, Ministry of Education and Health*

Dr. P. M. Bardi, *Director, Museum of São Paulo*

Sra. Dina Coelho, *Secretary General, São Paulo Bienal Foundation*

Mr. Alvin H. Cohen, *Cultural Affairs Officer, United States Consulate General, São Paulo*

Dr. Lygia da Fonseca Fernandes da Cunha, *Chief, Iconographic Section, National Library, Rio de Janeiro*

Dr. Adonias Filho, *Director General, National Library, Rio de Janeiro*

Srta. Dina Flüsser, *Division of Cultural Diffusion, Ministry of Foreign Affairs*

Prof. Alfredo Galvão, *Director, National Museum of Fine Arts, Rio de Janeiro*

Mr. George C. Huffard, *Rio de Janeiro*

Sra. Rosalina Leão, *Former Chief, Section of Plastic Arts, Ministry of Foreign Affairs*

Mr. James H. MacGillivray, *Cultural Affairs Officer, United States Embassy, Rio de Janeiro*

Dr. Josué Montelo, *Director, National Historical Museum, Rio de Janeiro*

Sr. Edson Motta, *Service of the National Artistic and Historic Patrimony, Ministry of Education*

Dr. Aloisio de Paula, *Director, Museum of Modern Art, Rio de Janeiro*

Dr. Ciro Poggi

Prof. Gerson Pompeu Pinhero, *Director, National School of Fine Arts*

Sra. Carmen Portinho, *Director, Museum of Modern Art, Rio de Janeiro*

Prof. Walter Zanini, *Director, Museum of Contemporary Art, University of São Paulo*


## Chile

Excmo. Sr. Gabriel Valdés Subercaseaux, *Minister of Foreign Affairs*

Excmo. Sr. Dr. Radomiro Tomic, *Ambassador to the United States*

Excmo. Sr. Dr. Juan Gómez Millas, *Minister of Education*

Excmo. Sr. Julio Philippi I., *Former Minister of Foreign Affairs*

Excmo. Sr. Alejandro Garretón Silva, *Former Minister of Education*

Excmo. Sr. Sergio Gutiérrez Olivos, *Former Ambassador to the United States*

Sr. Nemesio Antúnez, *Cultural Affairs Officer, Chilean Embassy, Washington, D.C.*

Sr. Federico Assler, *Curator-Secretary, Museum of Contemporary Art, Santiago de Chile*

Sra. María Eugenia Borowicz, *Extension Institute of Plastic Arts, University of Chile*

Sr. Jorge Elliott, *Director, Extension Institute of Plastic Arts, University of Chile*

Gral. Oscar Fuentes Pantoja, *Executive Vice President, National Commission for UNESCO*

Sr. Eugenio González Rojas, *Rector, University of Chile*

Maestro Carlos Pedraza, *Dean, Faculty of Fine Arts, University of Chile*

Sr. Tole Peralta, *Director, Casa del Arte, University of Concepción*

Sr. Ricardo Satander Batalla, *Director, Municipal Museum of Fine Arts, Viña del Mar*

Mr. Joseph J. Sibley

Mr. Philip A. Turner, *Cultural Affairs Officer, United States Embassy, Santiago*

Maestro Mario Valdivieso, *Director, School of Art, Catholic University of Chile*

Maestro Luis Vargas Rosas, *Director, National Museum of Fine Arts*

## Colombia

Excmo. Sr. Dr. Fernando Gómez Martínez, *Minister of Foreign Affairs*

Excmo. Sr. Dr. Pedro Gómez Valderrama, *Minister of Government*

Excmo. Sr. Dr. Daniel Arango, *Minister of National Education*

Excmo. Sr. Dr. Eduardo Uribe Botero, *Ambassador to the United States*

Excmo. y Rdmo. Sr. Cardenal Concha, *Archbishop of Bogotá*

Mr. George W. Arenas

Srta. Teresa Cuervo Borda, *Director, National Museum*

Mr. Spruille Braden, Jr.

Mr. Stanley R. Burke, Jr.

Dr. Jaime Duarte French, *Director, Luis Angel Arango Library*

Maestro Manuel Hernández, *Director, School of Fine Arts, National University of Colombia*

Sra. Marta Traba, *Director, Museum of Modern Art of Bogotá*

Srta. Mireya Zawadzky, *Chief, Fine Arts Section, Ministry of National Education*

Dr. Guillermo Hernández de Alba, *Director, 20th of July Museum, Bogotá*

Dr. Germán Botero de los Rios, *Sub-Gerente-Secretario, Bank of the Republic, Bogotá*

Mr. Francis E. Townsend, *Cultural Affairs Officer, United States Embassy, Bogotá*

## Ecuador

Excmo. Sr. Dr. Gonzalo Escudero, *Minister of Foreign Relations*

Excmo. Sr. Lic. Humberto Vacas-Gómez, *Minister of Education*

Excmo. Sr. Dr. Gustavo Larrea, *Ambassador to the United States*

Excmo. Sr. Dr. José Antonio Correa, *Former Ambassador to the United States*

Sr. Eloy Aviles Alfaro

Lic. Francisco Baquerizo

Sra. Germania Paz y Miño de Breilh, *Commission Member, Yale-Texas Exhibition, Quito*

Dr. Abél Romeo Castillo, *President, Casa de la Cultura Ecuatoriana, Núcleo del Guayas*

Sr. Rodrigo Chávez, *Director, Municipal Museum, Guayaquil*

Sr. Lic. Jaime Chávez Granja, *President, Casa de la Cultura Ecuatoriana*

Sra. Laura de Crespo, *Director, Library of the Casa de la Cultura Ecuatoriana, Quito*

Sr. Nicolás Delgado

Maestro Eduardo Kingman, *Director, National Museum of Colonial Art, Quito*

Srta. Neda Prpic

Fray José Maria Vargas, O.P., *Jijón y Caamaño Museum of Archaeology and History, Quito*

Capitan César Arturo Vinueza Moscoso

Mr. Andy G. Wilkinson, *Cultural Affairs Officer, United States Embassy, Quito*

## Guatemala

Excmo. Sr. Lic. Alberto Herrarte González, *Minister of Foreign Affairs*

Excmo. Sr. Col. Rolando Chinchilla Aguilar, *Minister of Public Education*

Excmo. Sr. Dr. Carlos García-Bauer, *Ambassador to the United States*

Srta. Aida Campo Asturias, *Director, General Direction of Fine Arts and Cultural Extension*

Prof. Daniel Contreras, *Director, National Museum of History and Fine Arts*

Miss Dorothy Dillon, *Cultural Affairs Officer, United States Embassy, Guatemala City*

Sr. Roberto González Goyri, *Member, Committee of Plastic Arts, General Direction of Fine Arts and Cultural Extension*

Sr. Willard T. Hodgsdon

## Mexico

Excmo. Sr. Antonio Carrillo Flores, *Secretary of Foreign Affairs*

Excmo. Sr. Lic. Agustín Yañez, *Secretary of Education*

Excmo. Sr. Hugo B. Margáin, *Ambassador to the United States*

Excmo. Sr. José Gorostiza, *Former Secretary of Foreign Affairs*

Excmo. Sr. Jaime Torres Bodet, *Former Secretary of Education*

Lic. Antonio Arriaga Ochoa, *Director, National Museum of History, Chapultepec*

Sra. Carmen Barreda, *Director, National Museum of Modern Art*

Dr. John E. Brown, *Cultural Affairs Officer, United States Embassy, Mexico, D.F.*

Dr. Ignacio Chávez, *Rector, National Autonomous University of Mexico*

Dr. Eusebio Dávalos Hurtado, *Director General, National Institute of Anthropology and History*

Sr. Horacio Flores-Sánchez, *Former Chief, Department of Plastic Arts, National Insitutute of Fine Arts*

Sra. Mary Urquidi de Franco

Maestro Fernando Gamboa, *Former Commissioner, Mexican Pavillion, New York World's Fair*

Sr. Celestino Gorostiza, *Former Director General, National Institute of Fine Arts*

Prof. Jorge Guerra Ruiz, *Director, Library of The National School of Plastic Arts*

Sr. Jorge Hernández Campos, *Chief, Department of Plastic Arts, National Institute of Fine Arts*

Sr. José Luis Martínez, *Director General, National Institute of Fine Arts*

Sra. Vera Gandara de Niro

Sra. Lola Olmedo de Olvera

Sr. Lino Picaceño, *Library of the National School of Plastic Arts*

Maestro Victor M. Reyes, *Former Assistant Technical Director, National Institute of Fine Arts*

Mr. McNeil S. Stringer, Jr.

Sr. Jesús R. Talavera, *Technical Director, Museum of the Palace of Fine Arts, National Institute of Fine Arts*

Sra. Ana María Icaza de Xirau

Sr. Lic. José Guadalupe Zuno, *Director, Museum of the State of Jalisco*

## Panama

Excmo. Sr. Ing. Fernando Eleta A., *Minister of Foreign Affairs*

Excmo. Sr. Lic. Rigoberto Paredes, *Minister of Education*

Excmo. Sr. Ricardo M. Arias E., *Ambassador to the United States*

Excmo. Sr. E. Arturo Morgan, *Vice-Minister of Foreign Affairs*

Excmo. Sr. Manuel Sisnett, *Vice-Minister of Education*

Excmo. Sr. Lic. Galileo Solís, *Former Minister of Foreign Affairs*

Excmo. Sr. Lic. Miguel J. Moreno, Jr., *Former Ambassador to the United States*

Excmo. Sr. Lic. Manuel Solís Palma, *Former Minister of Education*

Sr. Adolfo Arias E., *Former President, Panamanian Institute of Art*

Mr. John E. Heath

Lic. Ana María Jaén J., *Director, National Library of Panama*

Mr. Charles P. Lord

Mr. Charles R. Meyer, *Cultural Affairs Officer, United States Embassy, Panama City*

Sra. Olga Zubieta de Oller, *Executive Secretary, Panamanian Institute of Art*

## Peru

Excmo. Sr. Dr. Fernando Schwalb López-Aldana, *Chairman of the Cabinet of Ministers and Minister of Foreign Affairs*

Excmo. Sr. Gral. Ernesto Montagne, *Minister of Public Education*

Excmo. Sr. Dr. Celso Pastor de la Torre, *Ambassador to the United States*

Excmo. Sr. Dr. Francisco Miró Quesada Cantuarias, *Former Minister of Public Education*

Sr. José María Arguedas, *Director, Nacional Museum of the Republic and of History*

Dr. Gaylon L. Caldwell, *Former Cultural Affairs Officer, United States Embassy*

Mr. Richard Kaynor

Sra. Sara de LaValle, *Curator, Museum of Art*

Dr. Alvaro Llona Bernal

Arq. Luis Miró Quesada, *Dean, Faculty of Architecture, National University of Engineering*

Sr. José Monteverde

Mr. Everett C. Rompf

Dr. Román Saavedra S., *American Institute of Arts*

Sr. Luis T. Seminario García, *Pinacoteca Municipal "Ignacio Merino," Lima*

Mr. Derry U. Shaw

Dr. Fernando Silva Santistéban, *President, Casa de la Cultura del Perú*

Dr. Francisco Stastny, *Director, Museum of Art*

Maestro Juan Manuel Ugarte Eléspuru, *Director, National School of Fine Arts*

Dr. Luis E. Valcárcel, *Director, National Museum of Peruvian Culture*

## Uruguay

Excmo. Sr. Luis A. Vidal Zaglio, *Minister of Foreign Affairs*

Excmo. Sr. Juan E. Pivel Devoto, *Minister of Public Education and Social Welfare*

Excmo. Sr. Juan Felipe Yriart, *Ambassador to the United States*

Excmo. Sr. Alejandro Zorilla de San Martín, *Former Minister of Foreign Affairs*

Sr. Luis Mario Allés, *Director, Municipal Museum of Montevideo*

Srta. María Julia Ardau, *Acting Director, National Historical Museum*

Arq. Leopoldo Artuccio

Sr. Octavio Assunção

Mr. Lawrence Flood, *Assistant Cultural Affairs Officer, United States Embassy, Montevideo*

Sr. Angel Kalenberg, *Director, General Electric Institute*

Arq. Alberto Muñoz del Campo, *Director, National Museum of Fine Arts*

Sr. Dionisio Trillo Pays, *Director, National Library of Uruguay*

Sr. Juan Carlos Weigle, *Director, Juan Manuel Blanes Municipal Museum of Fine Arts, Montevideo*

## Venezuela

Excmo. Sr. Dr. Ignacio Iribarren Borges, *Minister of Foreign Affairs*

Excmo. Sr. Dr. Manuel Siso Martínez, *Minister of Education*

Excmo. Sr. Dr. Enrique Tejera Paris, *Ambassador to the United States*

Excmo. Sr. Dr. J. L. Salcedo-Bastardo, *President, National Institute of Culture and Fine Arts*

Excmo. Sr. Dr. Alberto Cuevas Picón, *President, Municipal Council of Caracas*

Sr. Miguel Arroyo, *Director, Museum of Fine Arts, Caracas*

Sr. Simón Alberto Consalvi, *Director, Central Office of Information, Republic of Venezuela*

Mr. Robert D. Cross, *Former Cultural Affairs Officer, United States Embassy, Caracas*

Mr. James Smith, *Acting Cultural Affairs Officer, United States Embassy, Caracas*

Regrettably, space does not permit mentioning the names of scores of other persons who have made substantial contributions to the national participations of their respective countries.

# Photographic Credits

Bodo Wuth (Quito): 45.

Hernán Díaz (Bogotá): 22, 65, 116.

Di Tella Institute – Alvarado (Buenos Aires): 8, 9, 10, 11, 13, 14, 24, 25, 48, 49, 63, 81, 89, 94, 97, 100.

Helga Studio (New York): 86.

Gautherot (Rio de Janeiro): 7, 12, 15, 17, 40, 52, 53, 62, 91, 107.

Irazábal (Caracas): 36, 50, 54, 68, 74, 78, 113.

Frank Lerner (New York): 21, 42, 88, 90, 114.

López Campos (Mexico): 1, 6, 16, 19, 37, 38, 39, 47, 57, 58, 75, 104.

José de Mesa (La Paz): 85, 101.

Muniz (Rio de Janeiro): 102.

Nelson (New York): 92.

Neumann (Lima): 2, 26, 29, 33, 43, 44, 55, 76, 95.

Pacheco (Quito): 32.

Scheier (São Paulo): 51, 69, 70, 73, 96, 103, 108, 110, 112.

Stallforth (Chile): 56.

L. Steiner (New York): 115.

Sunami (The Museum of Modern Art, New York): 87.

Testoni (Montevideo): 20, 27, 34, 35, 67, 79, 80, 84.

University of Chile – Montandón (Santiago): 30, 41, 46, 64, 93, 106, 109, 111.

Vázquez (Mexico): 98.

Yale University – Audio Visual Center (New Haven): 4, 31.

# Lenders to the Exhibition

Familia Andrade, São Paulo
Sr. Nemesio Antúnez, Santiago de Chile
Sr. Adolfo Arias Espinosa, Panamá
Sr. Miguel G. Arroyo C., Caracas
Arzobispado de Bogotá
Sr. Federico Assler, Santiago de Chile
Sr. and Sra. Octavio Assunção, Montevideo
Banco de Londres y Montreal, Guayaquil, Ecuador
Banco de México, Mexico, D.F.
Sr. Ernesto Barreda, Santiago de Chile
Mr. David Baumgarten, New York
Biblioteca de la Escuela Nacional de Artes Plásticas, Mexico, D.F.
Biblioteca "Luis Angel Arango", Bogotá
Biblioteca Nacional, Rio de Janeiro
Sr. Héctor Borda, La Paz
Familia Rodrigo Borja, Quito
Sr. Alfredo Boulton, Caracas
Sr. Armando Braun Menéndez, Buenos Aires
Sr. Pablo A. Burchard, Santiago de Chile
Sr. Horacio Butler, Buenos Aires
Sr. Mario Carreño, Santiago de Chile
Sr. Flavio de Carvalho, São Paulo
Casa del Arte, Universidad de Concepción, Chile
Casa de la Cultura Ecuatoriana, Quito
Casa de la Cultura Escuatoriana, Núcleo Guayas, Guayaquil, Ecuador
Casa Misional Espíritu Santo Medina y Pérez, Guayaquil, Ecuador
Centro de Artes Visuales, Instituto Torcuato di Tella, Buenos Aires
Sra. Lygia Clark, Rio de Janeiro
Srta. Julia Codesido, Lima
Sra. Rosa R. de Covarrubias, Mexico, D.F.
Sr. José Cúneo Perinetti, Montevideo
Srta. Dinora Doudtchitzky, Chile
Sr. Alberto Dutary, Panamá
Sr. Agustín Edwards, Santiago de Chile
Sra. Matías Errázuriz Gómez, Buenos Aires
Escola Nacional de Belas Artes, Rio de Janeiro
Escuela de Arte, Universidad Católica de Chile, Santiago de Chile
Sra. Marta Faz, Santiago de Chile

Sr. Gabriel Fernández Ledesma, Mexico, D.F.
Sr. Antenor Fernández Soler, Lima
Fundação Bienal de São Paulo
Galería de Arte Mexicano, Mexico, D.F.
Galería Bonino, Buenos Aires
Galería Bonino, New York
Galería Rubbers, Buenos Aires
Galería San Marcos, Lima
Galería Carmen Waugh, Santiago de Chile
Sr. Humberto Garavito Suasnávar, Guatemala
Arq. Graziano Gasparini V., Caracas
Sr. Carlos María Gelly y Obes, Buenos Aires
General Electric Institute, Montevideo
Srta. Gertrude Goldschmidt, Caracas
Sr. José Gómez Sicre, Washington, D.C.
Familia Roberto González Goyri, Guatemala City
Sr. Ricardo Grau, Lima
Sr. Walter Gross, Lima
Sra. Ana Güido de Icaza, Mexico, D.F.
Sr. Pedro Hanné Gallo, Bogotá
Sr. and Sra. João Hermes Pereira de Araujo, Buenos Aires
Sr. Gil Imaná Garrón, La Paz
Sr. Victor Manuel Infante, Córdoba, Argentina
Instituto Nacional de Antropología e Historia, Mexico, D.F.
Instituto Nacional de Bellas Artes, Mexico, D.F.
International Business Machines Corporation, New York
Captain Emil Lassen, Santiago de Chile
Sr. and Sra. Flavian Levine, Santiago de Chile
Sr. and Sra. Luiz Lópes Coelho, São Paulo
Sr. Victor Magariños D., Buenos Aires
Arq. Fernando Martínez, Bogotá
Sr. Carlos Mérida, Mexico, D.F.
Sr. Domingo E. Minetti, Rosario, Argentina
Ministerio de Educación, Quito
Srta. Marta Minujin, Buenos Aires
Familia Moncloa Ordóñez, Lima
Sr. A. Monllor, La Paz
Sr. Mario Müller Lewit, Quito
Museu de Arte Contemporânea, Universidade de São Paulo
Museo de Arte Contemporáneo, Santiago de Chile
Museo de Arte, Lima
Museo de Arte Moderno de la Ciudad de Buenos Aires

215

Museo de Arte Moderno, Bogotá
Museu de Arte Moderna, Rio de Janeiro
Museo de Artes Plásticas "Eduardo Sívori," Buenos Aires
Museo de Artes Plásticas de la Provincia de Buenos Aires,
    La Plata, Argentina
Museu de Arte de São Paulo
Museo de Bellas Artes de Caracas
Museo de Bellas Artes, Viña del Mar, Chile
Museo del Estado de Jalisco, Guadalajara, Mexico
Museo Histórico y Archivo Municipal, Montevideo
Museo Histórico Nacional, Buenos Aires
Museo Histórico Nacional, Montevideo
Museo Jijón y Caamaño, Quito
Museo Municipal, Guayaquil, Ecuador
Museo Municipal de Arte, La Paz
Museo Municipal de Bellas Artes "Juan B. Castagnino,"
    Rosario, Argentina
Museo Municipal "Juan Manuel Blanes," Montevideo
Museo Nacional, Bogotá
Museo Nacional de Arte, La Paz
Museo Nacional de Arte Colonial, Quito
Museo Nacional de Arte Moderno, Mexico, D.F.
Museo Nacional de Bellas Artes, Córdoba, Argentina
Museo Nacional de Bellas Artes, Buenos Aires
Museo Nacional de Bellas Artes, Montevideo
Museu Nacional de Belas Artes, Rio de Janeiro
Museo Nacional de Cultura Peruana, Lima
Museo Nacional de Historia, México, D.F.
Museo Nacional de Historia y Bellas Artes, Guatemala City
Museo Nacional de la República, Lima
Museo del Palacio de Bellas Artes, Mexico, D.F.
Museo Provincial de Bellas Artes "Emilio A. Caraffa,"
    Córdoba, Argentina
Museo Taurino, Sr. Fernando Berckemeyer, Lima
Museo 20 de Julio, Bogotá
The Museum of Modern Art, New York
Sra. Viuda del Dr. José Gabriel Navarro Enríquez, Quito
Sr. Hans Neumann, Caracas
Sr. Presley Norton, Guayaquil, Ecuador
Oficina de Planeamiento Urbano de la Municipalidad de
    Caracas
Arq. Juan O'Gorman, Mexico, D.F.
Familia Clemente Orozco, Mexico, D.F.
Familia José Clemente Orozco, Mexico, D.F.
Sr. Alejandro Otero, Caracas
Srta. Maria Luisa Pacheco, La Paz
Sra. Luisa Zuloaga de Palacios, Caracas

Srta. Isabel Palacios, Caracas
Sr. Román F. Pardo, Buenos Aires
Lic. Francísco Pérez de Salazar, Mexico, D.F.
Pinacoteca Dr. Felipe O. Pérez, Panamá
Pinacoteca Virreinal de San Diego, Mexico, D.F.
Sr. Manuel Porrúa, Mexico, D.F.
Sr. Marco Augusto Quiroa, Guatemala City
Sr. Eduardo Ramírez Villamizar, Bogotá
Sr. Jorge Reyes, Guayaquil, Ecuador
Srta. Ruth Rivera, Mexico, D.F.
Familia Rodríguez Padilla, Guatemala
Sr. Juan Antonio Rodríguez Roda, Bogotá
Arq. Germán Samper Gnecco, Bogotá
San Francisco Museum of Art, San Francisco
Sr. Antonio Santamarina, Buenos Aires
Sr. Alberto Sayago, Mexico, D.F.
Sr. Roberto Seminario, Guayaquil, Ecuador
Sr. Carlos Serex, Bogotá
Dr. William B. Shekter, Sausalito, California
Sr. Carlos Squirru, Buenos Aires
Sociedad Nacional de Bellas Artes, Santiago de Chile
Sr. Gerson Alves de Souza, Rio de Janeiro
Arq. Clorindo Testa, Buenos Aires
Sr. Alfredo Testoni, Montevideo
Srta. Ifigenia Torres, Montevideo
Sra. Manolita Piña de Torres García, Montevideo
Sra. Maria Luisa Zuloaga de Tovar, Caracas
Sra. Marta Traba, Bogotá
Sr. Guillermo Trujillo, Panamá
University Club, Mexico, D.F.
Sr. and Sra. Rafael Vasconés Hurtado, Quito
Sr. Germán Vergara Donoso, Santiago de Chile
Srta. María de los Angeles Vilas Gacén y Hernández, Mexico,
    D.F.
Arq. Carlos Raúl Villanueva, Caracas
Sr. Oswaldo Viteri, Quito
Arq. Amancio Williams, Buenos Aires
Sr. and Sra. Ernesto Wolf, São Paulo
Yale University Art Gallery, New Haven
Yale University Library, New Haven
Sr. Ricardo Yrarrázaval, Santiago de Chile
Srta. Elisa Elvira Zuloaga, Caracas
Familia Zuloaga Ramírez, Caracas

*In addition to the above, there are a number of lenders who
have chosen to remain anonymous.*

## Owners of works illustrated[†]

1 Pinacoteca Virreinal de San Diego, Mexico, D.F.
2 Museo Nacional de la República, Lima
3 Sr. Humberto Garavito Suasnávar, Guatemala City
4 Yale University Library, New Haven
5 Sr. Alfredo Boulton, Caracas
6 Museo Nacional de Historia, Mexico, D.F.
7 Museu Nacional de Belas Artes, Rio de Janeiro
8 Sr. and Sra. João Hermes Pereira de Araujo, Buenos Aires*
9 Museo Nacional de Bellas Artes, Buenos Aires
10 Museo Histórico Nacional, Buenos Aires
11 Sr. Domingo E. Minetti, Rosario, Argentina
12 Museu Nacional de Belas Artes, Rio de Janeiro
13 Museo Nacional de Bellas Artes, Buenos Aires
14 Sr. Domingo E. Minetti, Rosario, Argentina
15 Biblioteca Nacional, Rio de Janeiro
16 Banco de México, Mexico, D.F.*
17 Escola Nacional de Belas Artes, Rio de Janeiro
18 Arzobispado de Bogotá
19 University Club, Mexico, D.F.
20 Museo Histórico y Archivo Municipal, Montevideo
21 Sr. and Sra. Rafael Vasconés Hurtado, Quito
22 Biblioteca "Luis Angel Arango," Bogotá
23 Sr. and Sra. Octavio Assunção, Montevideo
24 Museo Nacional de Bellas Artes, Buenos Aires
25 Museo Histórico Nacional, Buenos Aires
26 Pinacoteca Municipal "Ignacio Merino," Lima*
27 Museo Histórico y Archivo Municipal, Montevideo
28 Casa del Arte, Universidad de Concepción, Chile
29 Museo Taurino, Sr. Fernando Berckemeyer, Lima
30 Sr. Germán Vergara Donoso, Santiago de Chile
31 Yale University Art Gallery, New Haven
32 Sra. Viuda del Dr. José Gabriel Navarro Enríquez, Quito
33 Museo Taurino, Sr. Fernando Berckemeyer, Lima*
34 Museo Municipal "Juan Manuel Blanes," Montevideo
35 Museo Municipal "Juan Manuel Blanes," Montevideo
36 Museo de Bellas Artes, Caracas

37 Banco de México, Mexico, D.F.
38 Museo Nacional de Historia, Mexico, D.F.*
39 Sra. Ana Güido de Icaza, Mexico, D.F.
40 Biblioteca Nacional, Rio de Janeiro
41 Biblioteca Nacional, Santiago de Chile*
42 Museo Nacional, Bogotá
43 Museo Nacional de la República, Lima
44 Pinacoteca Municipal "Ignacio Merino," Lima*
45 Museo Municipal de Quito*
46 Museo Nacional de Bellas Artes, Santiago de Chile*
47 Museo Nacional de Arte Moderno, Mexico, D.F.*
48 Museo Nacional de Bellas Artes, Buenos Aires
49 Museo Nacional de Bellas Artes, Buenos Aires
50 Museo de Bellas Artes, Caracas
51 Museu de Arte de São Paulo
52 Museu Nacional de Belas Artes, Rio de Janeiro
53 Museu Nacional de Belas Artes, Rio de Janeiro
54 Museo de Bellas Artes, Caracas
55 Museo de Arte, Lima
56 Casa del Arte, Universidad de Concepción, Chile
57 Instituto Nacional de Bellas Artes, Mexico, D.F.
58 Museo del Palacio de Bellas Artes, Mexico, D.F.*
59 International Business Machines Corporation, New York
60 Sr. Carlos María Gelly y Obes, Buenos Aires
61 San Francisco Museum of Art. Gift of Dr. Grace L. McCann Morley
62 Museu Nacional de Belas Artes, Rio de Janeiro*
63 Museo Nacional de Bellas Artes, Buenos Aires
64 Museo Nacional de Bellas Artes, Santiago de Chile*
65 Museo Nacional, Bogotá
66 Museo del Estado de Jalisco, Guadalajara, Mexico
67 Museo Nacional de Bellas Artes, Montevideo

†Numbers given in this list are plate numbers.

*Not included in the exhibition.

68 Sr. Alfredo Boulton, Caracas
69 Museu de Arte de São Paulo
70 Sr. Flávio de Carvalho, São Paulo
71 International Business Machines Corporation, New York
72 Museo del Estado de Jalisco, Guadalajara, Mexico
73 Srta. Tarsila do Amaral, São Paulo*
74 Museo de Bellas Artes, Caracas
75 Museo Nacional de Arte Moderno, Mexico, D.F.
76 Srta. Julia Codesido, Lima
77 San Francisco Museum of Art. Gift of Albert M. Bender as a Memorial to Caroline Walter
78 Museo de Bellas Artes, Caracas
79 Sra. Manolita Piña de Torres García, Montevideo
80 Sr. and Sra. Octavio Assunção, Montevideo
81 Museo Nacional de Bellas Artes, Buenos Aires
82 International Business Machines Corporation, New York
83 Sr. Victor Manuel Infante, Córdoba, Argentina
84 Museo Nacional de Bellas Artes, Montevideo
85 Sr. Héctor Borda, La Paz
86 International Business Machines Corporation, New York
87 The Museum of Modern Art, New York. Gift of Clemente Orozco
88 Sr. Nemesio Antúnez, Santiago de Chile
89 Museo Nacional de Bellas Artes, Buenos Aires
90 Sr. Alejandro Obregón, Barranquilla, Colombia
91 Museu de Arte Moderna, Rio de Janeiro

*Not included in the exhibition.

92 Galería Bonino, New York
93 Museo de Arte Contemporáneo, Santiago de Chile
94 Museo de Arte Moderno de la Cuidad de Buenos Aires
95 Sr. Walter Gross, Lima
96 Fundação Bienal de São Paulo
97 Galería Bonino, Buenos Aires
98 Mr. David Baumgarten, New York
99 Captain Emil Lassen, Santiago de Chile
100 Galería Rubbers, Buenos Aires
101 Museo Nacional de Arte, La Paz
102 Sr. Gerson Alves de Souza, Rio de Janeiro
103 Sr. Wesley Duke Lee, São Paulo
104 Museo Nacional de Cultura Peruana, Lima
105 Galería Carmen Waugh, Santiago de Chile
106 Sr. Pablo A. Burchard, Santiago de Chile
107 Biblioteca Nacional, Rio de Janeiro
108 Museu de Arte Contemporânea, Universidade de São Paulo
109 Galería Carmen Waugh, Santiago de Chile
110 Sr. and Sra. Ernesto Wolf, São Paulo
111 Galería Carmen Waugh, Santiago de Chile
112 Sr. and Sra. Ernesto Wolf, São Paulo
113 Sra. Luisa Zuloaga de Palacios, Caracas
114 Sr. Guillermo Trujillo, Panamá
115 Galería Bonino, New York
116 Sr. Pedro Hanné Gallo, Bogotá

# Works in the Exhibition

The works listed here are arranged alphabetically based on the artist's surname according to the usage of his country. Catalogue numbers are given at the beginning of each entry. In dimensions, height precedes width. Illustrations in the catalogue are identified by separate plate numbers included within the catalogue entries. Note that several works of art reproduced in the catalogue are not in the exhibition.

1. Abarca, Agustín (Chile, 1882–1953)
   *Landscape* (*Paisaje*). 1930
   Watercolor, 25 x 39 in.
   Sociedad Nacional de Bellas Artes, Santiago de Chile

2. Abramo, Livio (Brazil, 1903–    )
   *Paraguay*. 1962 (Plate 112)
   Wood engraving, 8¾ x 12⅜ in.
   Lent by Sr. and Sra. Ernesto Wolf, São Paulo

3. Abularach, Rodolfo (Guatemala, 1933–    )
   *Courtesan* (*Cortezã*). 1959 (Plate 108)
   Drawing, 39⅛ x 29½ in.
   Museu de Arte Contemporanea, Universidade de São Paulo

4. Acuña, Luis Alberto (Colombia, 1904–    )
   *Figures* (*Figuras*). 1952
   Oil on burlap, 35 x 27½ in.
   Museo de Arte Moderno, Bogotá

5. Adam, Alberto, after J. D. Dulin (active Buenos Aires, 1867)
   *A Slaughterhouse in the State of La Plata*
   (*Un Matadero en los Estados de La Plata*)
   Lithograph, 12¾ x 18¼ in.
   Museo Histórico Nacional, Buenos Aires

6. Alfaro Siqueiros, David (Mexico, 1898–    )
   *Moises Saenz*. 1931
   Lithograph, 21⅜ x 16⅛ in.
   The Museum of Modern Art, New York. Inter-American Fund

7. Alfaro Siqueiros, David (Mexico, 1898–    )
   *Portrait of Amado de la Cueva* (*Retrato de Amado de la Cueva*). 1920
   Oil on canvas, 49⅛ x 34 in.
   Museo del Estado de Jalisco, Guadalajara, Mexico

8. Alfaro Siqueiros, David (Mexico, 1898–    )
   *Victims of War* (*Víctimas de la guerra*). 1945
   Synthetic lacquer on composition board, 12 ft. ¾ in. x 8 ft. 1¼ in.
   Instituto Nacional de Bellas Artes, Mexico, D.F.

9. Amador, Manuel E. (Panama, 1869–1952)
   *Portrait of President Manuel Amador G.*
   (*Retrato del Presidente Manuel Amador G.*)
   Oil on canvas, 43 x 32¾ in.
   Pinacoteca Dr. Felipe O. Pérez, Panama

10. do Amaral, Tarsila (Brazil, active since 1920s)
    *The Negress* (*A Negra*)
    Oil on canvas, 39⁵⁄₁₆ x 32 in.
    Museu de Arte Contemporânea, Universidade de São Paulo

11. Américo de Figueiredo e Melo, Pedro (Italy, 1834–1905)
    *Peace and Concord* (*Paz e concordia*). 1895 (Plate 51)
    Oil on canvas, 16½ x 23½ in.
    Museu de Arte de São Paulo

12. Amoêdo, Rodolfo (Brazil, 1857–1941)
    *Marabá*. 1882 (Plate 52)
    Oil on canvas, 47½ x 67½ in.
    Museu Nacional de Belas Artes, Rio de Janeiro

13. Amoêdo, Rodolfo (Brazil, 1857–1941)
    *Bad News* (*Más noticias*). 1895 (Plate 53)
    Oil on canvas, 39¼ x 29 in.
    Museu Nacional de Belas Artes, Rio de Janeiro

14. Anonymous (Colombia)
    *La Pola Goes to the Gallows* (*La Pola marcha al
        cadalso*). c. 1823
    Oil on wood panel, 30 x 37½ in.
    Museo Nacional, Bogotá

15. Anonymous (Mexico)
    *Political Farce* (*Sainete político*)
    Lithograph, 10¾ x 16⅜ in.
    Lent by Sr. Manuel Porrúa, Mexico, D.F.

16. Anonymous (Xalapan, Mexico)
    *Portrait of Miguel Pérez Amador* (*Retrato de Miguel
        Pérez Amador*) (Plate 39)
    Oil on copper, 16 x 12 in.
    Lent by Sra. Ana Güido de Icaza, Mexico, D.F.

17. Anonymous (Mexico)
    *Solemn and Peaceful Entrance of the Trigarantine Army*
    (*Solemne y pacífica entrada del Ejército Trigarante*)
        (Plate 6)
    Oil on canvas, 32½ x 49¾ in.
    Museo Nacional de Historia, Mexico, D.F.

18. Anonymous (Peru)
    *Fruit Market* (*Frutería*)
    Watercolor, 7½ x 9½ in.
    Yale University Library, New Haven

19. Anonymous (Peru)
    *Fruit Seller*
    Watercolor, 9½ x 7½ in.
    Yale University Library, New Haven

20. Anonymous (Peru)
    *Piquantería*. c. 1810
    Watercolor, 9½ x 7½ in.
    Yale University Library, New Haven

21. Anonymous (Peru)
    *Square of Lima*
    Gouache, 12½ x 18 in.
    Yale University Library, New Haven

22. Anonymous (Uruguay)
    *Battle of Sarandi in 1825* (*Batalla de Sarandi en* 1825)
    Watercolor, 12⅞ x 19½ in.
    Museo Histórico y Archivo Municipal, Montevideo

23. Antúnez, Nemesio (Chile, 1918–     )
    *Composition: Sun* (*Composición: Sol*). 1965 (Plate 88)
    Oil on canvas, 50 x 50 in.
    Lent by the artist

24. Arnal, Enrique (Bolivia, 1932–     )
    *Tambo*. 1960 (Plate 101)
    Oil, 38³⁄₁₆ x 51³⁄₁₆ in.
    Museo Nacional de Arte, La Paz

25. Arnout, after Nebel, Karl (latter b. Germany, 1805–1855)
    *Interior of Mexico* (*Interior de México*)
    Lithograph, 10⅜ x 14 in.
    Lent by Banco de México, Mexico, D.F.

26. Arrieta, José Agustín (Mexico, 1802–1879)
    *Market Scene: The Surprise* (*Escena de mercado: la
        sorpresa*)
    Oil on canvas, 27¼ x 36¾ in.
    Museo Nacional de Historia, Mexico, D.F.

27. Arrieta, José Agustín (Mexico, 1802–1879)
    *Still Life* (*Naturaleza Muerta*)
    Oil on canvas, 35 x 26 in.
    Lent by Lic. Francisco Pérez de Salazar, Mexico, D.F.

28. Assler, Federico (Chile, 1929–     )
    *Florescence* (*Floración*). 1964
    Oil, 31⅞ x 55⅛ in.
    Lent by the artist

29. Baca-Flor, Carlos (Peru, 1867–1941)
    *Couple* (*Pareja*). 1900 (Plate 55)
    Oil on board, 10 x 6¾ in.
    Mueso de Arte, Lima

30. Bacle, César Hipólito (Argentine, b. Switzerland,
        1794–1838)
    *Lady of Buenos Aires, Ball Costume* (*Señora Porteña,
        traje de baile*). 1834–35
    Lithograph, 11⅜ x 8¼ in.
    Lent by Sr. Román F. Pardo, Buenos Aires

31. Barradas, Rafael Pérez (Uruguay, 1890–1928)
   *All at 0.65* (*Todo a 0.65*)
   Oil on canvas, 28¾ x 33 in.
   Museo Nacional de Bellas Artes, Montevideo

32. Barradas, Rafael Pérez (Uruguay, 1890–1928)
   *Miller from Aragón* (*Molinero de Aragón*) (Plate 67)
   Oil on canvas, 46¾ x 29 in.
   Museo Nacional de Bellas Artes, Montevideo

33. Barreda, Ernesto (Chilean, b. France, 1927–    )
   *Embrasure* (*Tronera*). 1964
   Oil, 44⅛ x 44⅛ in.
   Lent by the artist

34. Baz, Ignacio (Argentina, 1826–1887)
   *Gen. Juan Manuel de Rosas* (Plate 25)
   Pencil, 8⅞ x 7¾ in.
   Museo Histórico Nacional, Buenos Aires

35. Baz, Ignacio (Argentina, 1826–1887)
   *Gen. Juan Facundo Quiroga*
   Pencil, 8¼ x 7½ in.
   Museo Histórico Nacional, Buenos Aires

36. Bermúdez, José Ignacio (Cuba, 1922–    )
   *Microflora*. 1956
   Collage of paper with charcoal, pencil, tempera,
      19¾ x 25½ in.
   The Museum of Modern Art, New York. Inter-American
   Fund

37. Berni, Antonio (Argentina, 1905–    )
   *The Bull Fighter* (*El Torero*). 1964
   Woodcut, 30 x 19½ in.
   Lent by Galería Rubbers, Buenos Aires

38. Berni, Antonio (Argentina, 1905–    )
   *The Family* (*La Familia*). 1957
   Tempera and oil on canvas, 61 x 77 in.
   Lent by Galería Rubbers, Buenos Aires

39. Besnes e Yrigoyen, Juan Manuel (Spain, 1788–1865)
   *The Priest, Doctor Pérez Castellano* (*El Presbítero
      Doctor Pérez Castellano*) (Plate 20)
   Watercolor, 10½ x 7 in.
   Museo Histórico y Archivo Municipal, Montevideo

40. Blanes, Juan Manuel (Uruguay, 1830–1901)
   *Review of the Army of Gen. Oribe* (*Revista del Ejército
      del Gral. Oribe*). 1851
   Oil on canvas, 25½ x 30¼ in.
   Museo Municipal "Juan Manuel Blanes," Montevideo

41. Blanes, Juan Manuel (Uruguay, 1830–1901)
   *The Assassination of Gen. Benancio Flores* (*Asesinato del
      Gral. Benancio Flores*) (Plate 34)
   Oil on canvas, 11 x 14 in.
   Museo Municipal "Juan Manuel Blanes," Montevideo

42. Blanes, Juan Manuel (Uruguay, 1830–1901)
   *The Two Ways* (*Los dos caminos*) (Plate 35)
   Oil on canvas, 24½ x 36 in.
   Museo Municipal "Juan Manuel Blanes," Montevideo

43. Blanes Viale, Pedro (Uruguay, 1879–1926)
   *Palma de Mallorca*. 1915
   Oil on canvas, 48¾ x 63¾ in.
   Museo Nacional de Bellas Artes, Montevideo

44. Boari, Adamo (Italian, active in Mexico, 1903–1911)
   *Palacio de Bellas Artes, Mexico, D.F.* 1904–1934
   Architectural drawing
   Museo del Palacio de Bellas Artes, Mexico, D.F.

45. Boggio, Emilio (Venezuela, 1857–1920)
   *Landscape with Bridge* (*Paisaje con puente*)
   Oil on canvas on wood, 21 x 25¼ in.
   Museo de Bellas Artes de Caracas

46. Bonatti, Eduardo (Chile, contemporary)
   *Crucifixion*
   Engraving
   Lent by the artist

47. Bondat (Cuba, 19th century)
   *Battle of Pacocha* (*Combate de Pacocha*). 1877 (Plate 43)
   Oil on canvas, 55¹⁄₁₆ x 78¾ in.
   Museo Nacional de la República, Lima

48. Borda, Arturo (Bolivia, 1883–1955)
   *Leonor Gozálvez y José Borda* (Plate 85)
   Oil, 59¹⁄₁₆ x 52 in.
   Lent by Sr. Héctor Borda, La Paz

49. Botero, Fernando (Colombia, 1932–    )
   *Our Lady of Fatima* (*Virgen de Fátima*). 1963
   Oil on burlap, 71½ x 69¾ in.
   Museo de Arte Moderno, Bogotá

50. Bru, Roser (Spain, 1923–    )
*The Infinite Life* (*La infinita vida*). 1964
Etching and aquatint, 19 x 14⅞ in.
Lent by Sr. Agustín Edwards, Santiago de Chile

51. Burchard, Pablo (Chile, 1873–1960)
*Landscape* (*Paisaje*). 1960 (Plate 106)
Watercolor, 28¾ x 20¼ in.
Lent by Sr. Pablo A. Burchard, Santiago de Chile

52. Burchard, Pablo (Chile, 1873–1960)
*Owls* (*Los Buhos*)
Watercolor, 10⅜ x 9¼ in.
Lent by Sr. Pablo A. Burchard, Santiago de Chile

53. Burchard, Pablo (Chile, 1873–1960)
*Dandelion* (*Dientes de León*). 1940
Oil, 14⅝ x 20¾ in.
Lent by Sr. Pablo A. Burchard, Santiago de Chile

54. Burchard, Pablo A. (Chile, 1919–    )
*Sketch for Mural Painting, Cinema Huérfanos* (*Boceto para pintura, Mural Cine Huérfanos*)
Lent by the artist

55. Burchard Häberle, Teodoro (Chile, 19th century)
*Elevation of San Salvador a la Calle de los Huérfanos, Santiago de Chile.* 1874
Architectural drawing in ink and watercolor on paper mounted on cardboard
Lent by Sr. Pablo A. Burchard, Santiago de Chile

56. Burchard Häberle, Teodoro (Chile, 19th century)
*Longitudinal Section of San Salvador a la Calle de los Huérfanos, Santiago de Chile.* 1874
Architectural drawing in ink and watercolor on paper mounted on cardboard
Lent by Sr. Pablo A. Burchard, Santiago de Chile

57. Burle Marx, Roberto (Brazil, 1909–    )
*Detail No. 5 of Plan for Quadricentennial Gardens, Ibiripuera Park, São Paulo.* 1953
Gouache, 48 x 39⅛ in.
The Museum of Modern Art, New York. Inter-American Fund

58. Burle Marx, Roberto; Stoddart, J. Godfrey; Tabora, Fernando (contemporary)
*Eastern Park—General Plan of Reforestation, Caracas* (*Parque del Este—plano general de reforestación, Caracas*). 1964
Blueprint of architectural drawing
Lent by the architects, Caracas

59. Butler, Horacio (Argentina, 1897–    )
*The Farewell* (*La Despedida*). 1937
Oil on canvas, 31½ x 39⅜ in.
Lent by the artist.

60. Cabré, Manuel (Venezuela, 1890–    )
*Landscape of the Lake* (*Paisaje de la laguna*). 1947
Oil on canvas, 39½ x 30 in.
Museo de Bellas Artes de Caracas

61. Cabrera, Francisco (Guatemala, 1781–1845)
*Doña Teresa Alvora, Marquesa Viuda de Sinibaldi.* c. 1815
Watercolor on ivory, 2¾ x 2⅜ in. (oval)
Lent by Sr. Humberto Garavito Suasnávar, Guatemala City

62. Cabrera, Francisco (Guatemala, 1781–1845)
*Gobernador General Don José Bustamante y Guerra* (Plate 3)
Watercolor, 2⁹⁄₁₆ x 2⅛ in.
Lent by Sr. Humberto Garavito Suasnávar, Guatemala City

63. Cabrera, Francisco (Guatemala, 1781–1845)
*Self-portrait* (*Autorretrato*). c. 1840
Watercolor on ivory, 3½ x 2¾ in. (oval)
Lent by Sr. Humberto Garavito Suasnávar, Guatemala City

64. Calder, Alexander (U.S.A., 1898–    )
*Design for Ceiling of the Auditorium of the Central University of Venezuela* (*Diseño para el techo del aula de la Universidad Central de Venezuela*). c. 1952
Pencil, ink and crayon on paper, 21¹¹⁄₁₆ x 30⅜ in.
Lent by Arq. Carlos Raúl Villanueva, Caracas

65. Camino Brent, Enrique (Peru, 1909– c. 1960)
*De Tinta Bridge, Cuzco* (*Puente de Tinta, Cuzco*). 1937
Oil on canvas, 31⅛ x 31¼ in.
Lent by Familia Moncloa Ordóñez, Lima

66. Caride, Miguel P. (Argentina, 1920–    )
*Configuration (Configuración)* (Plate 100)
Oil on canvas, 17⅝ x 13¾ in.
Lent by Galería Rubbers, Buenos Aires

67. Carreño, Mario (Cuba, 1913–    )
*Homage to Fra Angelico (Homenaje a Fra Angélico).*
1960 (Plate 105)
Watercolor study for mosaic mural, San Ignacio School,
Santiago de Chile
Lent by Galería Carmen Waugh, Santiago de Chile

68. Carreño, Mario (Cuba, 1913–    )
*Petrified World.* 1965 (Plate 111)
Ink and watercolor, 21 x 15½ in.
Lent by Galería Carmen Waugh, Santiago de Chile

69. Carril, Delia del (Argentina, active 1950s and '60s)
*The Virgins (Las Vírgenes).* 1963
Engraving, 11¾ x 15½ in.
Lent by Galería Carmen Waugh, Santiago de Chile

70. Carvalho, Flávio de (Brazil, 1899–    )
*From the tragic series "My Dying Mother," No. 1 (Da
Série trágica "Minha mãe morrendo" No. 1.* 1947
Pencil on paper, 26 x 20 in.
Museu de Arte Contemporânea, Universidade de São
Paulo

71. Carvalho, Flávio de (Brazil, 1899–    )
*Portrait of Elsie Houston (Retrato de Elsie Houston).*
1932 (Plate 70)
Oil on canvas, 18⅛ x 14¾ in.
Lent by the artist

72. Carvalho, Flávio de (Brazil, 1899–    )
*Self-portrait (Autorretrato).* 1965
Oil on canvas, 35½ x 26⅜ in.
Lent by the artist

73. Castellanos, Julio (Mexico, 1905–1947)
*The Angel Kidnappers (Los Robachicos).* 1943
Oil on canvas, 22⅝ x 37⅜ in.
The Museum of Modern Art, New York. Inter-American
Fund

74. Castillo, José S. de (Colombia, first half, 19th century)
*Plaza Mayor de Bogotá.* c. 1832
Watercolor, 20 x 24½ in.
Museo 20 de Julio, Bogotá

75. Castillo, Teófilo (Peru, 1857–1922)
*Procession (Procesión del Corpus).* 1917
Oil on canvas, 16½ x 22¾ in.
Museo de Arte, Lima

76. Castro-Cid, Enrique (Chile, 1937–    )
*Poetical Information.* 1963
Crayon and pencil, 14 x 22 in.
The Museum of Modern Art, New York. Gift of
John S. Newberry

77. Catherwood, Frederick (England, 1799–1854)
*The Well at Bolonchén, Yucatán (El Pozo en Bolonchén,
Yucatán).* 1843 (Plate 31)
Brush and brown ink, brown wash, 18¼ x 13⅜ in.
Yale University Art Gallery, New Haven

78. Catherwood, Frederick (England, 1799–1854)
*General View of Las Monjas at Uxmal*
Color lithograph, 12 x 15¾ in.
Lent by the Banco de México, Mexico, D.F.

79. Cavalcanti, Emiliano di (Brazil, 1897–    )
*Drawing (Desenho).* 1941
Ink, 21¾ x 9 in.
Lent by Sr. and Sra. Ernesto Wolf, São Paulo

80. Cavalcanti, Emiliano di (Brazil, 1897–    )
*Fishermen (Pescadores).* 1942
Oil on canvas, 32 x 39¾ in.
Lent by Sr. and Sra. Luiz Lópes Coelho, São Paulo

81. Cavalcanti, Emiliano di (Brazil, 1897–    )
*Five Young Ladies from Guarantinguetá (Cinco Moças de
Guaratinguetá.* 1930 (Plate 69)
Oil on canvas, 35¼ x 27½ in.
Museu de Arte de São Paulo

82. Challamel, Jules Robert (France, 1813–  ?  ),
after Lauvergne, Berthélemy (France, 1805–1871)
*Cathedral of Guayaquil (Catedral de Guayaquil)*
Color lithograph, 8¼ x 11¼ in.
Lent by Banco de Londres y Montreal, Guayaquil

83. Chambelland, Simone (France, presently active in Chile)
*Litomorfosis I*
Mixed media, 22½ x 14¾ in.
Lent by the artist

223

84. Charon, Louis-François (France, 1783 – after 1831),
    after Martinet (French?)
    *Simón Bolívar*
    Engraving, 17½ x 11⅛ in.
    Museo Nacional, Bogotá

85. Chiappini, J. (Haiti, 1922–    )
    *Portrait of Toussaint L'Ouverture* (*Retrato de Toussaint
    L'Ouverture*). 1941 (Plate 74)
    Oil on wood panel, 21 x 15½ in.
    Museo de Bellas Artes de Caracas

86. Clark, Lygia (Brazil, 1920–    )
    *Contra-Relievo Number 2.* 1960?
    Oil on board, 39¾ x 39¼ in. (diagonal, 55½ in.)
    Lent by the artist

87. Clausell, Joaquín (Mexico, 1866–1935)
    *Trees* (*Arboles*)
    Oil on cardboard, 12½ x 6½ in.
    Museo del Estado de Jalisco, Guadalajara, Mexico

88. Codesido, Julia (Peru, 1892–    )
    *The Andes* (*Los Andes*). 1965?
    Oil on canvas, 39¾ x 32 in.
    Lent by the artist

89. Cordero, Juan (Mexico, 1824–1884)
    *The Sculptors Perez and Valero.* 1867
    Oil on canvas, 42 x 33½ in.
    Museo Nacional de Arte Moderno, Mexico, D.F.

90. Coronel, Rafael (Mexico, 1932–    )
    *All Together* (*Todos juntos*). 1965
    Oil on canvas, 47¼ x 47¼ in.
    Lent by Dr. William B. Shekter, Sausalito, California

91. Covarrubias, Miguel (Mexico, 1904–1957)
    *Project for a mural for The Museum of Modern Art,
    New York* (*Proyecto para mural del Museo de Arte
    Moderno de Nueva York*). 1940
    Watercolor, 15⅜ x 22½ in.
    Lent by Sra. Rosa R. de Covarrubias, Mexico, D.F.

92. Covarrubias, Miguel (Mexico, 1904–1957)
    *The Lindy Hop.* 1936 (Plate 82)
    Lithograph, 13½ x 11¼ in.
    Lent by International Business Machines Corporation,
    New York

93. Cravo, Jr., Mario (Brazil, 1923–    )
    *Studies for Sculpture with Duelling Figures.* 1956
    Watercolor, pen and ink, pencil and crayon, 13¼ x 9½ in.
    The Museum of Modern Art, New York. Inter-American
    Fund

94. Cuevas, José Luis (Mexico, 1933–    )
    *Self-portrait with Figures.* 1959
    Ink wash drawing, 22 x 28 in.
    Lent by Sr. José Gómez Sicre, Washington, D.C.

95. Cúneo Perinetti, José (Uruguay, 1889–    )
    *The Moon over the Ranch* (*Luna sobre el rancherío*).
    1934 (Plate 80)
    Oil on canvas, 57¼ x 44½ in.
    Lent by Sr. and Sra. Octavio Assunção, Montevideo

96. Darondeau, Henri Benoit (France, 1807–1841)
    *Costume for Church and Ball* (*Vestido de iglesia y de baile*)
    Watercolor, 9⅞ x 12⅞ in.
    Museo Histórico y Archivo Municipal, Montevideo

97. Debret, Jean Baptiste (France, 1768–1848)
    *Dance of the Savages from the Mission of Saint Joseph*
    (*Danse des sauvages de la Mission de St. Joseph*)
    (Plate 15)
    Lithograph, 8½ x 13 in.
    Biblioteca Nacional, Rio de Janeiro

98. Debret, Jean Baptiste (France, 1768–1848)
    *Landing of Dona Leopoldina, First Empress of Brazil*
    (*Desembarque de Dona Leopoldina 1ª*) (Plate 7)
    Oil on canvas, 16¼ x 27½ in.
    Museu Nacional de Belas Artes, Rio de Janeiro

99. Deira, Ernesto (Argentina, 1928–    )
    *Around Thought A* (*No. 2*) (*En torno al pensamiento A
    (No. 2)*). 1964 (Plate 97)
    Oil and enamel on canvas, 77 x 63¾ in.
    Lent by Galería Bonino, Buenos Aires

100. Delhez, Víctor (Argentine, b. Belgium, 1901–    )
     *Babilonia.* 1961
     Wood engraving, 16½ x 13½ in.
     Museo de Artes Plásticas "Eduardo Sívori," Buenos Aires

101. Della Valle, Angel (Argentina, 1852–1903)
     *The Return from the Raid* (*La Vuelta del malón*). 1892
     (Plate 49)
     Oil on canvas, 19⅝ x 31½ in.
     Museo Nacional de Bellas Artes, Buenos Aires

102. Demócrito II (Argentina, 2nd half of 19th century)
    *Don Quixote*. 1891 (Plate 60)
    Lithograph on newsprint. From *Don Quixote*, Buenos
        Aires, Oct. 25, 1891
    Lent by Sr. Carlos María Gelly y Obes, Buenos Aires

103. Descalzi, Cayetano (Italy, active Argentina after 1830)
    *Lady of Buenos Aires in front of the Mirror (Dama
        porteña ante el espejo)*. 1845 (Plate 11)
    Oil on canvas, 12¾ x 9⅝ in.
    Lent by Sr. Domingo E. Minetti, Rosario, Argentina

104. D'Hastrel, Adolphe (France, 1805–1870)
    *Market Scene (Vista del mercado)*
    Watercolor, 9¾ x 13⅝ in.
    Museo Histórico y Archivo Municipal, Montevideo

105. D'Hastrel, Adolphe (France, 1805–1870)
    *Porter (Changador o Esportillero)*
    Lithograph, 15½ x 9⅝ in.
    Museo Histórico y Archivo Municipal, Montevideo

106. D'Hastrel, Adolphe (France, 1805–1870)
    *Rooftops of Montevideo (Azoteas de Montevideo)*. 1840
    Watercolor, 7⅜ x 9¾ in.
    Museo Histórico y Archivo Municipal, Montevideo

107. D'Hastrel, Adolphe (France, 1805–1870)
    *The Ruins of the Citadel (Ruinas de la Ciudadela)*. 1840
    Watercolor, 8⅜ x 11⅜ in.
    Museo Histórico y Archivo Municipal, Montevideo

108. Dosamantes, Francisco (Mexico, 1911–     )
    *The Soldier*. c. 1940
    Lithograph, 17¾ x 17¾ in.
    Lent by International Business Machines Corporation,
        New York

109. Doudtchitzky, Dinora (Chilean, b. Ukraine, 1914–     )
    *Engraving I (Grabado I)*. 1964
    Engraving
    Lent by the artist

110. Doumic, N. (Argentina, active 1844)
    *Soldiers of the Army of Oribe (Soldados del Ejército del
        Oribe)*
    Drawing, 10 x 13⅝ in.
    Museo Histórico Nacional, Buenos Aires

111. Dutary, Alberto (Panama, 1932–     )
    *Tenderness (Ternura)*. 1961
    Oil, 49¼ x 35½ in.
    Pinacoteca Dr. Felipe O. Pérez, Panama

112. Egerton, Daniel Thomas (England, ? – 1842)
    *Real del Monte*. 1840 (Plate 37)
    Lithograph, 17½ x 24¼ in.
    Lent by Banco de México, Mexico, D.F.

113. Escalante, Constantino (Mexico, 1836–1868)
    *". . . What kind of hats are we going to buy when we have
        no heads to put them on!" (". . . Qué sombreros vamos
        a comprar cuando ni cabeza tenemos para eso!")*.
    Lithograph on newsprint, 11⁹⁄₁₆ x 8¹⁄₁₆ in. From *La
        Orquesta*, Mexico, Nov. 18, 1865
    Lent by Srta. María de los Angeles Vilas Gacén y
        Hernández, Mexico, D.F.

114. Espinosa, José María (Colombia, 1796–1883)
    *Store of the Rooster (Almacén del gallo)*. 1855?
    Watercolor, 5¾ x 3¾ in.
    Museo Nacional, Bogotá

115. Estrada, José María (Mexico, active c. 1830–1860)
    *Boy with Hat (Muchacho con gorro)*
    Oil on canvas, 31¼ x 20⅛ in.
    Instituto Nacional de Bellas Artes, Mexico, D.F.

116. Fader, Fernando (Argentina, 1882–1935)
    *The Morning – From the Series "The Life of a Day"
        (La Mañana – de la serie "La Vida de un día")*. 1917
    Oil on canvas, 31 x 39 in.
    Museo Municipal de Bellas Artes "Juan B. Castagnino",
        Rosario, Argentina

117. Fader, Fernando (Argentina, 1882–1935)
    *Shawls from Manila (Los Mantones de Manila)*
    Oil on canvas, 46 x 55¼ in.
    Museo Nacional de Bellas Artes, Buenos Aires

118. Fader, Fernando (Argentina, 1882–1935)
    *Self-portrait (Autorretrato)*
    Oil on canvas, 29½ x 25⅜ in.
    Museo Municipal de Bellas Artes "Juan B. Castagnino,"
        Rosario, Argentina

119. Faz, Carlos (Chile, 1931–1953)
    *Funeral*
    Etching, 13½ x 8 in.
    Lent by Sra. Marta Faz, Santiago de Chile

120. Faz, Carlos (Chile, 1931–1953)
*Stick Roast (Asado al palo).* 1952 (Plate 99)
Oil, 48 1/16 x 73 1/4 in.
Lent by Captain Emil Lassen, Santiago de Chile

121. Fernández Muro, José Antonio (Spain, 1920–    )
*Flag (Bandera).* 1963 (Plate 115)
Oil on aluminum, 65 x 65 in.
Lent by Galería Bonino, New York

122. Fernández Muro, José Antonio (Spain, 1920–    )
*Painting (Pintura)*
Oil on canvas, 38 1/4 x 28 1/4 in.
Museo Nacional de Bellas Artes, Buenos Aires

123. Fierro, Pancho (Peru, 1803–1879)
*Procession (Procesión)*
Watercolor, 11 x 8 1/2 in.
Museo Taurino, Sr. Fernando Berckemeyer, Lima

124. Figari, Pedro (Uruguayan, b. Argentina, 1861–1938)
*Barracks Women (Cuarteleras).* 1922
Oil on cardboard, 26 1/2 x 38 in.
Lent by Sr. Domingo E. Minetti, Rosario, Argentina

125. Figari, Pedro (Uruguayan, b. Argentina, 1861–1938)
*Sharp Tongue (La Pulla)*
Oil on board, 27 1/2 x 37 1/2 in.
Museo Histórico Nacional, Montevideo

126. Figueroa, José Luis (Mexico, active Guadalajara c. 1910–1940)
*Earthly Paradise (El Paraíso terrenal)*
Oil on canvas, 23 3/4 x 43 1/4 in.
Museo del Estado de Jalisco, Guadalajara, Mexico

127. Fisquet, Théodore (France, 1813–1890)
*Humble Dwellings by the Sea – Valparaiso (Casa pobre del campo – Valparaiso).* 1836 (Plate 30)
Watercolor, 8 1/4 x 11 1/8 in.
Lent by Sr. Germán Vergara Donoso, Santiago de Chile

128. Forte, Vicente (Argentina, 1912–    )
*Totem.* 1965
Oil on canvas, 59 1/8 x 39 1/4 in.
Lent by Galería Rubbers, Buenos Aires

129. Fossa, Juan (Argentina, active c. 1830–1850)
*Scene of the Civil War (Escena de la Guerra Civil)*
Watercolor, 13 1/8 x 25 in.
Museo Histórico Nacional, Buenos Aires

130. Frasconi, Antonio (Uruguayan, b. Argentina, 1919–    )
*Mother and Child.* 1947
Woodcut printed in black, 25 1/2 x 10 in. (composition)
The Museum of Modern Art, New York. Inter-American Fund

131. Gallino, Cayetano (Italy, 1804–1884)
*Portrait of Don Domingo González (Retrato de Don Domingo González)*
Oil on canvas, 39 x 30 in.
Museo Municipal "Juan Manuel Blanes," Montevideo

132. Gamarra, José (Uruguay, 1934–    )
*Painting (Pintura).* 1963
Mixed media, 24 1/4 x 32 1/4 in.
Lent by General Electric Institute, Montevideo

133. Garay, Epifanio (Colombia, 1849–1903)
*Portrait of a Lady (Retrato de una dama).* 1893 (Plate 42)
Oil, 47 1/4 x 40 15/16 in.
Museo Nacional, Bogotá

134. García del Molino, Fernando (Chile, 1813–1899)
*Portrait of a Lady (Retrato de una señora)*
Oil on canvas, 36 1/2 x 34 in.
Museo Nacional de Bellas Artes, Buenos Aires

135. Gego (Venezuelan, b. Germany, 1912–    )
*Vertical Engraving.* 1963
Etching, 10 15/16 x 4 5/8 in.
Lent by Srta. Gertrude Goldschmidt, Caracas

136. Gerzso, Gunther (Mexico, 1915–    )
*Mythological Personage (Personaje mitológico).* 1964 (Plate 98)
Oil on canvas, 39 1/2 x 28 3/4 in. (sight)
Lent by Mr. David Baumgarten, New York

137. Gil de Castro, José (Peru, ? – 1841?)
*Portrait of Bolívar (Retrato de Bolívar).* 1823 (Plate 5)
Oil on canvas, 25 1/2 x 20 3/4 in.
Lent by Sr. Alfredo Boulton, Caracas

138. Gil de Castro, José (Peru, ? – 1841?)
*Portrait of Gen. José de San Martín.* 1818
Oil on canvas, 48 1/2 x 33 1/16 in.
Museo Histórico Nacional, Buenos Aires

139. Gil de Castro, José (Peru, ? – 1841?)
*The Martyr Olaya* (*El Mártir Olaya*). 1823 (Plate 2)
Oil on canvas, 70⅞ x 53⅛ in.
Museo Nacional de la República, Lima

140. Goeldi, Oswaldo (Brazil, 1895–1961)
*Horseman* (*Cavaleiro*). c. 1942
Woodcut printed in color, 11½ x 9 in.
Biblioteca Nacional, Rio de Janeiro

141. Goeldi, Oswaldo (Brazil, 1895–1961)
*Old Age* (*Velhice*) (Plate 107)
Woodcut printed in color, 9 x 11½ in.
Biblioteca Nacional, Rio de Janeiro

142. Goitia, Francisco (Mexico, 1886–1960)
*Self-portrait* (*Autorretrato*)
Oil on canvas, 24¾ x 48¼ in.
Instituto Nacional de Bellas Artes, Mexico, D.F.

143. Gómez Cornet, Ramón (Argentina, 1898–1964)
*Doll* (*Muñeco*). 1931
Oil on canvas, 66¼ x 25½ in.
Museo de Artes Plásticas de la Provincia de Buenos Aires, La Plata, Argentina

144. Gómez-Quiroz, Juan (Chile, 1939– )
*Description of a Vehicle to Hunt Stars*. 1965
Color intaglio, 19⅜ x 26⁷⁄₁₆ (sheet)
The Museum of Modern Art, New York. Gift of the artist

145. González, Carlos (Uruguay, 1905– )
*Gauchos*. 1937
Woodcut printed in color, 25½ x 22¼ in.
Lent by Sr. and Sra. Octavio Assunção, Montevideo

146. González, Carlos (Uruguay, 1905– )
*The Death of Martín Aquino* (*La Muerta de Martín Aquino*). 1943 (Plate 84)
Woodcut, 15¼ x 18¾ in.
Museo de Bellas Artes, Montevideo

147. González, Jaime (Chile, 1943– )
*Cover I for "Altazor" of Vicente Huidobro* (*Portado I para "Altazor" de Vicente Huidobro*). 1961 (Plate 109)
Print, 8⅝ x 9¹³⁄₁₆ in.
Lent by Galería Carmen Waugh, Santiago de Chile

148. González, Jaime (Chile, 1943– )
*Illustration for "Exterior" of Vicente Huidobro* (*Ilustración para "Exterior" de Vicente Huidobro*)
Ink, 11½ x 9 in.
Lent by Sr. and Sra. Flavian Levine, Santiago de Chile

149. González, Juan Francisco (Chile, 1853–1933)
*Nude* (*Desnudo*). 1925
Pencil, 5 x 7⅞ in.
Lent by Sr. Germán Vergara Donoso, Santiago de Chile

150. González G., Fernando; called Zigo (Guatemala, 1894– )
*Canon José Matías Delgado* (*Canónigo José Matías Delgado*). 1939 (?)
Ink and watercolor, 15½ x 12 in.
Lent by Familia Roberto González Goyri, Guatemala City

151. González G., Fernando; called Zigo (Guatemala, 1894– )
*General Justo Rufino Barrios y Francisco Morazón*
Ink, 14 x 22 in.
Lent by Familia Roberto González Goyri, Guatemala City

152. Gordon, Arturo (Chile, 1883–1944)
*The Drunks* (*Los Borrachos*) (Plate 56)
Oil on canvas, 27⁹⁄₁₆ x 38⁹⁄₁₆ in.
Casa del Arte, Universidad de Concepción, Chile

153. Grandjean de Montigny, August Henri Victor (France, 1776–1850)
*Plan for the Exchange Building* (*Proyecto da Praça do Comérço*) *Rio de Janeiro* (Plate 17)
Architectural drawing, ink and wash, 16⅝ x 32 in.
Escola Nacional de Belas Artes, Rio de Janeiro

154. Grashof, Frederico Otto (Prussia, 1812–1876)
*Cathedral of Montevideo* (*Catedral de Montevideo*). 1853
Pencil on paper, 7½ x 11¾ in.
Lent by Sr. and Sra. Octavio Assunção, Montevideo

155. Grassmann, Marcelo (Brazil, 1925– )
*Untitled*. 1961 (Plate 110)
Ink on paper, 19¾ x 25¾ in.
Lent by Sr. and Sra. Ernesto Wolf, São Paulo

156. Grau, Enrique (Colombia, 1920– )
*La Cayetena*. 1962
Oil on canvas, 31½ x 26⅜ in.
Lent by Sra. Marta Traba, Bogotá

157. Grau, Ricardo (Peruvian, b. France, 1908–   )
*Portrait of a Woman* (*Retrato de mujer*)
Oil on canvas, 29½ x 23⅝ in.
Lent by the artist

158. Grau, Ricardo (Peruvian, b. France, 1908–   )
*Untitled* (*Sin titulo*). 1964?
Oil on canvas, 45¾ x 32 in.
Lent by the artist

159. Greco, Alberto (Argentina, 1931–   )
*Painting – Man* (*Pintura – Hombre*)
Oil on canvas, 67 x 47½ in.
Museo de Arte Moderno de la Ciudad de Buenos Aires

160. Grilo, Sarah (Argentina, 1921–   )
*Painting* (*Pintura*). 1958
Oil on canvas, 37⅛ x 37⅛ in.
Museo Nacional de Bellas Artes, Buenos Aires

161. Guayasamín, Oswaldo (Ecuador, 1919–   )
*Fatigue* (*Cansancio*). 1952
Oil on board, 44⅜ x 32⅝ in.
Lent by Casa de la Cultura Ecuatoriana, Quito

162. Guayasamín, Oswaldo (Ecuador, 1919–   )
*Portrait of José Gabriel Navarro*. 1942
Oil on burlap, 27½ x 34½ in.
Lent by Sra.Viuda del Dr. José Gabriel Navarro
   Enríquez, Quito

163. Guerrero, Agustín (Ecuador, 1820–1898)
*Against Such Weapons There's No Defense* (*Para estas
   ármas no hay defensa*). 1855
Pencil and wash drawing, 5¼ x 7⅝ in.
Lent by Familia Rodrigo Borja, Quito

164. Guerrero, Agustín (Ecuador, 1820–1898)
*Freedom of the Press* (*Libertad de imprenta*). 1855
Pencil drawing, 5¼ x 7⅝ in.
Lent by Familia Rodrigo Borja, Quito

165. Guerrero, Agustín (Ecuador, 1820–1898)
*The Dance of San Juan in Otavalo* (*El baile de San Juan
   en Otavalo*). 1857
Watercolor, 7¼ x 8¾ in.
Lent by Familia Rodrigo Borja, Quito

166. Guerrero, José E. (Ecuador, 1905–   )
*Mama Cuchara*. 1948
Oil on canvas, 39¼ x 31 in.
Lent by Casa de la Cultura Ecuatoriana, Quito

167. Gurvich, José (Lithuania, 1927–   )
*Plaster relief* (*Relieve en yeso*)
Plaster, 15¾ x 25¾ in.
Lent by Sr. Alfredo Testoni, Montevideo

168. Hanné Gallo, Pedro (Colombia, 1930–   )
*Maternity* (*Maternidad*). 1962 (Plate 116)
Wood engraving, 40¾ x 14¾ in.
Lent by the artist

169. Heath, William (England, 1795–1840)
*Attack on Montevideo* (*Asalto de Montevideo*)
Watercolor, 7⅜ x 10½ in.
Lent by Sr. and Sra. Octavio Assunção, Montevideo

170. Herrán, Alvaro (Colombia, 1937–   )
*Painting* (*Pintura*). 1962
Oil on canvas, 78¾ x 78¾ in.
Lent by Sr. Carlos Serex, Bogotá

171. Herrán, Saturnino (Mexico, 1887–1918)
*The Christ of the Pomegranates* (*El Cristo de las
   Granadas*) (Plate 57)
Charcoal and pastel on green paper, 21⅞ x 12¾ in.
Instituto Nacional de Bellas Artes, Mexico, D.F.

172. Herrera Toro, Antonio (Venezuela, 1856–1914)
*Portrait of a Woman* (*Retrato de mujer*). 1883
Watercolor, 5⅞ x 4¾ in.
Lent by Srta. Isabel Palacios, Caracas

173. Hlito, Alfredo (Argentina, 1923–   )
*Work* (*Obra*). 1959
Oil on canvas, 59 x 51¼ in.
Museo de Arte Moderno de la Ciudad de Buenos Aires

174. Imaná Garrón, Gil (Bolivia, 1933–   )
*Patio*. 1964
Oil, 44½ x 22¼ in.
Lent by the artist

175. Iriarte Hesiquio, after Pedro Gualdi (Mexico,
    19th century)
    *View of the Panorama of Mexico City from the Tower of
    San Agustin (Vista del panorama de México desde la
    torre de San Agustín)*
    Color lithograph, 14½ x 20 in.
    Lent by the University Club, Mexico, D.F.

176. Jimeno y Planes, Rafael (Spain, 1761–1825)
    *Portrait of Don Manuel Tolsá* (Plate 1)
    Oil on canvas, 40½ x 32½ in.
    Pinacoteca Virreinal de San Diego, Mexico, D.F.

177. Kingman Riofrío, Eduardo (Ecuador, 1913–      )
    *Los Guandos*. 1941
    Oil on canvas, 58½ x 77¾ in.
    Lent by Casa de la Cultura Ecuatoriana, Quito

178. Kraft, Guillermo (Germany, 1839–1893), after Emilio
    Landini
    *Grand Theater of the Opera (Gran Teatro de la Opera)*
    Lithograph, 13⅝ x 18⅝ in.
    Museo Histórico Nacional, Buenos Aires

179. Kratzenstein, Rodolfo (Active Argentina, 1822–1885)
    *German Evangelical Church (Iglesia Evangélica
    Alemana)*
    Lithograph, 15 x 16¼ in.
    Museo Histórico Nacional, Buenos Aires

180. Kratzenstein, Rodolfo (Active Argentina, 1822–1885)
    *Sacrifice of Camila O'Gorman and the Priest Gutierrez
    (Sacrificio de Camila O'Gorman y del sacerdote
    Gutiérrez)*
    Lithograph, 16¼ x 23 in.
    Museo Histórico Nacional, Buenos Aires

181. Lam, Wifredo (Cuba, 1902–      )
    *Figures in Black and White (Figuras en negro y blanco)*.
    1954
    Oil on canvas, 41⅞ x 35¼ in.
    Museo de Bellas Artes de Caracas

182. Lam, Wifredo (Cuba, 1902–      )
    *Still Life (Naturaleza Muerta)*. 1923
    Oil on canvas, 5⅜ x 7⅛ in.
    Lent by Sra. Luisa Zuloaga de Palacios, Caracas

183. Lamonica, Roberto de (Brazil, 1933–      )
    *Engraving (Gravura)*. 1961
    Etching, 24½ x 20⅛ in.
    Lent by Sr. and Sra. Ernesto Wolf, São Paulo

184. La Placa, Alfredo (Bolivia, 1929–      )
    *Abstraction (Abstracción)*. 1960
    Oil, 47¼ x 35¹³⁄₁₆ in.
    Museo Nacional de Arte, La Paz

185. Lara Centellas, Hugo (Bolivia, 1932–      )
    *Sleeping Figures (Figuras durmientes)*. 1960
    Oil on canvas, 30 x 43½ in.
    Museo Municipal de Arte, La Paz

186. Lasansky, Mauricio (Argentina, 1914–      )
    *Dinner (Cena)*. 1937 (Plate 83)
    Woodcut, 18 x 21 in.
    Lent by Sr. Victor Manuel Infante, Córdoba, Argentina

187. Lee, Wesley Duke (Brazil, 1931–      )
    *Porta Factum*. 1965 (Plate 103)
    Oil, 62 x 40 in.
    Lent by the artist

188. Léger, Fernand (France, 1881–1955)
    *Design for Mural for the Central University of Caracas*.
    1952
    Gouache on paper, 17¾ x 36³⁄₁₆ in.
    Lent by Arq. Carlos Raúl Villanueva, Caracas

189. Lepori (?) (Italy, 19th century)
    *Pictorial Design for Liberty Monument Project (Disegno
    pittorico del progetto)*
    Watercolor, 48 x 24¾ in.
    Lent by Casa Misional Espíritu Santo Medina y Pérez,
    Guayaquil, Ecuador

190. Leticia, Ana (Brazil, 1929–      )
    *Composition in Black and Terra-cotta (Composição em
    preto e terra-cota)*. 1962
    Engraving on metal, 20¼ x 12¾ in.
    Museu de Arte Moderna, Rio de Janeiro

191. Leufert, Gerd (Latvia, 1914–      )
    *Union Square 18*. 1964
    Oil on canvas, 40⅛ x 40 in.
    Lent by Srta. Gertrude Goldschmidt, Caracas

192. Loballuz (Mexico, 19th century)
*Stagecoach Hold-up* (*Asalto de una diligencia*).
Watercolor and pencil, 10½ x 16½ in.
Museo Nacional de Historia, Mexico, D.F.

193. López, Cándido (Argentina, 1840–1902)
*Landing of the Argentine Army in front of the Trenches
of Curuzu* (*Desembarco del ejército argentino frente a
las trincheras de Curuzu*). 1891
Oil on canvas, 19 x 60 in.
Museo Nacional de Bellas Artes, Buenos Aires

194. Lovera, Juan (Venezuela, 1778 ? –1841)
*Licenciado Francisco Antonio Paul-Coto*. c. 1820
Oil on canvas, 22¼ x 16½ in.
Lent by Sr. Alfredo Boulton, Caracas

195. Luque, Angel (Venezuelan, b. Spain, 1927– )
*One Has to Put Color into It* (*Hay que ponerle color a la
cosa*). 1964
Oil on canvas, 66¾ x 54½ in.
Museo de Bellas Artes, Caracas

196. Lynch, Alberto (Chile, 1851– ?)
*Reclining Lady* (*Dama acostada*)
Ink and tempera. 9¾ x 12¹¹⁄₁₆ in.
Lent by Sra. Matías Errázuriz de Gómez, Buenos Aires

197. Mabe, Manabu (Brazil, 1924– )
*Conquest of the Circle* (*Conquista del círculo*). 1963
(Plate 91)
Oil on canvas, 72¾ x 72¾ in.
Museu de Arte Moderna, Rio de Janeiro

198. Macció, Rómulo (Argentina, 1931– )
*To Live a Little Each Day* (*Vivir un poco cada día*).
1963 (Plates 89 and 89a)
Mixed media, 71 in. diam.
Museo Nacional de Bellas Artes, Buenos Aires

199. Magariños, Víctor (Argentina, 1924– )
*Pintura*. 1964
Oil on canvas, 54½ x 75 in.
Lent by the artist

200. Maldonado, Tomás (Argentina, 1922– )
*From a Sector* (*Desde un sector*)
Oil on canvas, 27¾ x 27¾ in.
Museo Nacional de Bellas Artes, Buenos Aires

201. Maldonado Thibault, G. (Panama, contemporary)
*The Heroes* (*Los Héroes*). 1961
Oil on canvas, 37 x 41½ in.
Pinacoteca Dr. Felipe O. Pérez, Panama

202. Malfatti, Anita (Brazil, 1896– )
*Mario de Andrade*. 1922
Oil on canvas, 20¼ x 17¼ in.
Lent by Familia Andrade, São Paulo

203. Malharro, Martín A. (Argentina, 1865–1911)
*The Trees* (*Los Arboles*)
Oil on canvas, 25⅛ x 31¼ in.
Museo de Artes Plásticas de la Provincia de Buenos Aires,
La Plata, Argentina

204. Manosalvas, Juan (Ecuador, 1840–1906)
*Four Scenes from Life in Quito*. 1865
Pencil, 5¼ x 7¾ in.
Lent by Sra. Viuda del Dr. José Gabriel Navarro
Enríquez, Quito

205. Mariaca Arguedas, Antonio (Bolivia, 1929– )
*Lady of the Lake* (*Virgen del lago*). 1960
Oil, 36¹⁄₁₆ x 25⅜ in.
Lent by Sr. A. Monllor, La Paz

206. Marisol Escobar (Venezuelan, b. Paris, 1930– )
*Untitled*. 1960
Colored crayon and pasted paper, 27¼ x 39½ in.
The Museum of Modern Art, New York. Gift of the artist

207. Mark, Eduardo (British, b. Spain, 1817–1895)
*Main Square – Bogotá* (*Plaza mayor – Bogotá*). 1846
(Plates 22 and 22a)
Watercolor, 15¾ x 25⅝ in.
Biblioteca "Luis Angel Arango," Bogotá

208. Mark, Eduardo (British, b. Spain, 1817–1895)
*Bridge over the Gualí*
Watercolor, 9½ x 11¾ in.
Biblioteca "Luis Angel Arango," Bogotá

209. Mark, Edward Walhouse (British, b. Spain, 1817–1895)
*Girl of Guaduas in Sunday Dress* (*Muchacha de
Guaduas en vestido de domingo*). 1846
Watercolor, 11¾ x 9½ in.
Biblioteca "Luis Angel Arango," Bogotá

210. Martens, Conrad (England, 1801–1871)
*Picnic near Montevideo* (*Pic Nic frente a Montevideo*)
Watercolor, 5¾ x 10 in.
Museo Histórico y Archivo Municipal, Montevideo

211. Martínez Pedro, Luis (Cuba, 1910–    )
*Composition 13.* 1957
Oil on canvas, 58⅛ x 38 in.
The Museum of Modern Art, New York. Gift of Mr. and
   Mrs. Joseph Cantor

212. Martins, Aldemir (Brazil, 1922–    )
*Woman* (*Mulher*). 1961
Lithograph, 25½ x 18⅜ in.
Lent by Sr. and Sra. Ernesto Wolf, São Paulo

213. Matta Echaurren, Sebastián Antonio (Chile, 1912–    )
*Birth of America* (*Nacimiento de América*) (Plate 93)
Oil on canvas, 82 x 115½ in.
Museo de Arte Contemporáneo, Santiago de Chile

214. Matta Echaurren, Sebastián Antonio (Chile, 1912–    )
*Condors and Carrion.* 1941
Pencil and crayon, 23 x 29 in.
The Museum of Modern Art, New York. Inter-American
   Fund

215. Méndez, Leopoldo (Mexico, 1903–    )
*The Great Entrance*, from *Melodic Incidents of the
   Irrational World* (*El gran recibimiento*, de *Incidentes
   melódicos del mundo irracional*). 1944–45
Wood engraving, 10⁵⁄₁₆ x 8 in. (comp.)
The Museum of Modern Art, New York. Inter-American
   Fund

216. Méndez, Leopoldo (Mexico, 1903–    )
*Vision* (*Visión*). 1945 (Plate 86)
Woodcut, 12½ x 7¼ in.
International Business Machines Corporation, New York

217. Méndez, Leopoldo (Mexico, 1903–    )
*All the Land for the Peasants*
Linoleum, 7⅝ x 5⅞ in.
The Museum of Modern Art, New York. Inter-American
   Fund

218. Méndez, Leopoldo (Mexico, 1903–    )
*The Social Gathering.* 1932
Composition, 6¼ x 5⁵⁄₁₆ in.
The Museum of Modern Art, New York. Gift of Dr. W.
   Andrew Archer

219. Mérida, Carlos (Guatemala, 1891–    )
*Landscape of Paris* (*Paisaje de París*). 1910
Oil on canvas, 13 x 16 in.
Museo Nacional de Historia y Bellas Artes,
   Guatemala City

220. Mérida, Carlos (Guatemala, 1891–    )
*Four Sketches for a Ceramic Mural* (*Cuatro Bocetos para
   mural cerámico, Guatemala*). 1963–65
Watercolor and pencil, 19¼ x 25⅜ in.
Lent by the artist

221. Mérida, Carlos (Guatemala, 1891–    )
*Urban Landscape, No. 1* (*Paisaje de urbe No. 1*). 1956
Oil on canvas, 30 x 39¼ in.
Galería de Arte Mexicano, Mexico, D.F.

222. Meza, Guillermo (Mexico, 1917–    )
*Polyphemus.* 1941
Pen and ink, 15¾ x 19⅝ in.
The Museum of Modern Art, New York. Inter-American
   Fund

223. Michelena, Arturo (Venezuela, 1863–1898)
*Sick Child* (*Niño enfermo*). 1886 (Plate 54)
Oil on canvas, 31½ x 33½ in.
Museo de Bellas Artes, Caracas

224. Milián, Raul (Cuba, 1914–    )
*Untitled.* 1960
Watercolor and ink, 15 x 11 in.
The Museum of Modern Art, New York. Gift of Emilio
   del Junco

225. Minujin, Marta (Argentina, 1941–    )
*Erotic Defeat in Technicolor* (*Erótico derrotismo en
   technicolor*). 1964
Canvas, foam rubber, and fluorescent paint,
   51³⁄₁₆ x 23⅝ in.
Lent by the artist

226. Monsanto, Antonio Edmundo (Venezuela, 1890–1947)
*Road* (*Camino*). 1918?
Oil on canvas, 16 x 13 in.
Museo de Bellas Artes, Caracas

227. Montenegro, Roberto (Mexico, 1885–    )
*Ego Sum*
Oil, 20½ x 15 in.
Museo del Estado de Jalisco, Guadalajara, Mexico

228. Monvoisin, Raymond Quinsac (France, 1790–1870)
*Portrait of Don Andres Lamas* (Plate 27)
Oil on canvas, 28½ x 23 in.
Museo Histórico y Archivo Municipal, Montevideo

229. Morales, Armando (Nicaragua, 1927– )
*Nude* (*Desnudo*). 1960
Engraving, 11 x 17½ in.
Lent by Sr. Alberto Dutary, Panama

230. Morales, Armando (Nicaragua, 1927– )
*Landscape* (*Paisaje*). 1964 (Plate 92)
Oil on canvas, 80 x 58 in.
Lent by Galería Bonino, New York

231. Morel, Carlos (Argentina, 1813–1894)
*Cavalry Battle* (*Combate de caballería*). 1830 (Plate 9)
Oil on canvas, 17¾ x 21¼ in.
Museo Nacional de Bellas Artes, Buenos Aires

232. Morel, Carlos (Argentina, 1813–1894)
*Portrait of Señorita Macedonia Escardo*. 1839
Oil on canvas, 29¼ x 29½ in.
Museo Nacional de Bellas Artes, Buenos Aires

233. Moulin, Hipólito (active Argentina, 1830s)
*Lady of Buenos Aires, Promenade Costume* (*Señora Porteña, traje de paseo*). 1834–1835
Lithograph, 11 x 7⅞ in.
Lent by Sr. Román F. Pardo, Buenos Aires

234. Müller-Lewit, Mario (Ecuador, 1940– )
*Painting – Cycle of the Earth* (*Pintura – Ciclo de la tierra*). 1962
Oil, 32¼ x 48 in.
Lent by the artist

235. Nebel, Karl (Germany, 1805–1855)
*The Pyramid of Cholula* (*Pirámide de Cholula*)
Lithograph, 9⅝ x 14 in.
Lent by Sr. Manuel Porrúa, Mexico, D.F.

236. Obregón, Alejandro (Colombia, 1920– )
*Carnivorous Flowers* (*Flores carnívoras*) (Plate 90)
Oil on canvas, 67 13/16 x 78⅝ in.
Lent by the artist

237. Odriozola, Fernando (Brazil, b. Spain, 1921– )
*Drawing* (*Desenho*)
Ink and gouache, 13¾ x 25 3/16 in. (sight)
Lent by Sr. and Sra. Ernesto Wolf, São Paulo

238. O'Gorman, Juan (Mexico, 1905– )
*Memory of Los Remedios* (*Recuerdo de Los Remedios*). 1943 (Plate 75)
Tempera on composition board, 18¼ x 28¼ in.
Museo Nacional de Arte Moderno, Mexico, D.F.

239. O'Gorman, Juan (Mexico, 1905– )
*Project for fresco mural "History of Michoacán," "Gertrudis Bocanegra" Library, Pátzcuaro, Michoacán, Mexico*. 1939
Drawing, 64 9/16 x 57⅞ in.
Lent by the artist

240. O'Gorman, Juan (Mexico, 1905– )
*Project for primary school, Tamaulipas, Mexico* (*Proyecto para escuela primaria, Tamaulipas, México*). 1932
Pencil on translucent paper
Lent by the architect

241. O'Gorman, Juan (Mexico, 1905– )
*Project for secondary school, Tamaulipas, Mexico* (*Proyecto para escuela secundaria, Tamaulipas, México*). 1932
Pencil on translucent paper
Lent by the architect

242. O'Gorman, Juan (Mexico, 1905– )
*Project for Telephone Workers Union Building, Mexico, D.F.* (*Proyecto para el edificio del Sindicato de Telefonistas, México, D.F.*). 1933
Pencil on translucent paper
Lent by the architect

243. O'Gorman, Juan (Mexico, 1905– )
*Project for the Exterior Mosaic Murals, Library of the Universidad Nacional Autónoma de México, South Wall* (*Proyecto para la Biblioteca de la Universidad Nacional Autónoma de México, muro sur*)
Drawing, 47⅝ x 41⅜ in.
Lent by the architect

244. O'Gorman, Juan (Mexico, 1905– )
*Projects for Exterior Mosaic Murals, Library of the Universidad Nacional Autónoma de México, East and West Walls* (*Proyecto para la Biblioteca de la Universidad Nacional Autónoma de México, muros oriente y poniente*).
Drawing, 46½ x 35¾ in.
Lent by the architect

245. Orozco, José Clemente (Mexico, 1883–1949)
*Composition for Gods of the Modern World*. 1932–34
Gouache, 18⅞ x 25⅞ in.
On extended loan to The Museum of Modern Art, New
York, from the artist's son, Clemente Orozco

246. Orozco, José Clemente (Mexico, 1883–1949)
*Head of Quetzalcoatl* (*Cabeza de Quetzalcoatl*).
1932–1934 (Plate 87)
Crayon on tracing paper, 32¼ x 24⅛ in.
The Museum of Modern Art, New York. Gift of
Clemente Orozco

247. Orozco, José Clemente (Mexico, 1883–1949)
*Hispano-America – Preliminary and revised versions*.
1932–1934
Pencil. L: (prelim. version) 18⅞ x 9¾ in. (sheet);
R: (revised version) 20 x 14 in. (sheet)
On extended loan to The Museum of Modern Art, New
York, from the artist's son, Clemente Orozco

248. Orozco, José Clemente (Mexico, 1883–1949)
*Composition for Anglo-America*. c. 1932–1934
Pencil, 19 x 20⅞ in. (sheet)
On extended loan to The Museum of Modern Art, New
York, from the artist's son, Clemente Orozco

249. Orozco, José Clemente (Mexico, 1883–1949)
*Male Torso*. 1923
Crayon on light brown paper, 25¼ x 18¾ in.
The Museum of Modern Art, New York. Gift of
Abby Aldrich Rockefeller

250. Orozco, José Clemente (Mexico, 1883–1949)
*The Trench – First Idea*. c. 1923
Pencil on cream paper, 24¹⁄₁₆ x 20¼ in.
Lent by Familia Clemente Orozco, Mexico, D.F.

251. Orozco, José Clemente (Mexico, 1883–1949)
*Six preliminary studies for "Dive Bomber and Tank."*
1940
Drawings in various media and dimensions
Lent by Familia Clemente Orozco, Mexico, D.F.

252. Ossaye Gallardo, Roberto (Guatemala, 1927–1954)
*The Breakfast* (*El Desayuno*). 1954
Oil on canvas, 37⅜ x 51³⁄₁₆ in.
Museo Nacional de Historia y Bellas Artes,
Guatemala City

253. Ostrower, Fayga (Brazilian, b. Poland, 1920–    )
*Gravura 6522-A*. 1965
Color woodcut, 14 x 30 in.
Lent by Sr. and Sra. Ernesto Wolf, São Paulo

254. Otero, Alejandro (Venezuela, 1921–    )
*Collage No. 31*. 1965
Pasted paper on wood, 28⅝ x 23⅝ in.
Lent by the artist

255. Otero, Alejandro (Venezuela, 1921–    )
*White Coffee Pot* (*Cafetera blanca*). 1948
Oil on canvas, 25½ x 21¼ in.
Lent by Sr. Miguel G. Arroyo C., Caracas

256. Otero, Alejandro (Venezuela, 1921–    )
*Colorhythm 68* (*Coloritmo 68*). 1960
Polished duco on wood, 79 x 21½ in.
Museo de Bellas Artes, Caracas

257. Paalen, Wolfgang (Mexican, b. Austria, 1905–1959)
*Fumage*. 1944–1945
Oil and candle soot on paper, 18¾ x 10¼ in.
The Museum of Modern Art, New York. Gift of
Samuel A. Berger

258. Pacheco, Maria Luisa (Bolivia, 1919–    )
*Idol*. 1965
Oil and corrugated cardboard on canvas, 38 x 30 in.
Lent by the artist

259. Pacheco Pereyra, Armando (Bolivian, b. Brazil,
1910–    )
*Head* (*Cabeza*). 1953
Oil, 26⅜ x 23½ in.
Museo Nacional de Arte, La Paz

260. Palacios, Luisa (Venezuela, 1923–    )
*Persistence of Rose* (*Duración de rosa*). 1964 (Plate 113)
Color engraving, 17½ x 14⅝ in.
Lent by the artist

261. Pallière, Juan León (Brazil, 1823–1887)
*Gaucho Lassoing on Foot* (*Gaucho enlazando de a pie*)
Watercolor, 13⅜ x 9⅝ in.
Lent by Sr. Antonio Santamarina, Buenos Aires

262. Pallière, Juan León (Brazil, 1823–1887)
    *Landscape of the Jungle of the Argentine Misiones
      Province.* (*Paisaje de la selva de las Misiones
      argentinas*). 1864 (Plate 23)
    Watercolor, 12⅜ x 15¼ in.
    Lent by Sr. and Sra. Octavio Assunção, Montevideo

263. Pallière, Juan León (Brazil, 1823–1887)
    *The Store* (*La Tienda*)
    Watercolor, 14 in. diam.
    Museo Nacional de Bellas Artes, Buenos Aires

264. Pardo, Mercedes (Venezuela, 1922–    )
    *Primordial détaillé en ustensiles.* 1962
    Ink rubbing on paper, 19½ x 25½ in.
    Lent by Sr. Hans Neumann, Caracas

265. Paredes, Diógenes (Ecuador, 1910–    )
    *Onion Carriers* (*Cebolleras*)
    Oil on canvas, 34¼ x 30½ in.
    Casa de la Cultura, Ecuatoriana, Núcleo Guayas,
      Guayaquil, Ecuador

266. Parsons, G., after Whiting, Daniel Powers (latter,
      U.S.A., 1808–1892)
    *Valley near Saltillo* (*Valle cercano a Saltillo*)
    Color lithograph
    Lent by Banco de México, Mexico, D.F.

267. Paternosto, César (Argentina, 1931–    )
    *Climax.* 1959
    Oil on canvas, 63 x 63 in.
    Museo de Arte Moderno de la Ciudad de Buenos Aires

268. Pellegrini, Carlos Enrique (Savoy, 1800–1875)
    *Minuet.* 1831
    Watercolor, 9¼ x 13½ in.
    Lent by Sr. Domingo E. Minetti, Rosario, Argentina

269. Pellegrini, Carlos Enrique (Savoy, 1800–1875)
    *Doña Agustina Rozas de Mansilla and Her Son Lucio*
      (Plate 10)
    Watercolor, 11¼ x 9⅛ in.
    Museo Histórico Nacional, Buenos Aires

270. Pellegrini, Carlos Enrique (Savoy, 1800–1875)
    *Don Manuel Bernardino Masculino* (Plate 24)
    Watercolor, 12 in. (oval)
    Museo Nacional de Bellas Artes, Buenos Aires

271. Petrés, Fray Domingo de (Spain, 1759–1811)
    *Longitudinal Section of the Cathedral Church of Santa Fe*
      (*Corte longitudinal de la Iglesia Catedral de Santa Fé,
      Bogotá*). c. 1805
    Architectural drawing in ink and wash, 26¼ x 18¾ in.
    Lent by the Arzobispado de Bogotá

272. Petrés, Fray Domingo de (Spain, 1759–1811)
    *Plan and Profile of the Cathedral Church of Santa Fe,
      Bogotá* (*Plan y perfil de la Iglesia Catedral de
      Santa Fé, Bogotá.*) (Plate 18)
    Architectural drawing in ink and wash, 17⅜ x 28¾ in.
    Lent by the Arzobispado de Bogotá

273. Pettoruti, Emilio (Argentina, 1892–    )
    *Man with Yellow Flower* (*El Hombre de la flor amarilla*).
      1932
    Oil on canvas, 32 x 25½ in.
    Museo Nacional de Bellas Artes, Buenos Aires

274. Pettoruti, Emilio (Argentina, 1892–    )
    *The Quintet* (*El Quinteto*). 1927 (Plate 61)
    Oil on plywood, 59 x 51½ in.
    San Francisco Museum of Art. Gift of
      Dr. Grace L. McCann Morley

275. Pinto, Joaquín (Ecuador, 1842–1906)
    *Study of a Bird* (*Estudio de un pájaro*) (Plate 32)
    Watercolor, 3½ x 5½ in.
    Lent by Sra. Viuda del Dr. José Gabriel Navarro
      Enríquez, Quito

276. Pissarro, Camille (French, b. St. Thomas, 1830–1903)
    *Landscape with Figures* (*Paisaje con figuras*)
    Pencil on paper drawing, 10¹⁄₁₆ x 13⅝ in.
    Museo de Bellas Artes, Caracas

277. Piza, Arthur Luiz (Brazil, 1928–    )
    *Untitled* (*Sem Titulo*). 1959
    Drypoint engraving, 29½ x 21⅞ in.
    Lent by Sr. and Sra. Ernesto Wolf, São Paulo

278. Plaza, Exequiel (Chile)
    *The Bohemian Painter* (*El Pintor bohemio*)
    Oil on canvas, 39⅜ x 25⁹⁄₁₆ in.
    Casa del Arte, Universidad de Concepción, Chile

279. Poleo, Héctor (Venezuela, 1918–    )
*Persistence of Memory* (*Persistencia de la memoria*).
   1963–1964
Casein on canvas, 51¼ x 51 in.
Lent by Sr. Hans Neumann, Caracas

280. Poleo, Héctor (Venezuela, 1918–    )
*The Three Commissioners* (*Los tres comisarios*). 1942
   (Plate 78)
Oil on canvas, 35⁷⁄₁₆ x 27¾ in.
Museo de Bellas Artes, Caracas

281. Polesello, Rogelio (Argentina, 1939–    )
*Indigenous Images* (*Imágenes indígenas*). 1962
Oil on canvas, 102¾ x 77 in.
Museo de Bellas Arte, Caracas

282. Ponce, Bernal (Chile, contemporary)
*The Flight* (*El Vuelo*)
Engraving
Lent by Galería Marta Faz, Santiago de Chile

283. Ponce de León, Fidelio (Cuba, 1895–1949)
*Two Women.* 1934
Oil on canvas, 39¼ x 39⅜ in.
The Museum of Modern Art, New York. Gift of
   Dr. C. M. Ramírez Corría

284. Portinari, Candido (Brazil, 1903–1961)
*Coffee* (*Café*). 1935
Oil on canvas, 50 x 76 in.
Museu Nacional de Belas Artes, Rio de Janeiro

285. Pôrto Alegre, Manuel de Araújo (Brazil, 1806–1879)
*Caricature of Justiniano José de Rocha.* 1837 (Plate 40)
Lithograph on newsprint, 13¾ x 17⅜ in.
Biblioteca Nacional, Rio de Janeiro

286. Portocarrero, René (Cuba, 1912–    )
*Cathedral* (*Catedral*). 1961 (Plate 96)
Oil, 46 x 27 in.
Fundação Bienal de São Paulo

287. Posada, José Guadalupe (Mexico, 1851–1913)
*Female Dandy* (Plate 59)
Relief etching on zinc, 5½ x 7¾ in.
Lent by International Business Machines Corporation,
   New York

288. Potyguara, Lazzarotto, called Poty (Brazil, 1924–    )
*The Brakeman.* c. 1944
Engraving (etching), 14¼ x 17¼ in.
Biblioteca Nacional, Rio de Janeiro

289. Pradier, Charles Simon (Switzerland, 1783–1847)
*Dom João VI.* c. 1818–1820
Engraving, 25⁹⁄₁₆ x 16⅛ in.
Biblioteca Nacional, Rio de Janeiro

290. Pucciarelli, Mario A. (Argentina, 1928–    )
*Composition,* (*Composición*). 1963
Oil on canvas, 51½ x 38¾ in.
Museo Nacional de Bellas Artes, Buenos Aires

291. Pueyrredón, Prilidiano (Argentina, 1823–1870)
*A Rest in the Country* (*Un Alto en el campo*). 1861
   (Plate 13)
Oil on canvas, 29¾ x 65½ in.
Museo Nacional de Bellas Artes, Buenos Aires

292. Pueyrredón, Prilidiano (Argentina, 1823–1870)
*A Sunday in the Suburbs of San Isidro* (*Un domingo en
   los suburbios de San Isidro*)
Watercolor, 10¾ x 22¾ in.
Museo Nacional de Bellas Artes, Buenos Aires

293. Pueyrredón, Prilidiano (Argentina, 1823–1870)
*Sra. Eastman de Barros.* 1865
Oil on canvas, 50 x 39⅜ in.
Museo Nacional de Bellas Artes, Buenos Aires

294. Quinquela Martín, Benito (Argentina, 1890–    )
*New Bridge* (*Puente nuevo*)
Etching, 25½ x 19¼ in.
Museo de Artes Plásticas "Eduardo Sívori," Buenos Aires

295. Quiroa, Marco Augusto (Guatemala, 1937–    )
*The Tatascan* (*El Tatascán*). 1963
Mixed media on composition board, 23⅝ x 31½ in.
Lent by the artist

296. Ramírez Rosales, Manuel (Chile, 1804–1877)
*Landscape with Palm Trees* (*Paisaje con palmeras*)
   (Plate 28)
Oil on canvas, 16⅛ x 13 in.
Casa del Arte, Universidad de Concepción, Chile

297. Ramírez Villamizar, Eduardo (Colombia, 1923–    )
*Black and White No. 1* (*Blanco y negro No.* 1). 1959
Oil on canvas, 59⁹⁄₁₆ x 50⅛ in.
Lent by the artist

298. Ramírez Villamizar, Eduardo (Columbia, 1923–      )
*Model for relief mural, Bank of the Republic, Cúcuta*
Painted wood relief, 53¹¹⁄₁₆ x 35⅛ in.
Lent by the artist

299. Ramos Martínez, Alfredo (Mexico, 1875–1946)
*Old Bretons (Viejas Bretonas)*
Ink and watercolor, 11 x 9 in.
Museo Nacional de Bellas Artes, Córdoba, Argentina

300. Renart, Emilio J. (Argentina, 1925–      )
*Untitled.* 1965 (Plate 94)
Ink and tempera, 30 x 34 in.
Museo de Arte Moderno de la Ciudad de Buenos Aires

301. Rendón, Manuel (France, 1894–      )
*Untitled*
Oil on paper, 25 x 19½ in.
Lent by Sr. Roberto Seminario, Guayaquil, Ecuador

302. Reschreiter, Rudolf (Germany, 19th century)
*Sangay.* 1904
Gouache, 20⅝ x 40 in.
Museo Municipal, Guayaquil, Ecuador

303. Reverón, Armando (Venezuela, 1889–1954)
*The Cave (La Cueva).* 1920
Oil on canvas, 39¾ x 61³⁄₁₆ in.
Lent by Sr. Alfredo Boulton, Caracas

304. Reverón, Armando (Venezuela, 1889–1954)
*Landscape (Paisaje).* 1929 (Plate 68)
Oil on canvas, 36 x 41¾ in.
Museo de Bellas Artes, Caracas

305. Rivera, Diego (Mexico, 1886–1957)
*Building the Palace of Cortés.* 1930
Pencil on buff paper, 18⅞ x 12½ in. (sheet)
The Museum of Modern Art, New York

306. Rivera, Diego (Mexico, 1886–1957)
*Design for the Anahuacalli.* c. 1950
Architectural drawing for
    Diego Rivera Memorial Museum, México, D.F.
Lent by Srta. Ruth Rivera, Mexico, D.F.

307. Rivera, Diego (Mexico, 1886–1957)
*Day of the Dead in the Country.* 1925
Charcoal and color chalk, 18¼ x 11¾ in. (sheet)
The Museum of Modern Art, New York

308. Rivera, Diego (Mexico, 1886–1957)
*Flower Vendor.* 1935 (Plate 77)
Oil on panel, 47¾ x 47¾ in.
San Francisco Museum of Art. Gift of Albert M. Bender
    as Memorial to Caroline Walter

309. Rivera, Diego (Mexico, 1886–1957)
*Man at the Crossroads.* 1932
Pencil on brown paper, 30¼ x 69¼ in.
The Museum of Modern Art, New York

310. Rivera, Diego (Mexico, 1886–1957)
*The New Freedom,* from "Portrait of America" series.
    1933
Fresco, 72 x 71 in.
Lent by the International Rescue Committee, Inc.,
    New York

311. Rivera, Diego (Mexico, 1886–1957)
*Portrait of a Man (Retrato de hombre).* 1913 (Plate 66)
Oil on canvas, 38³⁄₁₆ x 31¹⁄₁₆ in.
Museo del Estado de Jalisco, Guadalajara, Mexico

312. Rivera, Diego (Mexico, 1886–1957)
*Sleep.* 1932
Lithograph, 20⅛ x 14¹³⁄₁₆ in. (sheet)
The Museum of Modern Art, New York. Gift of
    Abby Aldrich Rockefeller

313. Roa, Israel (Chile, 1909–      )
*Cemetery of Saint Ines (Cementerio de Santa Inéz).*
Oil on canvas
Casa del Arte, Universidad de Concepción, Chile

314. Rodríguez Padilla, Rafael (Guatemala, 1890–1929)
*Still Life (Bodegón).* 1927
Oil on canvas, 22¹⁄₁₆ x 24 in.
Lent by Familia Rodríguez Padilla, from the custody of
    Museo Nacional de História y Bellas Artes,
    Guatemala City

315. Rodríguez Roda, Juan Antonio; called Roda (Colombian,
    b. Spain, 1921–      )
*Philip IV (Felipe IV).* 1965
Oil on canvas, 43 x 71 in.
Lent by the artist

316. Rojas, Cristóbal (Venezuela, 1858–1890)
*Study of the Balcony (Estudio del balcón)* (Plate 50)
Oil on canvas, 28⅝ x 23⅜ in.
Museo de Bellas Artes, Caracas

317. Rugendas, Johann Moritz (Bavaria, 1802–1858)
*Portrait of the Princess of Joinville* (*D. Francisca de Braganza, Princesa de Joinville*). 1846
Watercolor, 22½ x 15¾ in.
Lent by Sr. and Sra. João Hermes Pereira de Araujo, Buenos Aires

318. Rugendas, Johann Moritz (Bavaria, 1802–1858)
*Plaza de Armas.* (Plate 29)
Oil on canvas, 27 x 36¾ in.
Museo Taurino, Sr. Fernando Berckemeyer. Lima

319. Rugendas, Johann Moritz (Bavaria, 1802–1858)
*Return of Garibaldi after the Battle of San Antonio* (*Retorno de Garibaldi después del combate de San Antonio*).
Oil on canvas, 32¾ x 39½ in.
Museo Histórico y Archivo Municipal, Montevideo

320. Rugendas, Johann Moritz (Bavaria, 1802–1858)
*Valparaiso Fire* (*Incendio de Valparaiso*).
Watercolor, 9 x 12½ in.
Lent by Sr. Armando Braun Menéndez, Buenos Aires

321. Ruiz, Antonio (Mexico, 1897–    )
*The New Rich* (*Los nuevos ricos*). 1941
Oil on canvas, 12⅝ x 16⅝ in.
The Museum of Modern Art, New York. Inter-American Fund

322. Sabatier, after Lauvergne, Berthélemy (latter b. France, 1805–1871)
*Vue de port de Guayaquil*
Color lithograph, 7¾ x 11¼ in.
Lent by the Banco de Londres y Montreal, Guayaquil, Ecuador

323. Sabogal, José (Peru, 1888–1956)
*The Dealer in Antiques* (*El Anticuario*). 1949 (Plate 104)
Woodcut, 11½ x 9⅛ in.
Museo Nacional de Cultura Peruana, Lima

324. Sabogal, José (Peru, 1888–1956)
*Mulatto Tamale Vendor* (*Mulata Tamalera*). 1926
Oil on burlap, 27¾ x 25½ in.
Lent by Sr. Antenor Fernández Soler, Lima

325. Sáez, Carlos Federico (Uruguay, 1878–1900)
*Portrait of a Young Lady* (*Retrato de Señorita*)
Oil on canvas, 24 x 24 in.
Museo Nacional de Bellas Artes, Montevideo

326. St. Aulaire, Félix Achille, after Sarokins, S. (latter British?, 19th century)
*View of Veracruz* (*Vista de Veracruz*) (Plate 19)
Lithograph, 15 x 19 in.
Lent by the University Club, Mexico, D.F.

327. Salas, Rafael (Ecuador, 1830–1906)
*Quito.* 1860 (Plate 21)
Oil, 20¼ x 30½ in.
Lent by Sr. and Sra. Rafael Vasconés Hurtado, Quito

328. Sánchez Elía, F. Peralta Ramos, A. Agostini, and C. Testa (Argentina, contemporary)
*Bank of London and South America, Buenos Aires.*
*5 drawings: a. Perspective, b. Ground Floor Plan, c. Longitudinal Section, d. Transverse Section, e. South Elevation.* 1960
Ink on translucent drafting paper, various sizes
Lent by Arq. Clorindo Testa, Buenos Aires

329. Santa María, Andrés de (Colombia, 1860–1945)
*Portrait of a Lady* (*Retrato de una Mujer*) (Plate 65)
Oil on canvas, 24 x 19½ in.
Museo Nacional, Bogotá

330. Santa María, Andrés de (Colombia, 1860–1945)
*Still Life* (*El Bodegón*)
Oil on canvas, 60¼ x 63½ in.
Museo Nacional, Bogotá

331. Santos Chávez, José (Chile, 1934–    )
*Southern Images, Cover I* (*Imágenes del Sur, Portada I*)
Woodcut, 21¼ x 14⅝ in.
Lent by Galería Carmen Waugh, Santiago de Chile

332. Serpa, Ivan (Brazil, 1923–    )
*15th of March,* 1952 (*Mayo 15 de 1952*)
Oil on canvas, 51 1/16 x 63 in.
Museu de Arte Moderna, Rio de Janeiro

333. Sheridan, Enrique (Argentina, 1838–1863)
*A Street in San Isidro* (*Una Calle de San Isidro*)
Watercolor, 10¼ x 7½ in.
Lent by Sr. Antonio Santamarina, Buenos Aires

334. Simone, Alfredo de (Italy, 1898–1950)
*The Street* (*La Calle*)
Oil on burlap, 31¾ x 34 in.
Museo Nacional de Bellas Artes, Montevideo

335. Sinclair Ballesteros, Alfredo (Panama, 1916–     )
*Marañón – from the series "City without Lights"*
   (*Marañón – de la serie "Ciudad sin luces"*). 1963
Oil, 23½ x 35¼ in.
Lent by Sr. Adolfo Arias Espinosa, Panama

336. Sívori, Eduardo (Argentina, 1847–1918)
*Landscape "The Bather"* (*Paisaje "El Bañador"*).
Oil on canvas, 18½ x 13¾ in.
Lent by Sr. Domingo E. Minetti, Rosario, Argentina

337. Sívori, Eduardo (Argentina, 1847–1918)
*Portrait of the Artist's Wife* (*Retrato de la esposa del
   autor*) (Plate 48)
Oil on canvas, 35½ x 25½ in.
Museo Nacional de Bellas Artes, Buenos Aires

338. Soto, Jesús (Venezuela, 1923–     )
*Vibration* (*Vibración*). 1964
Wood, novopan, metal, and nylon, 40⁵⁄₁₆ x 67¾ in.
Lent by Sr. Hans Neumann, Caracas

339. Souza, Gerson Alves de (Brazil, 1926-     )
*Purgatory* (*Purgatorio*). 1965 (Plate 102)
Oil on composition board, 23⅝ x 23⅝ in.
Lent by the artist

340. Spilimbergo, Lino Eneas (Argentina, 1896–1964)
*Still Life* (*Naturaleza Muerta*)
Oil on burlap, 45 x 30 in.
Museo Municipal de Bellas Artes "Juan B. Castagnino,"
   Rosario, Argentina

341. Spilimbergo, Lino Eneas (Argentina, 1896–1964)
*Figures* (*Figuras*) (Plate 81)
Oil on canvas, 51³⁄₁₆ x 37⅜ in.
Museo Nacional de Bellas Artes, Buenos Aires

342. Squirru, Carlos (Argentina, 1934–     )
*Cancer*. 1957
Tempera, 23⅞ x 18 in.
The Museum of Modern Art, New York. Inter-American
   Fund

343. Squirru, Carlos (Argentina, 1934–     )
*Sectioned Hand* (*Mano seccionada*). 1964
Mixed media, 2 pieces: 39 x 23 in. (base)
   38⅝ x 34¼ in. (head)
Lent by the artist

344. Subercaseaux, Ramón (Chile, 1854–1936)
*The Mouth of the River at Viña del Mar*
   (*Desembocadura del estero de Viña del Mar*)
Oil on canvas, 19⅝ x 39⅜ in.
Museo de Bellas Artes, Viña del Mar, Chile

345. Szyszlo, Fernando de (Peru, 1925–     )
*Cajamarca*. 1963 (Plate 95)
Oil on canvas, 51½ x 39¼ in.
Lent by Sr. Walter Gross, Lima

346. Tabara, Ernesto (Ecuador)
*View of Guayaquil from the Airplane* (*Visión de
   Guayaquil desde el avión*). 1964
Oil on canvas, 32 x 39½ in.
Lent by Sr. Jorge Reyes, Guayaquil, Ecuador

347. Tamayo, Rufino (Mexico, 1899–     )
*The Fountain* (*La Fuente*). 1951
Oil on canvas, 31¾ x 39½ in.
Museo de Bellas Artes, Caracas

348. Tamayo, Rufino (Mexico, 1899–     )
*Homage to the Race* (*Homenaje a la raza*). 1952
Oil on composition board, approx. 16 x 12 ft.
Museo del Palacio de Bellas Artes, Mexico, D.F.

349. Tamayo, Rufino (Mexico, 1899–     )
*The Flute Player* (*El Flautero*). 1944 (Plate 71)
Oil on canvas, 45 x 37 in.
Lent by International Business Machines Corporation,
   New York

350. Tatis, José Gabriel (Colombia, 1813– ?)
*Self-portrait*. 1853
Watercolor. Title page for *Ensayos de Dibujo*.
Museo Nacional, Bogotá

351. Tatis, José Gabriel (Colombia, 1813– ?)
*Prominent Gentlemen of Bogotá*. 1853
Watercolor. From *Ensayos de Dibujo*.
Museo Nacional, Bogotá

352. Taunay, Nicolas Antoine (France, 1755–1830)
*Carioca Square in* 1816 (*O Largo da Carioca em* 1816)
Oil on canvas, 18 x 22 in.
Museu Nacional de Belas Artes, Rio de Janeiro

353. Taunay, Nicolas Antoine (France, 1755–1830)
*Jeanneton* (Plate 12)
Oil on canvas, 18⅛ x 14¹⁵⁄₁₆ in.
Museu Nacional de Belas Artes, Rio de Janeiro

354. Testa, Clorindo (Argentina, b. Naples, 1923–      )
*Painting* (*Pintura*). 1961
Mixed media, 63¾ x 63¾ in.
Centro de Artes Visuales, Instituto Torcuato di Tella,
     Buenos Aires

355. Tolsá, Manuel (Spain, 1757–1816)
*Plan for the School of Mines, Mexico City* (*Proyecto de la
     Escuela de Minería, Ciudad de México*). 1819(?)
Ink on paper, 19¾ x 27¾ in.
Biblioteca de la Academia de San Carlos, Mexico, D.F.

356. Toral, Mario (Chile, 1934–      )
*Untitled* (*Sin título*)
Watercolor, 24 x 19¼ in.
Lent by Galería Carmen Waugh, Santiago de Chile

357. Torres, Mariano de Jesús (Morelia, Mexico, 19th century)
*Closed Street of San Agustín, Morelia* (*Calle cerrada de
     San Agustín, Morelia*). 1874
Oil on canvas, 16½ x 25 in.
Museo Regional de Morelia, Mexico

358. Torres García, Joaquín (Uruguay, 1874–1949)
*Abstract Composition* (*Composición abstracta*). 1937
Tempera on cardboard, 32 x 40 in.
Lent by Srta. Ifigenia Torres, Montevideo

359. Torres García, Joaquín (Uruguay, 1874–1949)
*Constructive Ship "America"* (*Barco Constructivo
     "América"*). 1943 (Plate 79)
Oil on cardboard, 18¼ x 28¾ in.
Lent by Sra. Manolita Piña de Torres García, Montevideo

360. Torres García, Joaquín (Uruguay, 1874–1949)
*Portrait of Velázquez* (*Retrato de Velázquez*). 1945
Oil on cardboard, 19¾ x 16¼ in.
Lent by Sra. Manolita Piña de Torres García, Montevideo

361. Torres Méndez, Ramón (Colombia, 1809–1885)
*Country Types* (*Tipos de campesinos*)
Pencil drawing, 8¹⁄₁₆ x 9¾ in.
Museo Nacional, Bogotá

362. Tovar y Tovar, Martín (Venezuela, 1828–1902)
*Juana Verrue.* 1877 (Plate 36)
Oil on canvas, 25⁹⁄₁₆ x 21¼ in.
Museo de Bellas Artes, Caracas

363. Tovar y Tovar, Martín (Venezuela, 1828–1902)
*Self-portrait* (*Autorretrato*). 1855
Oil on canvas, 19⅝ x 12 in.
Lent by Familia Zuloaga Ramírez, Caracas

364. Troya, Rafael (Ecuador, 1845–1921)
*The Shore* (*El Litoral*). 1905
Museo Nacional de Arte Colonial, Quito

365. Trujillo, Guillermo (Panama, 1927–      )
*Mother Fury* (*La Madre Furia*). 1964
Ink drawing, 11 x 15 in.
Lent by the artist

366. Turner, Charles (England, 1773–1857), after
     Gil de Castro (Peru ? –1841?)
*Simón Bolívar.* 1830
Mezzotint, 20⅛ x 13 in.
Museo Nacional, Bogotá

367. Ugarte Eléspuru, Juan Manuel (Peru, 1911–      )
*Cartoon for Mural Painting in the Mercedes Cabello
     School, Lima* (*Bosquejo para pintura mural, Escuela
     Mercedes Cabello, Lima*). 1945
Watercolor and pencil on paper
Lent by Galería San Marcos, Dr. Luis Felipe Tello, Lima

368. Urteaga, Mario (Peru, 1875–1957)
*The Betrothed* (*Los Novios*). 1937 (Plate 76)
Oil on canvas, 20¼ x 16 in.
Lent by Srta. Julia Codesido, Lima

369. Urteaga, Mario (Peru, 1875–1957)
*Burial of an Illustrious Man.* 1936
Oil on canvas, 23 x 32½ in.
The Museum of Modern Art, New York. Inter-American
     Fund

370. Valencia, César (Ecuador, 1918–      )
*Caricature of José Gabriel Navarro* (*Caricatura de
     José Gabriel Navarro*). 1942
Watercolor, 18⅛ x 13¾ in.
Lent by Sra. Viuda del Dr. José Gabriel Navarro
     Enríquez, Quito

371. Valenti, Carlos (Guatemala, 1891–1912)
    *Jaime Sabartés*. 1911
    Charcoal, 23⅝ x 14 in. (sight)
    Lent by Sr. Humberto Garavito Suasnávar,
    Guatemala City

372. Vasarely, Victor (Hungary, 1908–     )
    *Mural for the Central University of Venezuela* (*Mural
        para la Universidad Central de Venezuela*). 1952
    India ink on paper, 9⁷⁄₁₆ x 25⅛ in.
    Lent by Arq. Carlos Raúl Villanueva, Caracas

373. Vega, Jorge Luis de la (Argentina, 1930–     )
    *Music Hall*. 1963
    Oil on canvas, 102¾ x 76 in.
    Lent by Galería Bonino, Buenos Aires

374. Velasco, José María (Mexico, 1840–1912)
    *The Valley of Mexico Seen from the Hill of Guadalupe*
        (*El Valle de México visto del Cerro de Guadalupe*).
        1905
    Oil on canvas, 30 x 41¾ in.
    Museo Nacional de Arte Moderno, Mexico, D.F.

375. Victorica, Miguel Carlos (Argentina, 1884–1955)
    *Nude* (*Desnudo de mujer*)
    Charcoal, 25 x 10⅞ in.
    Museo Municipal de Bellas Artes "Juan B. Castagnino,"
        Rosario, Argentina

376. Victorica, Miguel Carlos (Argentina, 1884–1955)
    *Nude* (*Desnudo*). 1923 (Plate 63)
    Oil on canvas, 45¼ x 57½ in.
    Museo Nacional de Bellas Artes, Buenos Aires

377. Vidal, Emeric Essex (England, 1791–1861)
    *Country Race* (*Carrera de campo*) (Plate 14)
    Watercolor, 10¼ x 18¾ in.
    Lent by Sr. Domingo E. Minetti, Rosario, Argentina

378. Vidal, Emeric Essex (England, 1791–1861)
    *Estancia Foreman of the Epoch of Artigas* (*Estanciero de
        la época de Artigas*)
    Watercolor, 12⁵⁄₁₆ x 9³⁄₁₆ in.
    Museo Histórico y Archivo Municipal, Montevideo

379. Vilches, Eduardo (Chile, 1932–     )
    *The Pérezes* (*Los Pérez*). 1964
    Woodcut, 11½ x 17½ in.
    Escuela de Arte, Universidad Católica de Chile, Santiago
        de Chile

380. Villacis, Aníbal (Ecuador, 1927–     )
    *Untitled* (*Sin Título*)
    Oil and metal on composition board, 47¾ x 40⅛ in.
    Lent by Sr. Jorge Reyes, Guayaquil, Ecuador

381. Villanueva, Carlos Raúl (England, 1900–     )
    4 *Preliminary Sketches for University City*, *Central
        University of Venezuela*, *Caracas*. c. 1946
    Ink, compressed charcoal (2), and yellow chalk;
        6⅝ x 9⅞, 8⅜ x 11½, 11¼ x 8⅜, and 14¼ x 14⅛ in.
        respectively
    Lent by the architect

382. Vinatea Reynoso, Jorge (Peru, 1900–1931)
    *San Martin*. 1921?
    Watercolor, 16⅝ x 10¼ in.
    Lent by Familia Moncloa Ordóñez, Lima

383. Vinatea Reynoso, Jorge (Peru, 1900–1931)
    *Straw Boats of Lake Titicaca* (*Balsas del Titicaca*). 1930
    Oil on burlap, 37¾ x 29¼ in.
    Lent by Familia Moncloa Ordóñez, Lima

384. Visconti, Elyseu D'Angelo (Italy, 1867–1944)
    *Sra. Nicolina Pinto do Couto*
    Oil on canvas, 39½ x 32 in.
    Museu Nacional de Belas Artes, Rio de Janeiro

385. Viteri, Oswaldo (Ecuador, 1931–     )
    *Still Life Painting in Maroon and Ochre* (*Naturaleza
        muerta – Pintura en marron y ocre*). 1960
    Oil on canvas, 48½ x 33 in.
    Casa de la Cultura Ecuatoriana, Quito

386. Williams, Amancio (Argentina, 1913–     )
    *Concert Hall* (*Sala de conciertos*); *Project*. Accoustical
        studies, 1941; project, 1942–45/1953. Drawing
        showing three sections.
    Colored ink and pasted paper, 42⅛ x 67¾ in.
    Lent by the architect

387. Williams, Amancio (Argentina, 1913–     )
    *Concert Hall* (*Sala de conciertos*); *Project*. Accoustical
        studies, 1941; project, 1942–45/1953. Drawing
        showing one section.
    Colored ink, gouache, and pasted paper, 29⅞ x 39⅜ in.
    Lent by the architect

388. Williams, Amancio (Argentina, 1913–    )
*Suspended Office Building* (*Edificio de oficinas suspendidas*); *Project*. 1946
Two drawings: elevation and plan. Ink on translucent paper, each 42⅛ x 31½ in.
Lent by the architect

389. Williams, Amancio (Argentina, 1913–    )
*House in Mar del Plata* (*Casa en Mar del Plata*). 1943–1945
Drawing: elevation. Ink on translucent paper, 42⅛ x 20 1/16 in.
Lent by the architect

390. Wulf, Lloyd (U.S.A., active Ecuador, 1940–1965)
*Two Men and Wine* (*Dos Hombres con vino*)
Ink drawing, 14¾ x 12½ in.
Lent by Sr. Presley Norton, Guayaquil, Ecuador

391. Wulf, Lloyd (U.S.A., active Ecuador, 1940–1965)
*Evocation of Trees* (*Evocación de árboles*)
Oil on canvas, 54¼ x 32 in.
Lent by Sr. Jorge Reyes, Guayaquil, Ecuador

392. Yrarrázaval, Ricardo (Chile, 1942–    )
*Standing Figure* (*Figura de pié*)
Oil, 51 9/16 x 38 3/16 in.
Lent by Galería Carmen Waugh, Santiago de Chile

393. Zachrisson, Julio (Panama, 1930 –    )
*Witch's Funeral* (*Funerales de la bruja*). 1963
(Plate 114)
Engraving, 19½ x 25 in.
Lent by Sr. Guillermo Trujillo, Panama

394. Zalce, Alfredo (Mexico, 1908–    )
*Parade of the Shoeshine Boys* (*Parada de limpiabotas*). 1941
Color lithograph, 15 x 19½ in.
Lent by International Business Machines Corporation, New York

395. Zañartu, Enrique (Chilean, b. Paris, 1921–    )
*Personages*. 1956
Oil on canvas, 39 x 32 in.
The Museum of Modern Art, New York. Inter-American Fund

# Index of artists by country

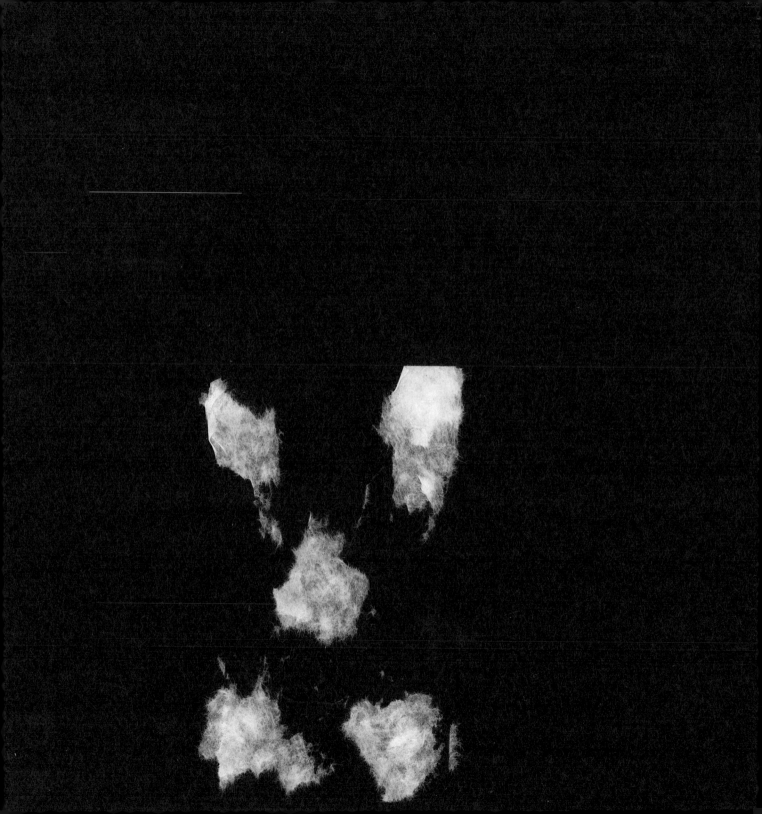